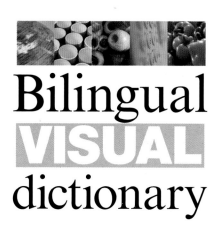

Bilingual
VISUAL
dictionary

Bilingual

VISUAL

dictionary

DK

LONDON, NEW YORK, MELBOURNE, MUNICH, DELHI

Senior Editor Angela Wilkes
Senior Art Editor Vicky Short
DTP Designer Deeraj Arora
DTP Coordinator Balwant Singh
Production Editor Lucy Baker
Production Controller Rita Sinha
Managing Art Editor Christine Keilty
US Editor Christine Heilman

Designed for Dorling Kindersley by WaltonCreative.com
Art Editor Colin Walton, assisted by Tracy Musson
Designers Peter Radcliffe, Earl Neish, Ann Cannings
Picture Research Marissa Keating

Language content for Dorling Kindersley by
g-and-w PUBLISHING
Managed by Jane Wightwick, Shuang Zou
Translation by Foreign Language
Teaching & Research Press
Pinyin transcription by Lin Jing

First American Edition, 2008

Published in the United States by
DK Publishing
375 Hudson Street
New York, New York 10014

20 19 18 17 16 15 14 13 12

024-BD587-April/08

Published in Great Britain by Dorling Kindersley Limited.

A catalog record for this book is available from
the Library of Congress.

ISBN 978-0-7566-3442-1

Printed by L. Rex Printing Co. Ltd, China

Discover more at
www.dk.com

目录 mùlù
contents

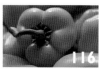

人 rén • people

外表 wàibiǎo • appearance

健康 jiànkāng • health

家居 jiājū • home

服务 fúwù • services

购物 gòuwù • shopping

食物 shíwù • food

外出就餐 wàichū jiùcān • eating out

词典介绍

about the dictionary

图片的应用经研究有助于对信息的理解和记忆。本着这个原则，这本有着丰富图片注释的英中双语词典包含了范围很广的词汇。

这本词典按照情景划分章节，从饮食到健身，从家居到工作，从太空到动物世界，包括了日常生活的所有细节。从这本词典中你也可以找到额外的常用词汇和词组以便口语练习和词汇量的扩大。

这本词典实用，生动，易用。对所有对语言有兴趣的人来说是一个重要的参考工具。

注意事项

本词典中的中文汉字同中华人民共和国官方汉字一样为简体汉字。

本词典为普通话注音，注音标记为拼音。拼音是中国人和中文学生最熟悉的一种音标。四声的变化也在拼音的结构中显示。

所有词语项都是以同样的顺序展示 – 文字，拼音，英文。例如：

午餐
wǔcān
lunch

安全带
ānquándài
seat belt

动词在英文词尾以 (v) 作为标记。例如：

收获 shōuhuò | harvest (v)

所有词汇在书后也有总目录可以查阅。在总目录里你可以通过查询英文，或者查询拼音找到相应的页数。这样可以很顺利地找到和拼音或英文相对应的中文文字翻译。

The use of pictures is proven to aid understanding and the retention of information. Working on this principle, this highly-illustrated English–Chinese bilingual dictionary presents a large range of useful current vocabulary.

The dictionary is divided thematically and covers most aspects of the everyday world in detail, from the restaurant to the gym, the home to the workplace, outer space to the animal kingdom. You will also find additional words and phrases for conversational use and for extending your vocabulary.

This is an essential reference tool for anyone interested in languages—practical, stimulating, and easy-to-use.

A few things to note

The Chinese in the dictionary is presented in simplified Chinese characters, as used in the People's Republic of China.

The pronunciation included for the Chinese is given in the Mandarin dialect and is shown in Pinyin, the standard romanization familiar to most native speakers and learners of Chinese. Accents showing the Chinese tones are included on the Pinyin.

The entries are always presented in the same order—Chinese, Pinyin, English—for example:

午餐
wǔcān
lunch

安全带
ānquándài
seat belt

Verbs are indicated by a (v) after the English—for example:

收获 shōuhuò | harvest (v)

Each language also has its own index at the back of the book. Here you can look up a word in either English or Pinyin and be referred to the page number(s) where it appears. To reference the Chinese characters for a particular word, look it up in the Pinyin or English index and then go to the page indicated.

使用说明

不论你学习语言的目的是工作，兴趣，为旅行做准备还是仅仅在已学语言的基础上扩大词汇量，这本词典都是你语言学习的重要工具。你可以多方面去运用它。

在学习一种新的语言的时候，注意同源词汇（即在不同语言中相似的词汇）和衍生词汇（即只在某种语言中有相似根源的词汇）。你可以发现语言和语言之间的联系。例如说，英文从中文中引用了一些关于食品的词汇，而同时也输出了一些关于科技和流行文化的词汇。

实用技巧
• 当你设身处地在家，工作场所或者学校的时候，试着看相对应自己所在环境的章节。这样一来你可以合上书，环视四周看看自己可以识别多少事物。
• 为自己做一些词汇卡片，一面英文一面中文和汉语拼音。时常携带这些卡片并且测试自己的记忆。记住每次测试之前要打乱卡片的顺序。
• 挑战自己尝试用某一页上的所有词汇写一个小故事，一封信或者一段对话。这样不但可以帮助你牢记这些词汇，而且可以帮助你记住它们的拼写。如果你想尝试写一篇长一点的文章，那么以至少含有2–3个词的句子为起点。
• 如果你有很强的视觉记忆，试着将书上的内容画出来或者在纸上诠释出来，然后合上书，在已有的图形下面填充词汇。
• 一但你变得更加自信，从中文目录中任意找一些词汇，检查自己是否在翻阅到相关页之前能知道其词意。

how to use this book

Whether you are learning a new language for business, pleasure, or in preparation for an overseas vacation, or are hoping to extend your vocabulary in an already familiar language, this dictionary is a valuable learning tool that you can use in a number of different ways.

When learning a new language, look out for cognates (words that are alike in different languages) and derivations (words that share a common root in a particular language). You can also see where the languages have influenced each other. For example, English has imported some terms for food from Chinese but, in turn, has exported some terms used in technology and popular culture.

Practical learning activities
• As you move around your home, workplace, or school, try looking at the pages that cover that setting. You could then close the book, look around you, and see how many of the objects and features you can name.
• Make flashcards for yourself with English on one side and Chinese/Pinyin on the other side. Carry the cards with you and test yourself frequently, making sure you shuffle them between each test.
• Challenge yourself to write a story, letter, or dialogue using as many of the terms on a particular page as possible. This will help you retain the vocabulary and remember the spelling. If you want to build up to writing a longer text, start with sentences incorporating 2–3 words.
• If you have a very visual memory, try drawing or tracing items from the book onto a piece of paper, then close the book and fill in the words below the picture.
• Once you are more confident, pick out words in the foreign language index and see if you know what they mean before turning to the relevant page to check if you were right.

人 rén
people

人体 réntǐ • body

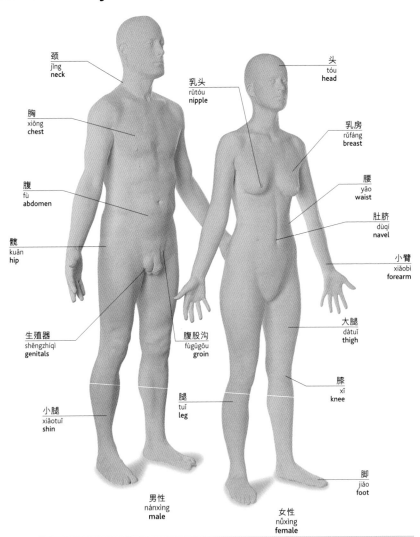

颈
jǐng
neck

乳头
rǔtóu
nipple

头
tóu
head

胸
xiōng
chest

乳房
rǔfáng
breast

腰
yāo
waist

腹
fù
abdomen

肚脐
dùqí
navel

髋
kuān
hip

小臂
xiǎobì
forearm

生殖器
shēngzhíqì
genitals

腹股沟
fùgǔgōu
groin

大腿
dàtuǐ
thigh

膝
xī
knee

小腿
xiǎotuǐ
shin

腿
tuǐ
leg

脚
jiǎo
foot

男性
nánxìng
male

女性
nǚxìng
female

中文 zhōngwén • english

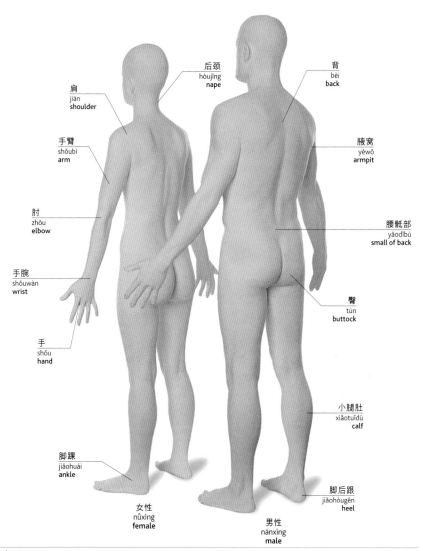

肩
jiān
shoulder

后颈
hòujǐng
nape

背
bèi
back

手臂
shǒubì
arm

腋窝
yèwō
armpit

肘
zhǒu
elbow

腰骶部
yāodǐbù
small of back

手腕
shǒuwàn
wrist

臀
tún
buttock

手
shǒu
hand

小腿肚
xiǎotuǐdù
calf

脚踝
jiǎohuái
ankle

脚后跟
jiǎohòugēn
heel

女性
nǚxìng
female

男性
nánxìng
male

面部 miànbù • face

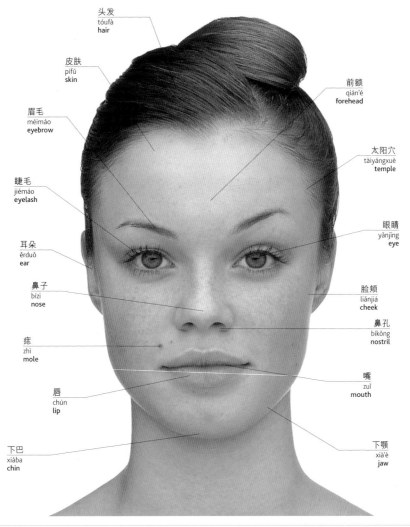

头发
tóufà
hair

皮肤
pífū
skin

眉毛
méimáo
eyebrow

睫毛
jiémáo
eyelash

耳朵
ěrduǒ
ear

鼻子
bízi
nose

痣
zhì
mole

唇
chún
lip

下巴
xiàba
chin

前额
qián'é
forehead

太阳穴
tàiyángxuè
temple

眼睛
yǎnjīng
eye

脸颊
liǎnjiá
cheek

鼻孔
bíkǒng
nostril

嘴
zuǐ
mouth

下颚
xià'è
jaw

皱纹
zhòuwén
wrinkle

雀斑
quèbān
freckle

毛孔
máokǒng
pore

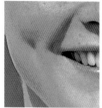

酒窝
jiǔwō
dimple

手 shǒu • hand

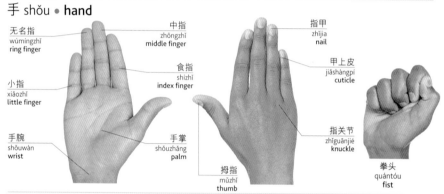

无名指
wúmíngzhǐ
ring finger

中指
zhōngzhǐ
middle finger

指甲
zhǐjia
nail

甲上皮
jiǎshàngpí
cuticle

食指
shízhǐ
index finger

小指
xiǎozhǐ
little finger

手腕
shǒuwàn
wrist

手掌
shǒuzhǎng
palm

指关节
zhǐguānjié
knuckle

拇指
mǔzhǐ
thumb

拳头
quántóu
fist

脚 jiǎo • foot

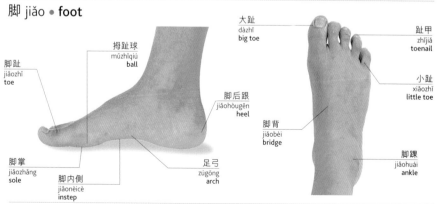

大趾
dàzhǐ
big toe

趾甲
zhǐjiǎ
toenail

拇趾球
mǔzhǐqiú
ball

脚趾
jiǎozhǐ
toe

脚后跟
jiǎohòugēn
heel

小趾
xiǎozhǐ
little toe

脚背
jiǎobèi
bridge

脚掌
jiǎozhǎng
sole

脚内侧
jiǎonèicè
instep

足弓
zúgōng
arch

脚踝
jiǎohuái
ankle

肌肉 jīròu • muscles

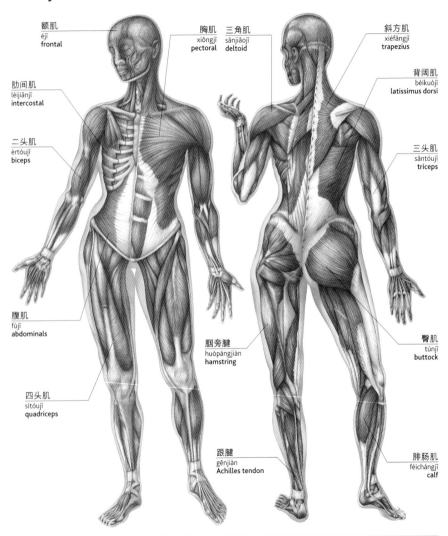

额肌
éjī
frontal

胸肌
xiōngjī
pectoral

三角肌
sānjiǎojī
deltoid

斜方肌
xiéfāngjī
trapezius

肋间肌
lèijiānjī
intercostal

背阔肌
bèikuòjī
latissimus dorsi

二头肌
èrtóujī
biceps

三头肌
sāntóujī
triceps

腹肌
fùjī
abdominals

腘旁腱
huòpángjiàn
hamstring

臀肌
túnjī
buttock

四头肌
sìtóujī
quadriceps

跟腱
gēnjiàn
Achilles tendon

腓肠肌
féichángjī
calf

骨骼 gǔgé • skeleton

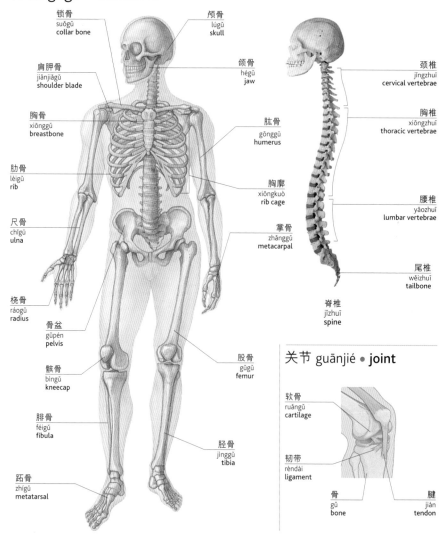

锁骨
suǒgǔ
collar bone

颅骨
lúgǔ
skull

肩胛骨
jiānjiǎgǔ
shoulder blade

颌骨
hégǔ
jaw

胸骨
xiōnggǔ
breastbone

肱骨
gōnggǔ
humerus

肋骨
lèigǔ
rib

胸廓
xiōngkuò
rib cage

尺骨
chǐgǔ
ulna

掌骨
zhǎnggǔ
metacarpal

桡骨
ráogǔ
radius

骨盆
gǔpén
pelvis

髌骨
bìngǔ
kneecap

股骨
gǔgǔ
femur

腓骨
féigǔ
fibula

胫骨
jìnggǔ
tibia

跖骨
zhígǔ
metatarsal

颈椎
jīngzhuī
cervical vertebrae

胸椎
xiōngzhuī
thoracic vertebrae

腰椎
yāozhuī
lumbar vertebrae

尾椎
wěizhuī
tailbone

脊椎
jǐzhuī
spine

关节 guānjié • joint

软骨
ruǎngǔ
cartilage

韧带
rèndài
ligament

骨
gǔ
bone

腱
jiàn
tendon

内脏 nèizàng • internal organs

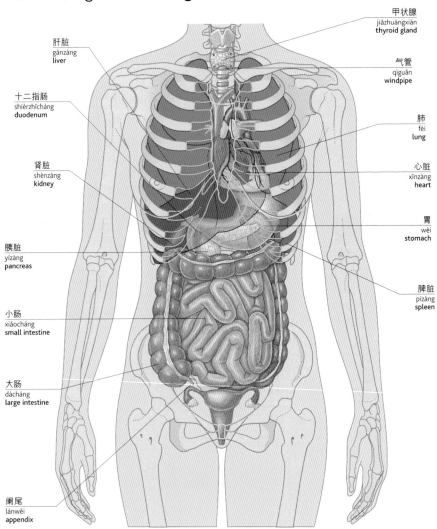

甲状腺
jiǎzhuàngxiàn
thyroid gland

气管
qìguǎn
windpipe

肝脏
gānzàng
liver

十二指肠
shíèrzhǐcháng
duodenum

肺
fèi
lung

肾脏
shènzàng
kidney

心脏
xīnzàng
heart

胃
wèi
stomach

胰脏
yízàng
pancreas

脾脏
pízàng
spleen

小肠
xiǎocháng
small intestine

大肠
dàcháng
large intestine

阑尾
lánwěi
appendix

头部 tóubù • **head**

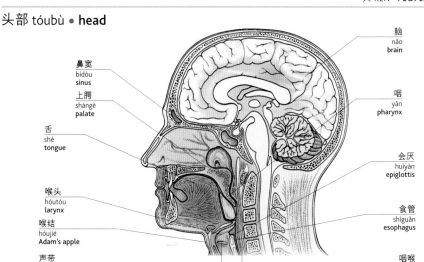

鼻窦
bídòu
sinus

上腭
shàngè
palate

舌
shé
tongue

喉头
hóutóu
larynx

喉结
hóujié
Adam's apple

声带
shēngdài
vocal cords

脑
nǎo
brain

咽
yān
pharynx

会厌
huìyàn
epiglottis

食管
shíguǎn
esophagus

咽喉
yānhóu
throat

人体系统 réntǐxìtǒng • **body systems**

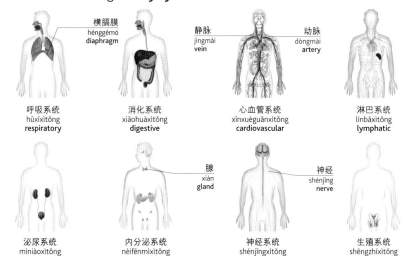

横膈膜
hénggémó
diaphragm

呼吸系统
hūxīxìtǒng
respiratory

消化系统
xiāohuàxìtǒng
digestive

静脉
jìngmài
vein

动脉
dòngmài
artery

心血管系统
xīnxuèguǎnxìtǒng
cardiovascular

淋巴系统
línbāxìtǒng
lymphatic

泌尿系统
mìniàoxìtǒng
urinary

腺
xiàn
gland

内分泌系统
nèifēnmìxìtǒng
endocrine

神经
shénjīng
nerve

神经系统
shénjīngxìtǒng
nervous

生殖系统
shēngzhíxìtǒng
reproductive

生殖器官 shēngzhíqìguān • reproductive organs

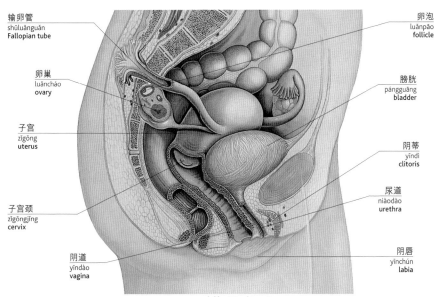

输卵管
shūluǎnguǎn
Fallopian tube

卵巢
luǎncháo
ovary

子宫
zǐgōng
uterus

子宫颈
zǐgōngjīng
cervix

阴道
yīndào
vagina

卵泡
luǎnpāo
follicle

膀胱
pángguāng
bladder

阴蒂
yīndì
clitoris

尿道
niàodào
urethra

阴唇
yīnchún
labia

女性 nǚxìng | female

生殖 shēngzhí • reproduction

精子
jīngzǐ
sperm

卵子
luǎnzǐ
egg

受精 shòujīng | fertilization

词汇 cíhuì • vocabulary

荷尔蒙 hé'ěrméng hormone	阳痿 yángwěi impotent	有生殖能力的 yǒushēngzhínénglìde fertile
排卵 páiluǎn ovulation	怀孕 huáiyùn conceive	月经 yuèjīng menstruation
不育 bùyù infertile	性交 xìngjiāo intercourse	性病 xìngbìng sexually transmitted infection

中文 zhōngwén • english

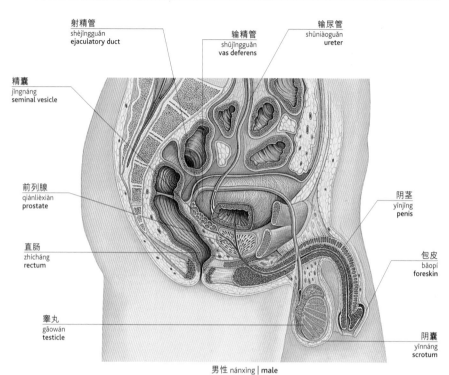

射精管
shèjīngguǎn
ejaculatory duct

输精管
shūjīngguǎn
vas deferens

输尿管
shūniàoguǎn
ureter

精囊
jīngnáng
seminal vesicle

前列腺
qiánlièxiàn
prostate

直肠
zhícháng
rectum

睾丸
gāowán
testicle

阴茎
yīnjīng
penis

包皮
bāopí
foreskin

阴囊
yīnnáng
scrotum

男性 nánxìng | male

避孕 bìyùn · contraception

子宫托
zǐgōngtuō
cap

阴道隔膜
yīndàogémó
diaphragm

避孕套
bìyùntào
condom

宫内避孕器
gōngnèibìyùnqì
IUD

避孕药
bìyùnyào
pill

家庭 jiātíng • family

祖母
zǔmǔ
grandmother

祖父
zǔfù
grandfather

姑父
gūfu
uncle

姑妈
gūmā
aunt

父亲
fùqīn
father

母亲
mǔqīn
mother

表兄弟
biǎoxiōngdì
cousin

兄弟
xiōngdì
brother

姊妹
zǐmèi
sister

妻子
qīzi
wife

儿媳
érxí
daughter-in-law

儿子
érzi
son

女儿
nǚér
daughter

女婿
nǚxù
son-in-law

孙子
sūnzi
grandson

孙女
sūnnǚ
granddaughter

丈夫
zhàngfu
husband

词汇 cíhuì • vocabulary

亲戚 qīnqi **relatives**	父母 fùmǔ **parents**	孙子女 / 外孙子女 sūnzǐnǚ / wàisūnzǐnǚ **grandchildren**	继母 jìmǔ **stepmother**	继子 jìzǐ **stepson**	配偶 pèiǒu **partner**
世代 shìdài **generation**	孩子 háizi **children**	祖父母 / 外祖父母 zǔfùmǔ / wàizǔfùmǔ **grandparents**	继父 jìfù **stepfather**	继女 jìnǚ **stepdaughter**	双胞胎 shuāngbāotāi **twins**

岳母
yuèmǔ
mother-in-law

岳父
yuèfù
father-in-law

妻妹(姐)夫
qīmèi(jiě)fū
brother-in-law

妻妹(姐)
qīmèi(jiě)
sister-in-law

外甥女
wàishēngnǚ
niece

外甥
wàishēng
nephew

太太
tàitài
Mrs.

称谓 chēngwèi • titles

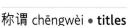

先生
xiānshēng
Mr.

小姐
xiǎojiě
Miss

成长阶段 chéngzhǎngjiēduàn • stages

婴儿
yīng'ér
baby

儿童
értóng
child

男孩
nánhái
boy

女孩
nǚhái
girl

青少年
qīngshàonián
teenager

成年人
chéngniánrén
adult

男人
nánrén
man

女人
nǚrén
woman

人际关系 rénjìguānxì • relationships

经理
jīnglǐ
manager

助理
zhùlǐ
assistant

生意伙伴
shēngyìhuǒbàn
business partner

雇主
gùzhǔ
employer

雇员
gùyuán
employee

同事
tóngshì
colleague

办公室 bàngōngshì | office

邻居
línjū
neighbor

朋友
péngyǒu
friend

熟人
shúrén
acquaintance

笔友
bǐyǒu
pen pal

男朋友
nánpéngyǒu
boyfriend

女朋友
nǚpéngyǒu
girlfriend

未婚夫
wèihūnfū
fiancé

未婚妻
wèihūnqī
fiancée

情侣 qínglǚ | couple

未婚夫妻 wèihūnfūqī | engaged couple

情感 qínggǎn • emotions

微笑
wēixiào
smile

快乐
kuàilè
happy

悲伤
bēishāng
sad

兴奋
xīngfèn
excited

无聊
wúliáo
bored

皱眉
zhòuméi
frown

惊讶
jīngyà
surprised

惊恐
jīngkǒng
scared

愤怒
fènnù
angry

困惑
kùnhuò
confused

忧虑
yōulǜ
worried

紧张
jǐnzhāng
nervous

自豪
zìháo
proud

自信
zìxìn
confident

尴尬
gāngà
embarrassed

羞涩
xiūsè
shy

词汇 cíhuì • vocabulary

烦躁 fánzào **upset**	笑 xiào **laugh (v)**	叹息 tànxī **sigh (v)**	叫喊 jiàohǎn **shout (v)**
震惊 zhènjīng **shocked**	哭 kū **cry (v)**	晕倒 yūndǎo **faint (v)**	打哈欠 dǎhāqian **yawn (v)**

人生大事 rénshēngdàshì • life events

出生
chūshēng
be born (v)

入学
rùxué
start school (v)

交友
jiāoyǒu
make friends (v)

毕业
bìyè
graduate (v)

就业
jiùyè
get a job (v)

恋爱
liàn'ài
fall in love (v)

结婚
jiéhūn
get married (v)

生子
shēngzǐ
have a baby (v)

婚礼 hūnlǐ | wedding

离婚
líhūn
divorce

葬礼
zànglǐ
funeral

词汇 cíhuì • vocabulary

洗礼
xǐlǐ
christening

纪念日
jì'niànrì
anniversary

移民
yímín
emigrate (v)

退休
tuìxiū
retire (v)

死亡
sǐwáng
die (v)

立遗嘱
lìyízhǔ
make a will (v)

出生证明
chūshēng zhèngmíng
birth certificate

婚宴
hūnyàn
wedding reception

蜜月
mìyuè
honeymoon

犹太男孩成人(13岁)仪式
yóutài nánhái chéngrén
(shísānsuì)yíshì
bar mitzvah

节庆 jiéqìng • celebrations

生日聚会
shēngrìjùhuì
birthday party

贺卡
hèkǎ
card

礼物
lǐwù
present

生日
shēngrì
birthday

圣诞节
shèngdànjié
Christmas

节日 jiérì • festivals

逾越节
yúyuèjié
Passover

新年
xīnnián
New Year

狂欢节 / 嘉年华会
kuánghuānjié / jiā'niánhuáhuì
carnival

游行
yóuxíng
procession

斋月
zhāiyuè
Ramadan

缀带
duàndài
ribbon

感恩节
gǎn'ēnjié
Thanksgiving

复活节
fùhuójié
Easter

万圣节
wànshèngjié
Halloween

排灯节
páidēngjié
Diwali

外表 wàibiǎo
appearance

童装 tóngzhuāng • children's clothing

婴儿 yīng'ér • baby

儿童防雪装
értóng fángxuězhuāng
snowsuit

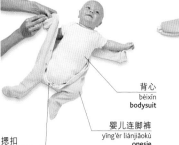

背心
bèixīn
bodysuit

婴儿连脚裤
yīng'ér liánjiăokù
onesie

婴儿睡衣
yīng'érshuìyī
sleeper

连衫裤
liánshānkù
romper

围嘴
wéizuĭ
bib

摁扣
ènkòu
snap

婴儿手套
yīng'érshŏutào
mittens

婴儿鞋
yīng'érxié
booties

绒布尿布
róngbù niàobù
cloth diaper

一次性尿布
yícixìng niàobù
disposable diaper

塑料尿裤
sùliào niàokù
plastic pants

幼儿 yòuér • toddler

T恤衫
Txùshān
T-shirt

工装裤
gōngzhuāngkù
overalls

遮阳帽
zhēyángmào
sun hat

短裤
duănkù
shorts

裙子
qúnzi
skirt

围兜
wéidōu
apron

儿童 értóng • child

连衣裙
liányīqún
dress

风帽
fēngmào
hood

凉鞋
liángxié
sandals

牛仔裤
niúzăikù
jeans

背包
bēibāo
backpack

棒形纽扣
bàngxíng
niŭkòu
toggle

围巾
wéijīn
scarf

滑雪衫
huáxuěshān
parka

长筒橡胶靴
chángtŏng
xiàngjiāoxuē
rain boots

夏天
xiàtiān
summer

雨衣
yŭyī
raincoat

秋天
qiūtiān
fall

粗呢外套
cūní wàitào
duffle coat

冬天
dōngtiān
winter

室内便袍
shìnèi biànpáo
bathrobe

标识
biāoshí
logo

运动鞋
yùndòngxié
athletic shoes

儿童睡衣
értóng shuìyī
nightgown

拖鞋
tuōxié
slippers

睡衣
shuìyī
nightwear

足球球衣
zúqiú qiúyī
soccer uniform

运动服
yùndòngfú
jogging suit

儿童保暖裤
értóngbăonuănkù
leggings

词汇 cíhuì • vocabulary

天然纤维
tiānrán xiānwéi
natural fiber

合成的
héchéngde
synthetic

这可以机洗吗？
zhèkěyĭ jīxĭ ma?
Is it machine-washable?

这适合两岁的孩子穿吗？
zhè shíhé liăngsuìde háizi chuān ma?
Will this fit a two-year-old?

男装 nánzhuāng • men's clothing

衣领
yīlǐng
collar

领带
lǐngdài
tie

腰带
yāodài
belt

翻领
fānlǐng
lapel

扣眼儿
kòuyǎn'ér
buttonhole

袖口
xiùkǒu
cuff

口袋
kǒudài
pocket

上装
shàngzhuāng
jacket

裤子
kùzi
pants

纽扣
niǔkòu
button

西装
xīzhuāng
business suit

外套
wàitào
coat

衬里
chènlǐ
lining

皮鞋
píxié
leather
shoes

词汇 cíhuì • vocabulary

衬衫 chènshān shirt	晨衣 chényī bathrobe	运动服 yùndòngfú jogging suit	长 cháng long
羊毛衫 yángmáoshān cardigan	内衣裤 nèiyīkù underwear	雨衣 yǔyī raincoat	短 duǎn short

有没有大／小一点儿的尺寸？
yǒuméiyǒu dà/xiǎo yìdiǎn de chǐcùn?
Do you have this in a larger/smaller size?

我可以试穿一下吗？
wǒ kěyǐ shìchuān yíxià ma?
May I try this on?

v型领
Vxínglǐng
V-neck

圆领
yuánlǐng
round neck

休闲上衣
xiūxián shàngyī
blazer

粗呢夹克
cūnijiákè
sport coat

马甲
mǎjiǎ
vest

T恤衫
Txùshān
T-shirt

滑雪衫
huáxuěshān
parka

运动衫
yùndòngshān
sweatshirt

防风夹克
fángfēngjiákè
windbreaker

运动裤
yùndòngkù
sweatpants

套头毛衣
tàotóumáoyī
sweater

睡衣
shuìyī
pajamas

背心
bèixīn
tank top

便装
biànzhuāng
casual wear

短裤
duǎnkù
shorts

三角内裤
sānjiǎonèikù
briefs

短衬裤
duǎnchènkù
boxer shorts

袜子
wàzi
socks

女装 nǚzhuāng • women's clothing

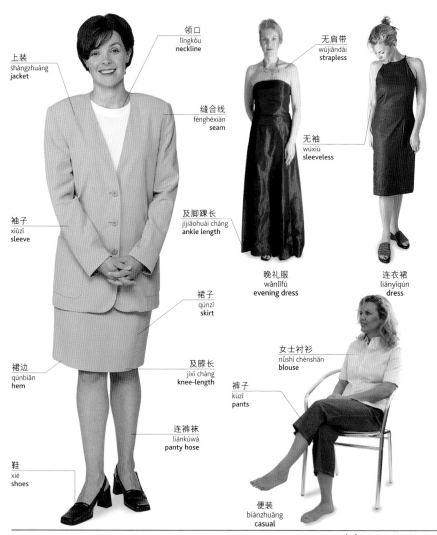

上装
shàngzhuāng
jacket

领口
lǐngkǒu
neckline

无肩带
wújiāndài
strapless

缝合线
fénghéxiàn
seam

无袖
wúxiù
sleeveless

袖子
xiùzǐ
sleeve

及脚踝长
jíjiǎohuái cháng
ankle length

晚礼服
wǎnlǐfú
evening dress

连衣裙
liányīqún
dress

裙子
qúnzǐ
skirt

女士衬衫
nǚshì chènshān
blouse

裙边
qúnbiān
hem

及膝长
jíxī cháng
knee-length

裤子
kùzǐ
pants

连裤袜
liánkùwà
panty hose

鞋
xié
shoes

便装
biànzhuāng
casual

女用内衣 nǚyòng nèiyī • lingerie

婚礼 hūnlǐ • wedding

女用长睡衣
nǚyòng cháng shuìyī
negligée

衬裙
chènqún
slip

肩带
jiāndài
strap

紧身内衣
jǐnshēn nèiyī
bra camisole

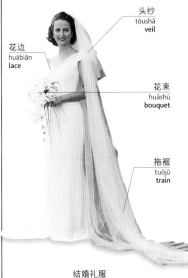

花边
huābiān
lace

头纱
tóushā
veil

花束
huāshù
bouquet

拖裾
tuōjū
train

结婚礼服
jiéhūn lǐfú
wedding dress

女式短上衣
nǚshì duǎnshàngyī
bustier

吊袜带
diàowàdài
garters

长筒袜
chángtǒngwà
stockings

连裤袜
liánkùwà
tights

背心
bèixīn
camisole

胸罩
xiōngzhào
bra

女用内裤
nǚyòng nèikù
panties

女睡衣
nǚshuìyī
nightgown

词汇 cíhuì • vocabulary

束腹 shùfù **corset**	剪裁考究 jiǎncái kǎojiu **tailored**
松紧袜带 sōngjǐn wàdài **suspenders**	露背装 lòubèizhuāng **halter neck**
垫肩 diànjiān **shoulder pad**	内有金属丝的(胸罩) nèiyǒu jīnshǔsīde (xiōngzhào) **underwired**
腰带 yāodài **waistband**	运动胸罩 yùndòng xiōngzhào **sports bra**

配饰 pèishì · accessories

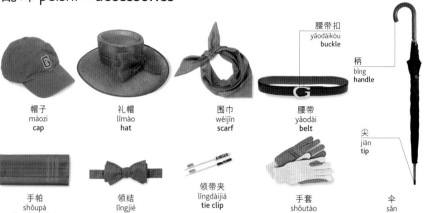

帽子
màozi
cap

礼帽
lǐmào
hat

围巾
wéijīn
scarf

腰带扣
yāodàikòu
buckle

腰带
yāodài
belt

柄
bǐng
handle

尖
jiān
tip

手帕
shǒupà
handkerchief

领结
lǐngjié
bow tie

领带夹
lǐngdàijiá
tie clip

手套
shǒutào
gloves

伞
sǎn
umbrella

首饰 shǒushì · jewelry

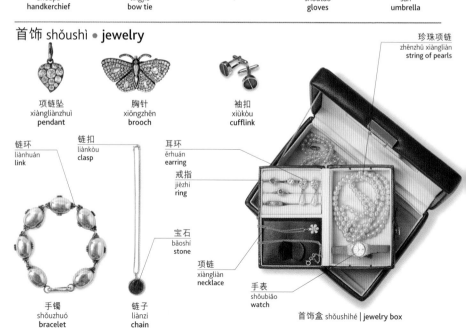

珍珠项链
zhēnzhū xiàngliàn
string of pearls

项链坠
xiàngliànzhuì
pendant

胸针
xiōngzhēn
brooch

袖扣
xiùkòu
cufflink

链环
liànhuán
link

链扣
liànkòu
clasp

耳环
ěrhuán
earring

戒指
jièzhi
ring

宝石
bǎoshí
stone

项链
xiàngliàn
necklace

手表
shǒubiǎo
watch

手镯
shǒuzhuó
bracelet

链子
liànzi
chain

首饰盒 shǒushìhé | **jewelry box**

包 bāo • bags

扣环
kòuhuán
fastening

背带
bēidài
shoulder strap

提手
tíshǒu
handles

钱夹
qiánjiá
wallet

钱包
qiánbāo
purse

挎包
kuàbāo
shoulder bag

旅行袋
lǚxíngdài
duffel bag

公文包
gōngwénbāo
briefcase

手提包
shǒutíbāo
handbag

背包
bēibāo
backpack

鞋 xié • shoes

鞋眼
xiéyǎn
eyelet

鞋带
xiédài
lace

鞋舌
xiéshé
tongue

鞋底
xiédǐ
sole

鞋跟
xiégēn
heel

步行靴
bùxíngxuē
hiking boot

运动鞋
yùndòngxié
athletic shoe

系带鞋
xìdàixié
lace-up

皮鞋
píxié
leather shoe

平底人字拖鞋
píngdǐ rénzi tuōxié
flip-flop

高跟鞋
gāogēnxié
high-heeled shoe

厚底鞋
hòudǐxié
platform shoe

凉鞋
liángxié
sandal

无带便鞋
wúdài biànxié
slip-on

镂花皮鞋
lòuhuā píxié
wingtip

头发 tóufà · hair

发梳
fàshū
comb

梳头
shūtóu
comb (v)

发刷
fàshuā
brush

刷头发 shuātóufà | brush (v)

冲洗
chōngxǐ
rinse (v)

美发师
měifàshī
hair stylist

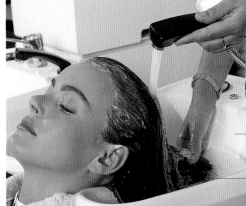

洗头盆
xǐtóupén
sink

顾客
gùkè
client

洗 xǐ | wash (v)

剪
jiǎn
cut (v)

罩衫
zhàoshān
cape

吹干
chuīgān
blow dry (v)

定型
dìngxíng
set (v)

美发用品 měifà yòngpǐn · accessories

吹风机
chuīfēngjī
hairdryer

卷发钳
juǎnfàqián
curling iron

洗发水
xǐfàshuǐ
shampoo

护发素
hùfàsù
conditioner

发胶
fàjiāo
gel

定型水
dìngxíngshuǐ
hairspray

剪刀
jiǎndāo
scissors

发箍
fàgū
hairband

卷发夹子
juǎnfà jiāzi
curler

发卡
fàqiǎ
bobby pin

发型 fàxíng · styles

丝带
sīdài
ribbon

马尾辫	麻花辫	法式盘头	发髻	小辫
mǎwěibiàn	máhuābiàn	fǎshì pántóu	fàjì	xiǎobiàn
ponytail	**braid**	**French braid**	**bun**	**pigtails**

女式短发	短发	卷发	烫发	直发
nǚshì duǎnfà	duǎnfà	juǎnfà	tàngfà	zhífà
bob	**crop**	**curly**	**perm**	**straight**

发根
fāgēn
roots

挑染	秃顶	假发
tiāorǎn	tūdǐng	jiǎfà
highlights	**bald**	**wig**

发色 fàsè · colours

金色	深褐色	红褐色	红棕色
jīnsè	shēnhèsè	hónghèsè	hóngzōngsè
blonde	**brunette**	**auburn**	**red**

黑色	灰色	白色	染色的
hēisè	huīsè	báisè	rǎnsède
black	**gray**	**white**	**dyed**

词汇 cíhuì · vocabulary

修剪 xiūjiǎn **trim (v)**	油性(发质) yóuxìng (fàzhì) **greasy**
拉直 lāzhí **straighten (v)**	干性(发质) gānxìng (fàzhì) **dry**
理发师 lǐfàshī **barber**	中性(发质) zhōngxìng (fàzhì) **normal**
头皮屑 tóupíxiè **dandruff**	头皮 tóupí **scalp**
发梢分叉 fàshāo fēnchà **split ends**	发带 fàdài **hair tie**

美容 měiróng • beauty

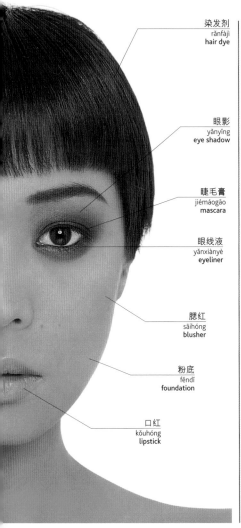

染发剂
rǎnfàjì
hair dye

眼影
yǎnyǐng
eye shadow

睫毛膏
jiémáogāo
mascara

眼线液
yǎnxiànyè
eyeliner

腮红
sāihóng
blusher

粉底
fěndǐ
foundation

口红
kǒuhóng
lipstick

化妆 huàzhuāng • makeup

眉笔
méibǐ
eyebrow pencil

眉刷
méishuā
eyebrow brush

眉夹
méijiá
tweezers

唇彩
chúncǎi
lip gloss

唇刷
chúnshuā
lip brush

唇线笔
chúnxiànbǐ
lip liner

化妆刷
huàzhuāngshuā
brush

遮瑕膏
zhēxiágāo
concealer

化妆镜
huàzhuāngjìng
mirror

粉饼
fěnbǐng
face powder

粉扑
fěnpū
powder puff

粉盒 fěnhé | compact

美容护理 měirónghùlǐ • beauty treatments

面膜
miànmó
facial mask

紫外线浴床
zǐwàixiàn yùchuáng
sunbed

面部护理
miànbùhùlǐ
facial

去死皮
qù sǐpí
exfoliate (v)

热蜡脱毛
rèlàtuōmáo
wax

趾甲护理
zhǐjiǎ hùlǐ
pedicure

化妆用品 huàzhuāng yòngpǐn • toiletries

洁面水
jiémiànshuǐ
cleanser

爽肤水
shuǎngfūshuǐ
toner

保湿霜
bǎoshīshuāng
moisturizer

黑肤霜
hēifūshuāng
self-tanning cream

香水
xiāngshuǐ
perfume

淡香水
dànxiāngshuǐ
cologne

指甲护理 zhǐjia hùlǐ • manicure

洗甲水
xǐjiǎshuǐ
nail polish remover

指甲锉
zhǐjiacuò
nail file

指甲油
zhǐjiayóu
nail polish

指甲剪
zhǐjiajiǎn
nail scissors

指甲刀
zhǐjiadāo
nail clippers

词汇 cíhuì • vocabulary

肤色 fūsè **complexion**	油性(皮肤) yóuxìng(pífū) **oily**	棕褐色皮肤 zōnghèsè pífū **tan**
皮肤白皙 pífū báixī **fair**	敏感性的 mǐngǎnxìngde **sensitive**	纹身 wénshēn **tattoo**
肤色较深 fūsè jiàoshēn **dark**	低变应原的 dībiànyìngyuánde **hypoallergenic**	抗皱 kàngzhòu **antiwrinkle**
干性(皮肤) gànxìng(pífū) **dry**	色调 sèdiào **shade**	棉球 miánqiú **cotton balls**

健康 jiànkāng
health

疾病 jíbìng · illness

发烧 fāshāo | fever

气雾剂
qìwùjì
inhaler

头痛
tóutòng
headache

鼻血
bíxiě
nosebleed

咳嗽
késou
cough

喷嚏
pēnti
sneeze

感冒
gǎnmào
cold

流感
liúgǎn
flu

哮喘
xiàochuǎn
asthma

痉挛
jìngluán
cramps

恶心
ěxin
nausea

水痘
shuǐdòu
chickenpox

皮疹
pízhěn
rash

词汇 cíhuì · vocabulary

中风 zhòngfēng **stroke**	糖尿病 tángniàobìng **diabetes**	湿疹 shīzhěn **eczema**	寒战 hánzhàn **chill**	呕吐 ǒutù **vomit (v)**	腹泻 fùxiè **diarrhea**
血压 xuèyā **blood pressure**	过敏 guòmǐn **allergy**	传染 chuánrǎn **infection**	胃痛 wèitòng **stomachache**	癫痫 diānxián **epilepsy**	麻疹 mázhěn **measles**
心肌梗塞 xīnjī gěngsè **heart attack**	枯草热 kūcǎorè **hayfever**	病毒 bìngdú **virus**	昏厥 hūnjué **faint (v)**	偏头痛 piāntóutòng **migraine**	腮腺炎 sāixiànyán **mumps**

医生 yīshēng · doctor
诊断 zhěnduàn · office visit

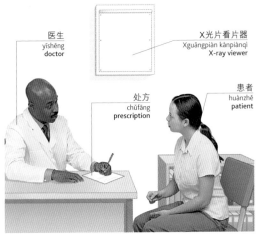

医生
yīshēng
doctor

X光片看片器
Xguāngpiàn kànpiànqì
X-ray viewer

处方
chǔfāng
prescription

患者
huànzhě
patient

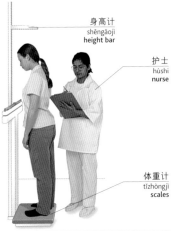

身高计
shēngāojì
height bar

护士
hùshi
nurse

体重计
tǐzhòngjì
scales

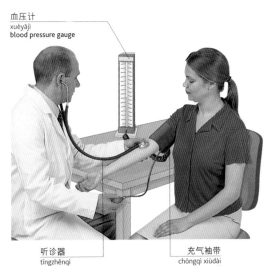

血压计
xuèyājì
blood pressure gauge

听诊器
tīngzhěnqì
stethoscope

充气袖带
chōngqì xiùdài
cuff

词汇 cíhuì · vocabulary

预约
yùyuē
appointment

接种
jiēzhòng
inoculation

诊疗室
zhěnliáoshì
doctor's office

体温计
tǐwēnjì
thermometer

候诊室
hòuzhěnshì
waiting room

体检
tǐjiǎn
medical
examination

我需要看医生。
wǒ xūyào kànyīshēng.
I need to see a doctor.

这儿疼。
zhè'er téng.
It hurts here.

创伤 chuāngshāng · injury

医用吊带
yīyòng
diàodài
sling

颈托
jīngtuō
neck brace

扭伤 niǔshāng | sprain

骨折
gǔzhé
fracture

头颈部损伤
tóujǐngbù sǔnshāng
whiplash

割伤
gēshāng
cut

擦伤
cāshāng
graze

淤伤
yūshāng
bruise

刺伤
cìshāng
splinter

晒伤
shàishāng
sunburn

烧伤
shāoshāng
burn

咬伤
yǎoshāng
bite

蜇伤
zhēshāng
sting

词汇 cíhuì · vocabulary

事故 shìgù **accident**	大出血 dàchūxuè **hemorrhage**	中毒 zhòngdú **poisoning**	他/她没事吧? tā/tā méishì ba? **Will he/she be all right?**
紧急情况 jǐnjí qíngkuàng **emergency**	水泡 shuǐpào **blister**	电击 diànjī **electric shock**	哪里疼? nǎli téng? **Where does it hurt?**
伤口 shāngkǒu **wound**	脑震荡 nǎozhèndàng **concussion**	头部损伤 tóubù sǔnshāng **head injury**	请叫救护车。 qǐngjiào jiùhùchē. **Please call an ambulance.**

急救 jíjiù · **first aid**

药膏
yàogāo
ointment

创可贴
chuàngkětiē
adhesive bandage

安全别针
ānquán biézhēn
safety pin

绷带
bēngdài
bandage

止痛药
zhǐtòngyào
painkillers

消毒湿巾
xiāodú shījīn
antiseptic wipe

镊子
nièzǐ
tweezers

剪刀
jiǎndāo
scissors

消毒剂
xiāodújì
antiseptic

急救箱 jíjiùxiāng | **first aid kit**

纱布
shābù
gauze

包扎
bāozā
dressing

医用夹板 yīyòngjiābǎn | **splint**

橡皮膏
xiàngpígāo
adhesive tape

复苏术
fùsūshù
resuscitation

词汇 cíhuì · **vocabulary**

休克 xiūkè **shock**	脉搏 màibó **pulse**	窒息 zhìxī **choke (v)**
不省人事 bùxǐng rénshì **unconscious**	呼吸 hūxī **breathing**	无菌 wújūn **sterile**

您能帮帮我吗?
nín néng bāngbāng wǒ ma?
Can you help?

你会急救吗?
nǐ huì jíjiù ma?
Do you know first aid?

医院 yīyuàn · hospital

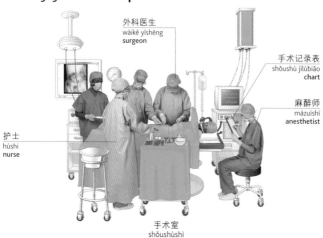

外科医生
wàikē yīshēng
surgeon

手术记录表
shǒushù jìlùbiǎo
chart

麻醉师
mázuìshī
anesthetist

护士
hùshi
nurse

手术室
shǒushùshì
operating room

验血
yànxuè
blood test

注射
zhùshè
injection

X光
Xguāng
X-ray

移动病床
yídòng bìngchuáng
gurney

呼叫按钮
hūjiào ànniǔ
call button

急诊室
jízhěnshì
emergency room

病房
bìngfáng
hospital room

轮椅
lúnyǐ
wheelchair

CT扫描
CT sǎomiáo
scan

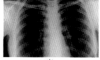

词汇 cíhuì · vocabulary

手术 shǒushù **operation**	出院 chūyuàn **discharged**	探视时间 tànshì shíjiān **visiting hours**	儿童病房 értóng bìngfáng **children's ward**	加护病房 jiāhù bìngfáng **intensive care unit**
收治的 shōuzhìde **admitted**	诊所 zhěnsuǒ **clinic**	产科病房 chǎnkē bìngfáng **maternity ward**	单人病房 dānrén bìngfáng **private room**	门诊病人 ménzhěn bìngrén **outpatient**

科室 kēshì · **departments**

耳鼻喉科
ěrbíhóukē
ear, nose, and throat (ENT)

心脏病科
xīnzàngbìngkē
cardiology

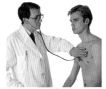

整形外科
zhěngxíngwàikē
orthopedics

妇科
fùkē
gynecology

理疗科
lǐliáokē
physiotherapy

皮肤科
pífūkē
dermatology

儿科
érkē
pediatrics

放射科
fàngshèkē
radiology

外科
wàikē
surgery

产科
chánkē
maternity

精神科
jīngshénkē
psychiatry

眼科
yǎnkē
ophthalmology

词汇 cíhuì · **vocabulary**

神经科 shénjīngkē **neurology**	泌尿科 mìniàokē **urology**	内分泌科 nèifēnmìkē **endocrinology**	病理科 bìnglǐkē **pathology**	结果 jiéguǒ **result**
肿瘤科 zhǒngliúkē **oncology**	矫形外科 jiǎoxíngwàikē **plastic surgery**	转诊 zhuǎnzhěn **referral**	检查 jiǎnchá **test**	专科医生 zhuānkē yīshēng **consultant**

牙医 yáyī • dentist

牙齿 yáchǐ • tooth

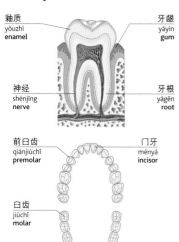

釉质
yòuzhì
enamel

牙龈
yáyín
gum

神经
shénjīng
nerve

牙根
yágēn
root

前臼齿
qiánjiùchǐ
premolar

门牙
ményá
incisor

臼齿
jiùchǐ
molar

犬齿
quǎnchǐ
canine

词汇 cíhuì • vocabulary

牙痛 yátòng toothache	牙钻 yázuàn drill
牙菌斑 yájūnbān plaque	牙线 yáxiàn dental floss
龋齿 qǔchǐ decay	拔牙 báyá extraction
填充物 tiánchōngwù filling	齿冠 chǐguàn crown

检查 jiǎnchá • checkup

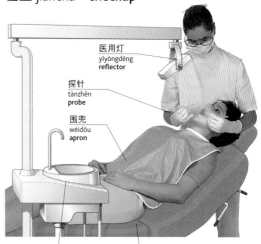

医用灯
yīyòngdēng
reflector

探针
tànzhēn
probe

围兜
wéidōu
apron

漱口池
shùkǒuchí
sink

牙科椅
yákēyǐ
dentist's chair

用牙线洁齿
yòng yáxiàn jiéchǐ
floss (v)

刷牙
shuāyá
brush

畸齿矫正器
jīchǐ jiǎozhèngqì
braces

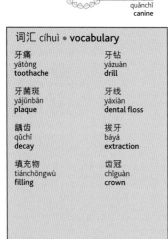

口腔光
kǒuqiāngguāng
dental X-ray

牙片
yápiàn
X-ray film

假牙
jiǎyá
dentures

配镜师 pèijìngshī · optician

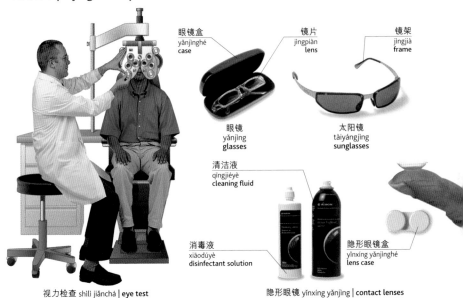

眼镜盒
yǎnjìnghé
case

镜片
jìngpiàn
lens

镜架
jìngjià
frame

眼镜
yǎnjìng
glasses

太阳镜
tàiyángjìng
sunglasses

清洁液
qīngjiéyè
cleaning fluid

消毒液
xiāodúyè
disinfectant solution

隐形眼镜盒
yǐnxíng yǎnjìnghé
lens case

视力检查 shìlì jiǎnchá | eye test

隐形眼镜 yǐnxíng yǎnjìng | contact lenses

眼睛 yǎnjīng · eye

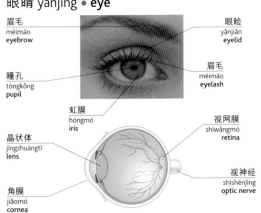

眉毛
méimáo
eyebrow

眼睑
yǎnjiǎn
eyelid

瞳孔
tóngkǒng
pupil

眉毛
méimáo
eyelash

虹膜
hóngmó
iris

视网膜
shìwǎngmó
retina

晶状体
jīngzhuàngtǐ
lens

视神经
shìshénjīng
optic nerve

角膜
jiǎomó
cornea

词汇 cíhuì · vocabulary

视力
shìlì
vision

散光
sǎnguāng
astigmatism

屈光度
qūguāngdù
diopter

远视
yuǎnshì
far-sightedness

眼泪
yǎnlèi
tear

近视
jìnshì
near-sightedness

白内障
báinèizhàng
cataract

双光的
shuāngguāngde
bifocal

怀孕 huáiyùn • pregnancy

护士
hùshi
nurse

妊娠检查
rènshēn jiǎnchá
pregnancy test

B超
Bchāo
scan

胎盘
tāipán
placenta

子宫颈
zǐgōngjǐng
cervix

脐带
qídài
umbilical cord

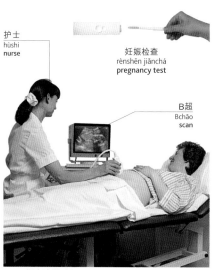

超声波(检查) chāoshēngbō(jiǎnchá) | **ultrasound**

子宫
zǐgōng
uterus

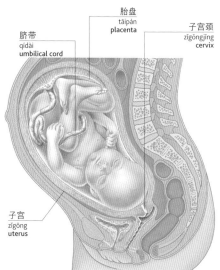

胎儿 tāi'ér | **fetus**

词汇 cíhuì • vocabulary

排卵 páiluǎn **ovulation**	出生前 chūshēngqián **prenatal**	宫缩 gōngsuō **contraction**	扩张术 kuòzhǎngshù **dilation**	分娩 fēnmiǎn **delivery**	逆产 nìchǎn **breech**
怀孕 huáiyùn **conception**	胚胎 pēitāi **embryo**	破羊水 pòyángshuǐ **break waters (v)**	硬膜外麻醉 yìngmó wài mázuì **epidural**	出生 chūshēng **birth**	早产的 zǎochǎnde **premature**
怀孕的 huáiyùnde **pregnant**	子宫 zǐgōng **womb**	羊水 yángshuǐ **amniotic fluid**	外阴切开术 wàiyīn qiēkāishù **episiotomy**	流产 liúchǎn **miscarriage**	妇科医生 fùkē yīshēng **gynecologist**
待产的 dàichǎnde **expecting**	怀孕三个月 huáiyùnsāngèyuè **trimester**	羊水穿刺诊断 yángshuǐ chuāncì zhěnduàn **amniocentesis**	剖腹产 pōufùchǎn **cesarean section**	缝合 fénghé **stitches**	产科医生 chǎnkē yīshēng **obstetrician**

分娩 fēnmiǎn • childbirth

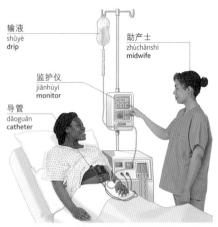

输液
shūyè
drip

助产士
zhùchǎnshì
midwife

监护仪
jiānhùyí
monitor

导管
dǎoguǎn
catheter

引产 yǐnchǎn | induce labor (v)

育婴箱 yùyīngxiāng | incubator

婴儿秤
yīng'érchèng
scales

出生时体重 chūshēngshí tǐzhòng | birth weight

产钳
chǎnqián
forceps

吸杯
xībēi
suction cup

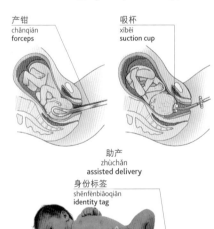

助产
zhùchǎn
assisted delivery

身份标签
shēnfènbiāoqiān
identity tag

新生儿 xīnshēng'ér | newborn baby

哺乳 bǔrǔ • nursing

吸乳器
xīrǔqì
breast pump

哺乳胸罩
bǔrǔ xiōngzhào
nursing bra

喂母乳
wèi mǔrǔ
breastfeed (v)

乳垫
rǔdiàn
pads

替代疗法 tìdài liáofǎ • **alternative therapy**

辅导教师
fǔdǎo jiàoshī
teacher

按摩
ànmó
massage

指压按摩
zhǐyā ànmó
shiatsu

瑜伽 yújiā | **yoga**

垫子
diànzi
mat

脊柱按摩法
jǐzhù ànmófǎ
chiropractic

整骨疗法
zhěnggǔ liáofǎ
osteopathy

足底反射疗法
zúdǐ fǎnshè liáofǎ
reflexology

冥想
míngxiǎng
meditation

顾问
güwèn
counselor

集体治疗
jítǐ zhìliáo
group therapy

灵气疗法
língqì liáofǎ
reiki

针灸
zhēnjiǔ
acupuncture

印度草药疗法
yìndù cǎoyào liáofǎ
ayurveda

催眠疗法
cuīmián liáofǎ
hypnotherapy

精油
jīngyóu
essential oils

本草疗法
běncǎo liáofǎ
herbalism

芳香疗法
fāngxiāng liáofǎ
aromatherapy

顺势疗法
shùnshì liáofǎ
homeopathy

指压疗法
zhǐyā liáofǎ
acupressure

治疗师
zhìliáoshī
therapist

精神疗法
jīngshén liáofǎ
psychotherapy

词汇 cíhuì • vocabulary

营养品 yíngyǎngpǐn supplement	自然疗法 zìrán liáofǎ naturopathy	放松 fàngsōng relaxation	药草 yàocǎo herb
水疗 shuǐliáo hydrotherapy	风水 fēngshuǐ feng shui	压力 yālì stress	水晶疗法 shuǐjīng liáofǎ crystal healing

家居 *jiājū*
home

房屋 fángwū • house

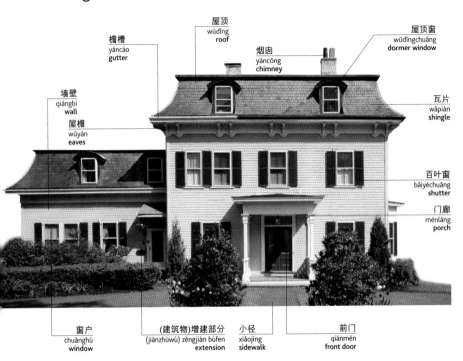

屋顶
wūdǐng
roof

檐槽
yáncáo
gutter

屋顶窗
wūdǐngchuāng
dormer window

烟囱
yāncōng
chimney

墙壁
qiángbì
wall

屋檐
wūyán
eaves

瓦片
wǎpiàn
shingle

百叶窗
bǎiyèchuāng
shutter

门廊
ménláng
porch

窗户
chuānghù
window

(建筑物)增建部分
(jiànzhùwù) zēngjiàn bùfen
extension

小径
xiǎojìng
sidewalk

前门
qiánmén
front door

词汇 cíhuì • vocabulary

独立式 dúlìshì **single-family**	房客 fángkè **tenant**	车库 chēkù **garage**	信箱 xìnxiāng **mailbox**	防盗警报 fángdào jǐngbào **burglar alarm**	租用 zūyòng **rent (v)**
半独立式 bàndúlìshì **duplex**	平房 píngfáng **bungalow**	阁楼 gélóu **attic**	门廊灯 ménlángdēng **porch light**	庭院 tíngyuàn **courtyard**	房租 fángzū **rent**
独栋住宅 dúdòngzhùzhái **townhouse**	地下室 dìxiàshì **basement**	房间 fángjiān **room**	房东 fángdōng **landlord**	楼层 lóucéng **floor**	连排式 liánpáishì **row house**

入口 rùkǒu · entrance

公寓 gōngyù · apartment

扶手
fúshǒu
hand rail

楼梯
lóutī
staircase

楼梯平台
lóutī píngtái
landing

楼梯栏杆
lóutī lángān
banister

门厅
méntīng
hallway

门铃
ménlíng
doorbell

门垫
méndiàn
doormat

门环
ménhuán
door knocker

门链
ménliàn
door chain

锁
suǒ
lock

钥匙
yàoshi
key

门闩
ménshuān
bolt

阳台
yángtái
balcony

公寓楼
gōngyùlóu
apartment building

对讲器
duìjiǎngqì
intercom

电梯
diàntī
elevator

室内系统 shìnèi xìtǒng • utilities

暖器片
nuǎnqìpiàn
radiator

电暖器
diànnuǎnqì
space heater

扇叶
shànyè
blade

风扇
fēngshàn
fan

对流式电暖器
duìliúshì diànnuǎnqì
portable heater

电 diàn • electricity

灯丝
dēngsī
filament

接地
jiēdì
ground prong

灯泡接口
dēngpào jiēkǒu
thread

灯泡 dēngpào | light bulb

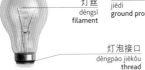

插片
chāpiàn
prong

插头 chātóu | plug

零线
língxiàn
neutral

火线
huǒxiàn
live

电线 diànxiàn | wires

词汇 cíhuì • vocabulary

电压 diànyā voltage	保险丝 bǎoxiǎnsī fuse	插座 chāzuò outlet	直流电 zhíliúdiàn direct current (DC)	停电 tíngdiàn power outage
安培 ānpéi amp	保险盒 bǎoxiǎnhé fuse box	开关 kāiguān switch	变压器 biànyāqì transformer	供电系统 gōngdiàn xìtǒng domestic supply
电力 diànlì power	发电机 fādiànjī generator	交流电 jiāoliúdiàn alternating current (AC)	电表 diànbiǎo electric meter	

中文 zhōngwén • english

管道装置 guǎndào zhuāngzhì • plumbing

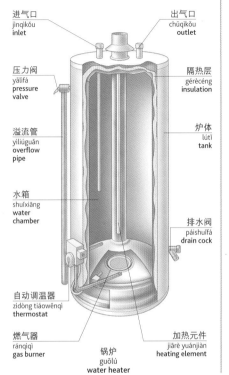

进气口
jìnqìkǒu
inlet

出气口
chūqìkǒu
outlet

压力阀
yālìfá
pressure
valve

隔热层
gérècéng
insulation

溢流管
yìliúguǎn
overflow
pipe

炉体
lútǐ
tank

水箱
shuǐxiāng
water
chamber

排水阀
páishuǐfá
drain cock

自动调温器
zìdòng tiáowēnqì
thermostat

燃气器
ránqìqì
gas burner

锅炉
guōlú
water heater

加热元件
jiārè yuánjiàn
heating element

洗涤槽 xǐdícáo • sink

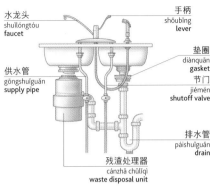

水龙头
shuǐlóngtóu
faucet

手柄
shǒubǐng
lever

供水管
gōngshuǐguǎn
supply pipe

垫圈
diànquān
gasket

节门
jiémén
shutoff valve

排水管
páishuǐguǎn
drain

残渣处理器
cánzhā chǔlìqì
waste disposal unit

抽水马桶 chōushuǐ mǎtǒng • toilet

贮水箱
zhùshuǐxiāng
tank

浮球
fúqiú
float ball

马桶座
mǎtǒngzuò
seat

桶身
tǒngshēn
bowl

污水管
wūshuǐguǎn
waste pipe

垃圾处理 lājīchǔlǐ • waste disposal

瓶子
píngzǐ
bottle

踏板
tàbǎn
pedal

盖子
gàizi
lid

垃圾回收箱
lājī huíshōuxiāng
recycling bin

垃圾桶
lājītǒng
trash can

分类箱
fēnlèixiāng
sorting unit

有机废物
yǒujī fèiwù
organic waste

起居室 qǐjūshì · living room

画
huà
painting

画框
huàkuàng
frame

灯
dēng
lamp

壁灯
bìdēng
wall light

钟表
zhōngbiǎo
clock

天花板
tiānhuābǎn
ceiling

储物柜
chǔwùguì
cabinet

沙发
shāfā
sofa

靠垫
kàodiàn
cushion

茶几
chájī
coffee table

地板
dìbǎn
floor

镜子
jìngzi
mirror

花瓶
huāpíng
vase

壁炉台
bìlútái
mantel

壁炉
bìlú
fireplace

挡火板
dǎnghuǒbǎn
screen

蜡烛
làzhú
candle

书架
shūjià
bookshelf

沙发床
shāfāchuáng
sofabed

地毯
dìtǎn
rug

窗帘
chuānglián
curtain

窗幔
chuāngmàn
sheer curtain

百叶窗
bǎiyèchuāng
Venetian blind

卷帘
juǎnlián
window shade

装饰脚线
zhuāngshì jiǎoxiàn
molding

扶手椅
fúshǒuyǐ
armchair

书房 shūfáng | study

餐厅 cāntīng • dining room

胡椒粉
hújiāofěn
pepper

盐
yán
salt

餐桌
cānzhuō
table

陶瓷餐具
táocí cānjù
crockery

餐具
cānjù
cutlery

椅子
yǐzi
chair

椅背
yǐbèi
back

座位
zuòwèi
seat

椅子腿
yǐzituǐ
leg

词汇 cíhuì • vocabulary

摆桌子 bǎizhuōzǐ set the table (v)	饿 è hungry	午餐 wǔcān lunch	饱 bǎo full	主人 zhǔrén host	请再给我加一些，好吗？ qǐng zàigěi wǒ jiā yìxiē, hǎoma? Can I have some more, please?
上菜 shàngcài serve (v)	桌布 zhuōbù tablecloth	晚餐 wǎncān dinner	一份 yīfèn portion	女主人 nǚzhǔrén hostess	我吃饱了，谢谢。 wǒ chībǎole, xièxiè. I've had enough, thank you.
吃 chī eat (v)	早餐 zǎocān breakfast	餐具垫 cānjùdiàn placemat	饭菜 fàncài meal	客人 kèrén guest	很好吃。 hěn hàochī. That was delicious.

餐具 cānjù • crockery and flatware

马克杯
mǎkèbēi
mug

咖啡杯
kāfēibēi
coffee cup

茶杯
chábēi
teacup

茶匙
cháchí
teaspoon

盘子
pánzi
plate

碗
wǎn
bowl

咖啡壶
kāfēihú
cafetière

茶壶
cháhú
teapot

带柄水壶
dàibǐngshuǐhú
pitcher

蛋杯
dànbēi
egg cup

酒杯
jiǔbēi
wine glass

平底玻璃杯
píngdǐbōlíbēi
tumbler

玻璃器皿
bōlí qìmǐn
glassware

餐巾套环
cānjīn tàohuán
napkin ring

甜点盘
tiándiǎnpán
side plate

正餐用盘
zhèngcān
yòngpán
dinner plate

汤盆
tāngpén
soup bowl

汤匙
tāngchí
soup spoon

餐巾
cānjīn
napkin

餐叉
cānchā
fork

餐具摆放
cānjù bǎifàng
place setting

餐匙
cānchí
spoon

餐刀
cāndāo
knife

厨房 chúfáng · **kitchen**

抽油烟机
chōuyóuyānjī
extractor fan

搁架
gējià
shelves

防溅挡板
fángjiàn dǎngbǎn
backsplash

陶瓷炉台
táocí lútái
ceramic stovetop

水龙头
shuǐlóngtóu
faucet

操作台
cāozuòtái
countertop

洗涤槽
xǐdícáo
sink

烤箱
kǎoxiāng
oven

抽屉
chōutì
drawer

橱柜
chúgui
cabinet

厨房电器 chúfáng diànqì · appliances

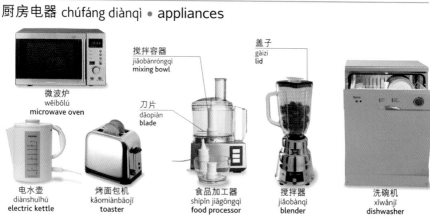

微波炉
wēibōlú
microwave oven

搅拌容器
jiǎobànróngqì
mixing bowl

盖子
gàizi
lid

刀片
dāopiàn
blade

电水壶
diànshuǐhú
electric kettle

烤面包机
kǎomiànbāojī
toaster

食品加工器
shípǐn jiāgōngqì
food processor

搅拌器
jiǎobànqì
blender

洗碗机
xǐwǎnjī
dishwasher

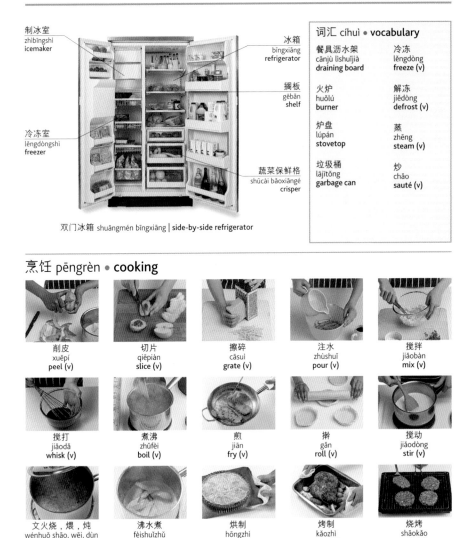

制冰室
zhìbīngshì
icemaker

冰箱
bīngxiāng
refrigerator

搁板
gēbǎn
shelf

冷冻室
lěngdòngshì
freezer

蔬菜保鲜格
shūcài bǎoxiāngé
crisper

词汇 cíhuì • vocabulary

餐具沥水架
cānjù lìshuǐjià
draining board

火炉
huǒlú
burner

炉盘
lúpán
stovetop

垃圾桶
lājītǒng
garbage can

冷冻
lěngdòng
freeze (v)

解冻
jiědòng
defrost (v)

蒸
zhēng
steam (v)

炒
chǎo
sauté (v)

双门冰箱 shuāngmén bīngxiāng | side-by-side refrigerator

烹饪 pēngrèn • cooking

削皮
xuēpí
peel (v)

切片
qiēpiàn
slice (v)

擦碎
cāsuì
grate (v)

注水
zhùshuǐ
pour (v)

搅拌
jiǎobàn
mix (v)

搅打
jiǎodǎ
whisk (v)

煮沸
zhǔfèi
boil (v)

煎
jiān
fry (v)

擀
gǎn
roll (v)

搅动
jiǎodòng
stir (v)

文火烧，煨，炖
wénhuǒ shāo, wēi, dùn
simmer (v)

沸水煮
fèishuǐzhǔ
poach (v)

烘制
hōngzhì
bake (v)

烤制
kǎozhì
roast (v)

烧烤
shāokǎo
grill (v)

厨具 chújù • kitchenware

案板
ànbǎn
cutting board

面包刀
miànbāodāo
bread knife

厨刀
chúdāo
kitchen knife

切肉刀
qiēròudāo
cleaver

磨刀器
módāoqì
knife sharpener

松肉槌
sōngròuchuí
meat tenderizer

串肉扦
chuànròuqiān
skewer

研杵
yánchǔ
pestle

削皮刀
xuēpídāo
peeler

苹果去核器
píngguǒ qùhéqì
apple corer

礤床
cǎchuáng
grater

研钵
yánbō
mortar

捣泥器
dǎoníqì
masher

开罐器
kāiguànqì
can opener

开瓶器
kāipíngqì
bottle opener

压蒜器
yāsuànqì
garlic press

分餐匙
fèncānchí
serving spoon

煎鱼铲
jiānyúchǎn
food turner

滤锅
lǜguō
colander

刮铲
guāchǎn
spatula

木勺
mùsháo
wooden spoon

漏勺
lòusháo
slotted spoon

长柄勺
chángbǐngsháo
ladle

切肉叉
qiēròuchā
carving fork

深口圆匙
shēnkǒu yuánchí
scoop

打蛋器
dǎdànqì
whisk

滤网
lǜwǎng
strainer

锅盖
guōgài
lid

不粘锅
bùzhānguō
non-stick

煎锅
jiānguō
frying pan

长柄深平底锅
chángbǐng shēn píngdǐguō
saucepan

烤架盘
kǎojiàpán
grill pan

炒锅
chǎoguō
wok

陶制炖锅
táozhìdùnguō
earthenware dish

玻璃
bōlí
glass

耐热
nàirè
ovenproof

搅拌碗
jiǎobànwǎn
mixing bowl

雪花酥模子
xuěhuāsū múzi
soufflé dish

烘烤菜肴盘
hōngkǎo càiyáopán
gratin dish

干酪蛋糕模
gānlào dàngāomú
ramekin

砂锅
shāguō
casserole dish

蛋糕制作 dàngāo zhìzuò • baking cakes

秤
chèng
scales

量壶
liánghú
measuring jug

蛋糕烤模
dàngāo kǎomú
cake tin

馅饼烤模
xiànbǐng kǎomú
pie tin

奶油蛋糕烤模
nǎiyóudàngāo kǎomú
flan tin

面粉刷 miànfěnshuā
pastry brush

擀面杖 gǎnmiànzhàng | rolling pin

蛋糕裱花袋 dàngāo
biǎohuādài | piping bag

松饼烤盘
sōngbing kǎopán
muffin tray

烤盘
kǎopán
baking tray

冷却架
lěngquèjià
cooling rack

烤箱手套
kǎoxiāng shǒutào
oven glove

围裙
wéiqún
apron

卧室 wòshì · **bedroom**

衣橱
yīchú
wardrobe

床头灯
chuángtóudēng
bedside lamp

床头板
chuángtóubǎn
headboard

床头柜
chuángtóugui
nightstand

五斗橱
wǔdǒuchú
chest of drawers

抽屉
chōuti
drawer

床
chuáng
bed

床垫
chuángdiàn
mattress

床罩
chuángzhào
bedspread

枕头
zhěntóu
pillow

暖水袋
nuǎnshuǐdài
hot-water bottle

时钟收音机
shízhōng shōuyīnjī
clock radio

闹钟
nàozhōng
alarm clock

纸巾盒
zhǐjīnhé
box of tissues

衣架
yījià
coathanger

床上用品 chuángshàng yòngpǐn • bed linen

枕套
zhěntào
pillowcase

床单
chuángdān
sheet

床帷
chuángwéi
dust ruffle

镜子
jìngzi
mirror

梳妆台
shūzhuāngtái
dressing table

羽绒被
yǔróngbèi
comforter

棉被
miánbèi
quilt

毯子
tǎnzi
blanket

地板
dìbǎn
floor

词汇 cíhuì • vocabulary

单人床 dānrénchuáng **twin bed**	床脚板 chuángjiǎobǎn **footboard**	失眠 shīmián **insomnia**	醒来 xǐnglái **wake up (v)**	设定闹钟 shèdìng nàozhōng **set the alarm (v)**
双人床 shuāngrénchuáng **full bed**	弹簧 tánhuáng **spring**	上床睡觉 shàngchuáng shuìjiào **go to bed (v)**	起床 qǐchuáng **get up (v)**	打鼾 dǎhān **snore (v)**
电热毯 diànrètǎn **electric blanket**	地毯 dìtǎn **carpet**	入睡 rùshuì **go to sleep (v)**	整理床铺 zhěnglǐ chuángpù **make the bed (v)**	内嵌式衣橱 nèiqiànshì yīchú **closet**

浴室 yùshì • bathroom

毛巾架
máojīnjià
towel bar

淋浴隔门
línyù gémén
shower door

冷水龙头
lěngshuǐ lóngtóu
cold faucet

热水龙头
rèshuǐ lóngtóu
hot faucet

淋浴喷头
línyù pēntóu
shower head

洗手池
xǐshǒuchí
washbasin

塞子
sāizi
plug

淋浴
línyù
shower

地漏
dìlòu
drain

马桶座
mǎtǒngzuò
toilet seat

抽水马桶
chōushuǐ mǎtǒng
toilet

马桶刷
mǎtǒngshuā
toilet brush

浴缸
yùgāng
bathtub

净身盆 jìngshēnpén | bidet

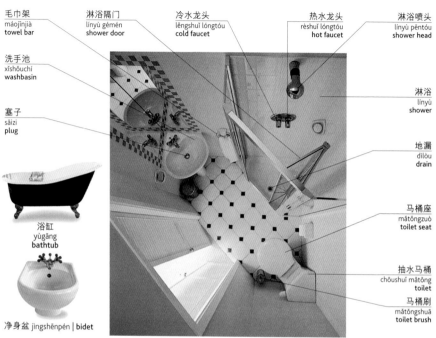

词汇 cíhuì • vocabulary

家用药箱
jiāyòng yàoxiāng
medicine cabinet

浴室防滑垫
yùshì fánghuádiàn
bath mat

卫生纸
wèishēngzhǐ
toilet paper

淋浴隔帘
línyù gélián
shower curtain

洗淋浴
xǐlínyù
take a shower (v)

洗澡
xǐzǎo
take a bath (v)

口腔卫生 kǒuqiāng wèishēng • dental hygiene

牙刷
yáshuā
toothbrush

牙线
yáxiàn
dental floss

牙膏
yágāo
toothpaste

漱口液
shùkǒuyè
mouthwash

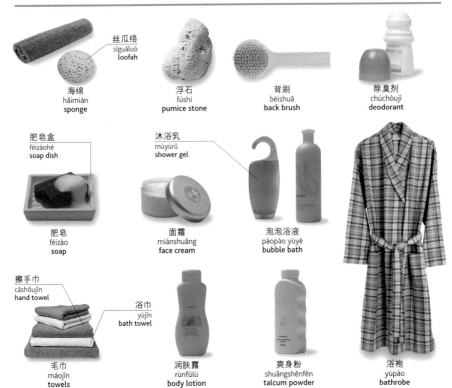

丝瓜络
sīguāluò
loofah

海绵
hǎimián
sponge

浮石
fúshí
pumice stone

背刷
bèishuā
back brush

除臭剂
chúchòujì
deodorant

肥皂盒
féizàohé
soap dish

沐浴乳
mùyùrǔ
shower gel

肥皂
féizào
soap

面霜
miànshuāng
face cream

泡泡浴液
pàopào yùyè
bubble bath

擦手巾
cāshǒujīn
hand towel

浴巾
yùjīn
bath towel

毛巾
máojīn
towels

润肤露
rùnfūlù
body lotion

爽身粉
shuǎngshēnfěn
talcum powder

浴袍
yùpáo
bathrobe

剃须 tìxū • shaving

电动剃须刀
diàndòng tìxūdāo
electric razor

剃须泡沫
tìxūpàomò
shaving foam

一次性剃须刀
yícìxìng tìxūdāo
disposable razor

剃刀刀片
tìdāo dāopiàn
razor blade

须后水
xūhòushuǐ
aftershave

育婴室 yùyīngshì · baby's room

婴儿护理 yīng'ér hùlǐ · baby care

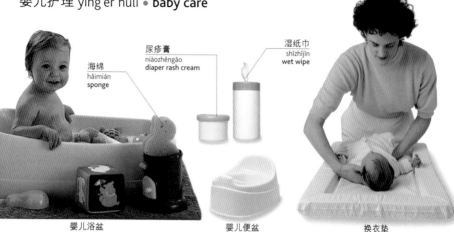

海绵
hǎimián
sponge

尿疹膏
niàozhěngāo
diaper rash cream

湿纸巾
shīzhǐjīn
wet wipe

婴儿浴盆
yīng'ér yùpén
baby bath

婴儿便盆
yīng'ér biànpén
potty

换衣垫
huànyīdiàn
changing mat

睡眠 shuìmián · sleeping

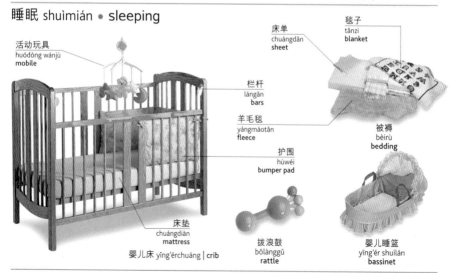

活动玩具
huódòng wánjù
mobile

床单
chuángdān
sheet

毯子
tǎnzi
blanket

栏杆
lángān
bars

羊毛毯
yángmáotǎn
fleece

被褥
bèirù
bedding

护围
hùwéi
bumper pad

床垫
chuángdiàn
mattress

婴儿床 yīng'érchuáng | **crib**

拨浪鼓
bōlànggǔ
rattle

婴儿睡篮
yīng'ér shuìlán
bassinet

游戏 yóuxì • playing

娃娃
wáwa
doll

长毛绒玩具
chángmáorón gwánjù
soft toy

娃娃屋
wáwáwū
dollhouse

玩具屋
wánjùwū
playhouse

长毛绒玩具熊
chángmáoróng wánjùxióng
teddy bear

玩具
wánjù
toy

玩具篮
wánjùlán
toy basket

球
qiú
ball

游戏围栏
yóuxì wéilán
playpen

安全 ānquán • safety

儿童安全锁
értóng ānquánsuǒ
child lock

婴儿监视器
yīng'ér jiānshìqì
baby monitor

楼梯门栏
lóutī ménlán
stair gate

饮食 yǐnshí • eating

高脚椅
gāojiǎoyǐ
high chair

奶嘴
nǎizuǐ
nipple

婴儿杯
yīng'érbēi
drinking cup

奶瓶
nǎipíng
bottle

外出 wàichū • going out

遮阳篷
zhēyángpéng
hood

折叠式婴儿车
zhédiéshì yīng'érchē
stroller

卧式婴儿车
wòshìyíng'érchē
baby carriage

尿布
niàobù
diaper

手提式婴儿床
shǒutíshì yīng'érchuáng
infant carrier

婴儿衣物袋
yīng'ér yīwùdài
diaper bag

婴儿吊带
yīng'ér diàodài
baby sling

洗衣间 xǐyījiān • utility room

洗涤 xǐdí • laundry

脏衣物
zāngyīwù
dirty laundry

干净衣物
gānjìng yīwù
clean clothes

洗衣篮
xǐyīlán
laundry basket

洗衣机
xǐyījī
washing machine

洗衣干衣机
xǐyī gānyījī
washer-dryer

滚筒式烘干机
gǔntǒngshì hōnggānjī
tumble dryer

衣物篮
yīwùlán
laundry basket

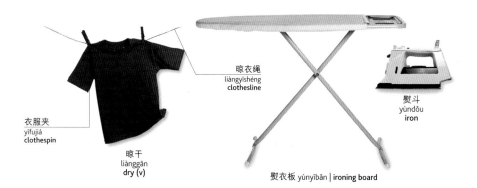

晾衣绳
liàngyīshéng
clothesline

衣服夹
yīfujiá
clothespin

熨斗
yùndǒu
iron

晾干
liànggān
dry (v)

熨衣板 yùnyībǎn | **ironing board**

词汇 cíhuì • vocabulary

装入 zhuāngrù **load (v)**	甩干 shuǎigàn **spin (v)**	熨烫 yùntàng **iron (v)**	洗衣机怎么用? xǐyījī zěnmeyòng? **How do I operate the washing machine?**
漂洗 piǎoxǐ **rinse (v)**	甩干机 shuǎigànjī **spin dryer**	织物柔顺剂 zhīwù róushùnjì **fabric conditioner**	如何设定洗染色/白色衣物? rúhé shèdìng xǐ rǎnsè/báisè yīwù? **What is the setting for colors/whites?**

清洁用具 qīngjiéyòngjù · cleaning equipment

吸管
xīguǎn
suction hose

短柄扫帚
duǎnbǐng sàozhou
brush

簸箕
bòji
dustpan

漂白剂
piǎobáijì
bleach

水桶
shuǐtǒng
pail

去污粉
qùwūfěn
powder

洗涤液
xǐdíyè
liquid

抹布
mābù
dustcloth

吸尘器
xīchénqì
vacuum cleaner

拖把
tuōbǎ
mop

清洁剂
qīngjiéjì
detergent

上光剂
shàngguāngjì
polish

扫除 sǎochú · activities

擦
cā
clean (v)

洗
xǐ
wash (v)

擦拭
cāshì
wipe (v)

刷洗
shuāxǐ
scrub (v)

刮除
guāchú
scrape (v)

长柄扫帚
chángbǐng sàozhou
broom

清扫
qīngsǎo
sweep (v)

除尘
chúchén
dust (v)

上光
shàngguāng
polish (v)

工作间 gōngzuòjiān • workshop

钻夹头
zuànjiátóu
chuck

先端部钻头
xiānduānbù
zuàntóu
drill bit

电池盒
diànchíhé
battery pack

镂花锯
lòuhuājù
jigsaw

充电式电钻
chōngdiànshì diànzuàn
rechargeable drill

电钻
diànzuàn
electric drill

胶枪
jiāoqiāng
glue gun

夹钳
jiáqián
clamp

刃
rèn
blade

台钳
táiqián
vise

打磨机
dǎmójī
sander

圆锯
yuánjù
circular saw

工作台
gōngzuòtái
workbench

木材胶
mùcáijiāo
wood glue

工具架
gōngjùjià
tool rack

槽刨
cáopáo
router

手摇曲柄钻
shǒuyáo
qūbǐngzuàn
bit brace

刨花
bàohuā
wood shavings

电源箱延长线
diànyuánxiāng
yánchángxiàn
extension cord

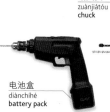

技艺 jìyì · techniques

切割
qiēgē
cut (v)

锯
jù
saw (v)

钻孔
zuànkǒng
drill (v)

钉
dìng
hammer (v)

刨 páo | plane (v)

车削 chēxiāo | turn (v)

雕刻 diāokè | carve (v)

焊锡
hànxī
solder

焊接 hànjiē | solder (v)

材料 cáiliào · materials

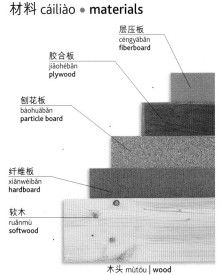

胶合板
jiāohébǎn
plywood

层压板
céngyābǎn
fiberboard

刨花板
bàohuābǎn
particle board

纤维板
xiānwéibǎn
hardboard

软木
ruǎnmù
softwood

木头 mùtóu | wood

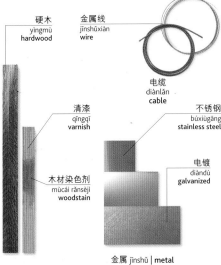

硬木
yìngmù
hardwood

金属线
jīnshǔxiàn
wire

电缆
diànlǎn
cable

清漆
qīngqī
varnish

木材染色剂
mùcái rǎnsèjì
woodstain

不锈钢
búxiùgāng
stainless steel

电镀
diàndù
galvanized

金属 jīnshǔ | metal

工具箱 gōngjùxiāng • toolbox

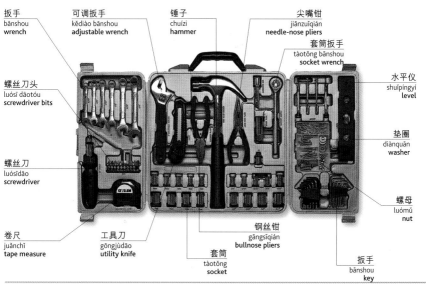

扳手
bānshou
wrench

可调扳手
kědiào bānshou
adjustable wrench

锤子
chuízi
hammer

尖嘴钳
jiānzuǐqián
needle-nose pliers

套筒扳手
tàotǒng bānshou
socket wrench

水平仪
shuǐpíngyí
level

螺丝刀头
luósī dāotóu
screwdriver bits

垫圈
diànquān
washer

螺丝刀
luósīdāo
screwdriver

螺母
luómǔ
nut

卷尺
juǎnchǐ
tape measure

工具刀
gōngjùdāo
utility knife

钢丝钳
gāngsīqián
bullnose pliers

套筒
tàotǒng
socket

扳手
bānshou
key

钻头 zuàntóu • drill bits

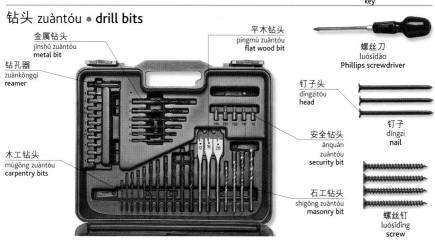

金属钻头
jīnshǔ zuàntóu
metal bit

平木钻头
píngmù zuàntóu
flat wood bit

螺丝刀
luósīdāo
Phillips screwdriver

钻孔器
zuànkǒngqì
reamer

钉子头
dīngzitóu
head

安全钻头
ānquán
zuàntóu
security bit

钉子
dīngzi
nail

木工钻头
mùgōng zuàntóu
carpentry bits

石工钻头
shígōng zuàntóu
masonry bit

螺丝钉
luósīdīng
screw

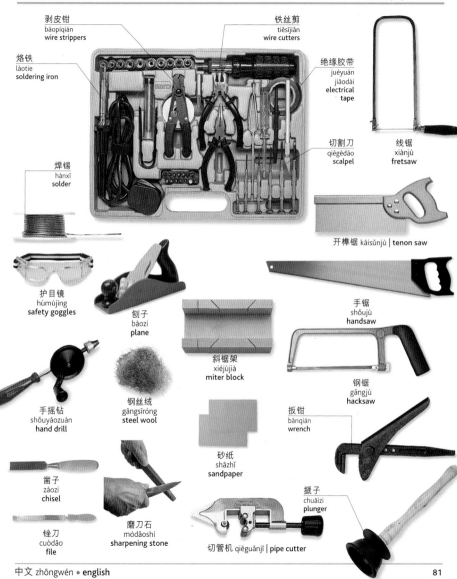

剥皮钳
bāopíqián
wire strippers

铁丝剪
tiěsījiǎn
wire cutters

烙铁
làotie
soldering iron

绝缘胶带
juéyuán
jiāodài
electrical
tape

焊锡
hànxī
solder

切割刀
qiēgēdāo
scalpel

线锯
xiànjù
fretsaw

开榫锯 kāisǔnjù | tenon saw

护目镜
hùmùjìng
safety goggles

刨子
bàozi
plane

斜锯架
xiéjùjià
miter block

手锯
shǒujù
handsaw

手摇钻
shǒuyáozuàn
hand drill

钢丝绒
gāngsīróng
steel wool

钢锯
gāngjù
hacksaw

扳钳
bānqián
wrench

凿子
záozi
chisel

砂纸
shāzhǐ
sandpaper

搋子
chuāizi
plunger

锉刀
cuòdāo
file

磨刀石
módāoshí
sharpening stone

切管机 qiēguǎnjī | pipe cutter

装修 zhuāngxiū · decorating

剪刀
jiǎndāo
scissors

工艺刀
gōngyìdāo
utility knife

铅锤线
qiānchuíxiàn
plumb line

刮刀
guādāo
scraper

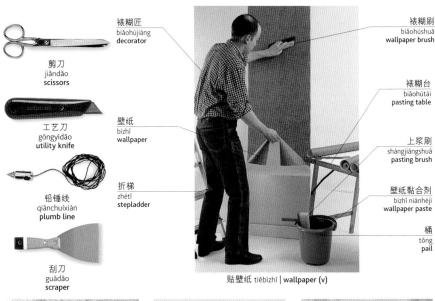

裱糊匠
biǎohújiàng
decorator

壁纸
bìzhǐ
wallpaper

折梯
zhétī
stepladder

裱糊刷
biǎohúshuā
wallpaper brush

裱糊台
biǎohútái
pasting table

上浆刷
shàngjiāngshuā
pasting brush

壁纸黏合剂
bìzhǐ niánhéjì
wallpaper paste

桶
tǒng
pail

贴壁纸 tiēbìzhǐ | wallpaper (v)

铲掉 chǎndiào | strip (v)

抹 mǒ | fill (v)

用砂纸打磨 yòng shāzhǐ dǎmó
sand (v)

粉刷 fěnshuā | plaster (v)

贴(墙纸) tiē(qiángzhǐ) | hang (v)

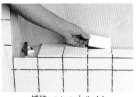

铺砖 pūzhuān | tile (v)

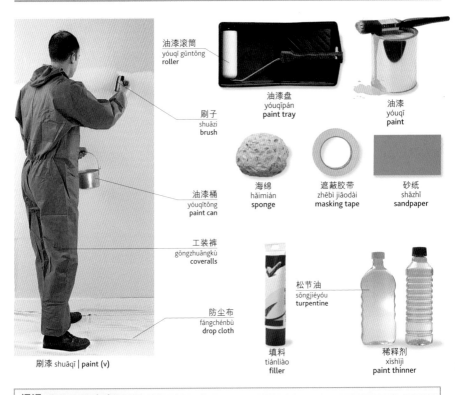

油漆滚筒
yóuqī gǔntǒng
roller

刷子
shuāzi
brush

油漆盘
yóuqīpán
paint tray

油漆
yóuqī
paint

海绵
hǎimián
sponge

遮蔽胶带
zhēbì jiāodài
masking tape

砂纸
shāzhǐ
sandpaper

油漆桶
yóuqītǒng
paint can

工装裤
gōngzhuāngkù
coveralls

松节油
sōngjiéyóu
turpentine

防尘布
fángchénbù
drop cloth

填料
tiánliào
filler

稀释剂
xīshìjì
paint thinner

刷漆 shuāqī | paint (v)

词汇 cíhuì • vocabulary

石膏 shígāo plaster	有光泽 yǒuguāngzé gloss	压花纸 yāhuāzhǐ embossed paper	内涂层 nèitúcéng undercoat	密封剂 mìfēngjì sealant
清漆 qīngqī varnish	无光泽 wúguāngzé mat	衬纸 chènzhǐ lining paper	外涂层 wàitúcéng topcoat	溶剂 róngjì solvent
无光漆 wúguāngqī latex	花样模板 huāyàng múbǎn stencil	底漆 dǐqī primer	防腐剂 fángfǔjì preservative	薄胶浆 báojiāojiāng grout

花园 huāyuán • garden

花园风格 huāyuánfēnggé • garden styles

内院 nèiyuàn | patio garden

法式花园 fǎshì huāyuán | formal garden

乡间花园
xiāngjiān huāyuán
cottage garden

香草花园
xiāngcǎo huāyuán
herb garden

屋顶花园
wūdǐng huāyuán
roof garden

岩石园
yánshíyuán
rock garden

庭院 tíngyuàn | courtyard

水景花园
shuǐjǐng huāyuán
water garden

花园装饰 huāyuán zhuāngshì • garden features

吊篮
diàolán
hanging basket

花格屏 huāgépíng | trellis

藤架
téngjià
arbor

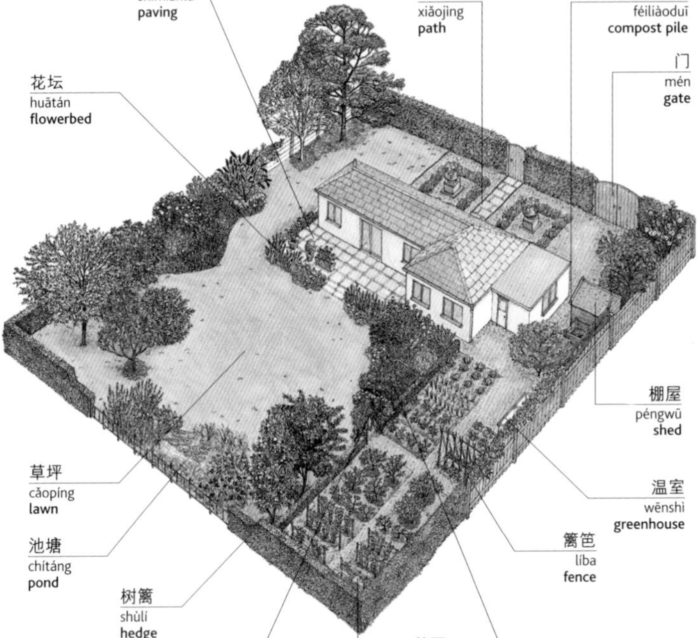

石面路
shímiànlù
paving

小径
xiǎojìng
path

肥料堆
féiliàoduī
compost pile

门
mén
gate

花坛
huātán
flowerbed

棚屋
péngwū
shed

温室
wēnshì
greenhouse

篱笆
líba
fence

草坪
cǎopíng
lawn

池塘
chítáng
pond

树篱
shùlí
hedge

拱门
gǒngmén
arch

菜圃
càipǔ
vegetable garden

绿草带
lǜcǎodài
herbaceous border

土壤 tǔrǎng
● soil

表层土
biǎocéngtǔ
topsoil

沙土
shātǔ
sand

石灰石
shíhuīshí
chalk

淤泥
yūní
silt

黏土
niántǔ
clay

铺面
pùmiàn
deck

喷泉 pēnquán | fountain

花园植物 huāyuánzhíwù • garden plants

植物种类 zhíwùzhǒnglèi • types of plants

一年生(植物)
yìniánshēng (zhíwù)
annual

二年生(植物)
èrniánshēng (zhíwù)
biennial

多年生(植物)
duōniánshēng (zhíwù)
perennial

球茎植物
qiújīng zhíwù
bulb

蕨类植物
juélèi zhíwù
fern

灯心草
dēngxīncǎo
rush

竹子
zhúzi
bamboo

杂草
zácǎo
weed

药草
yàocǎo
herb

水生植物
shuǐshēng zhíwù
water plant

树
shù
tree

落叶(植物)
luòyè (zhíwù)
deciduous

棕榈
zōnglú
palm

针叶树
zhēnyèshù
conifer

常绿(植物)
chánglǜ (zhíwù)
evergreen

灌木修剪
guànmù xiūjiǎn
topiary

高山植物
gāoshān zhíwù
alpine

肉质植物
ròuzhì zhíwù
succulent

仙人掌
xiānrénzhǎng
cactus

盆栽植物
pénzāi zhíwù
potted plant

阴地植物
yīndì zhíwù
shade plant

攀缘植物
pānyuán zhíwù
climber

开花灌木
kāihuā guànmù
flowering shrub

地被植物
dìbèi zhíwù
ground cover

匍匐植物
púfú zhíwù
creeper

观赏(植物)
guānshǎng
(zhíwù)
ornamental

草
cǎo
grass

园艺工具 yuányì gōngjù · garden tools

搂草耙
lōucǎopá
lawn rake

堆肥
duīféi
compost

种子
zhǒngzi
seeds

骨粉
gǔfěn
bone meal

铲
chǎn
spade

叉
chā
fork

长柄修篱剪
chángbǐng xiūlíjiǎn
long-handled shears

耙子
pázi
rake

锄头
chútou
hoe

碎石
suìshí
gravel

草袋
cǎodài
grass bag

马达
mǎdá
motor

把手
bǎshou
handle

浅底篮
qiǎndǐlán
tote

防护盘
fánghùpán
shield

支架
zhījià
stand

剪草器
jiǎncǎoqì
trimmer

剪草机
jiǎncǎojī
lawnmower

独轮手推车
dúlún shǒutuīchē
wheelbarrow

手叉
shǒuchā
hand fork

修枝剪
xiūzhījiǎn
pruners

园艺手套
yuányì shǒutào
gardening gloves

合股线
hégǔxiàn
twine

签条
qiāntiáo
labels

移植铲
yízhíchǎn
trowel

刃
rèn
blade

育苗盘
yùmiáopán
seed tray

捆绑细丝
kǔnbǎng xìsī
twist ties

固枝环
gùzhīhuán
ring ties

支撑杆
zhīchēnggān
canes

修篱剪
xiūlíjiǎn
shears

筛子
shāizǐ
sieve

杀虫剂
shāchóngjì
pesticide

花盆
huāpén
plant pot

橡胶靴
xiàngjiāoxuē
rubber boots

手锯
shǒujù
hand saw

浇灌 jiāoguàn · watering

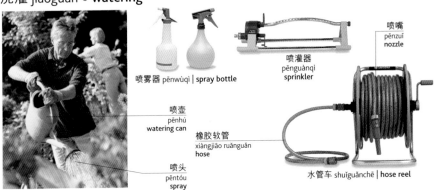

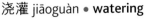

喷雾器 pēnwùqì | spray bottle

喷灌器
pēnguànqì
sprinkler

喷嘴
pēnzuǐ
nozzle

喷壶
pēnhú
watering can

橡胶软管
xiàngjiāo ruǎnguǎn
hose

喷头
pēntóu
spray

水管车 shuǐguǎnchē | hose reel

园艺 yuányì • gardening

草地
cǎodì
lawn

树篱
shùlí
hedge

花坛
huātán
flowerbed

割草机
gēcǎojī
lawnmower

树木支桩
shùmù zhīzhuāng
stake

割草 gēcǎo | mow (v)

铺草皮
pūcǎopí
sod (v)

钉
dīng
spike (v)

耙
pá
rake (v)

修枝
xiūzhī
trim (v)

挖
wā
dig (v)

播种
bōzhǒng
sow (v)

土表施肥
tǔbiǎo shīféi
top-dress (v)

浇水
jiāoshuǐ
water (v)

支撑杆
zhīchēnggān
cane

整枝
zhěngzhī
train (v)

摘除枯花
zhāichú kūhuā
deadhead (v)

喷水
pēnshuǐ
spray (v)

插条
chātiáo
cutting

嫁接
jiàjiē
graft (v)

插技
chājì
propagate (v)

修剪
xiūjiǎn
prune (v)

用杆支撑
yònggǎn zhīchēng
stake (v)

移植
yízhí
transplant (v)

清除杂草
qīngchú zácǎo
weed (v)

加护盖物
jiā hùgàiwù
mulch (v)

收获
shōuhuò
harvest (v)

词汇 cíhuì ● vocabulary

栽培 zāipéi cultivate (v)	园艺设计 yuányì shèjì landscape (v)	施肥 shīféi fertilize (v)	筛 shāi sieve (v)	有机(栽培)的 yǒujī(zāipéi)de organic	秧苗 yāngmiáo seedling	底土 dǐtǔ subsoil
护理 hùlǐ tend (v)	把...种于盆内 bǎ...zhòng yú pénnèi pot (v)	采摘 cǎizhāi pick (v)	松土 sōngtǔ aerate (v)	排水 páishuǐ drainage	肥料 féiliào fertilizer	除草剂 chúcǎojì weedkiller

服务 fúwù
services

急救 jíjiù • emergency services

救护车 jiùhùchē • ambulance

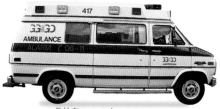

救护车 jiùhùchē | ambulance

担架
dānjià
stretcher

急救人员 jíjiù rényuán | paramedic

警察 jǐngchá • police

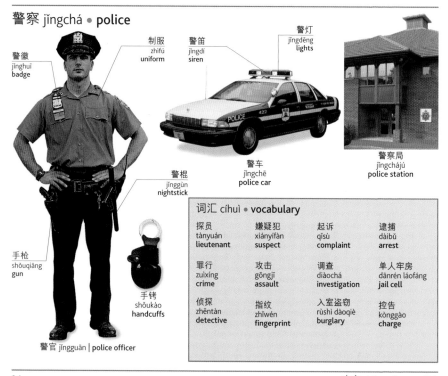

警徽
jǐnghuī
badge

制服
zhìfú
uniform

警笛
jǐngdí
siren

警灯
jǐngdēng
lights

警棍
jǐnggùn
nightstick

警车
jǐngchē
police car

警察局
jǐngchájú
police station

手枪
shǒuqiāng
gun

手铐
shǒukào
handcuffs

警官 jǐngguān | police officer

词汇 cíhuì • vocabulary

探员 tànyuán lieutenant	嫌疑犯 xiányífàn suspect	起诉 qǐsù complaint	逮捕 dàibǔ arrest
罪行 zuìxíng crime	攻击 gōngjī assault	调查 diàochá investigation	单人牢房 dānrén láofáng jail cell
侦探 zhēntàn detective	指纹 zhǐwén fingerprint	入室盗窃 rùshì dàoqiè burglary	控告 kònggào charge

消防队 xiāofángduì · fire department

头盔
tóukuī
helmet

烟
yān
smoke

水龙
shuǐlóng
hose

吊篮
diàolán
basket

消防队员
xiāofángduìyuán
firefighters

水柱
shuǐzhù
water jet

悬臂
xuánbì
boom

消防梯
xiāofángtī
ladder

驾驶室
jiàshǐshì
cab

火情 huǒqíng | fire

消防站
xiāofángzhàn
fire station

消防通道
xiāofángtōngdào
fire escape

消防车
xiāofángchē
fire engine

烟雾报警器
yānwù bàojǐngqì
smoke alarm

火灾警报器
huǒzāi jǐngbàoqì
fire alarm

消防斧
xiāofángfǔ
ax

灭火器
mièhuǒqì
fire extinguisher

消防栓
xiāofángshuān
hydrant

我需要警察/消防队/救护车。 wǒ xūyào jǐngchá/xiāofángduì/ jiùhùchē. **I need the police/fire department/** **an ambulance.**	在…有火情。 zài…yǒu huǒqíng. **There's a fire at…**	发生了事故。 fāshēngle shìgù. **There's been an accident.**	报警! bàojǐng! **Call the police!**

银行 yínháng · bank

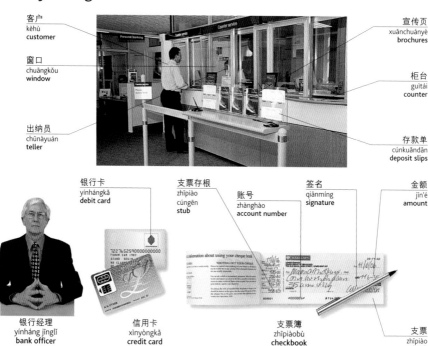

客户
kèhù
customer

窗口
chuāngkǒu
window

出纳员
chūnàyuán
teller

宣传页
xuānchuányè
brochures

柜台
guìtái
counter

存款单
cúnkuǎndān
deposit slips

银行卡
yínhángkǎ
debit card

支票存根
zhīpiào
cúngēn
stub

账号
zhànghào
account number

签名
qiānmíng
signature

金额
jīn'é
amount

银行经理
yínháng jīnglǐ
bank officer

信用卡
xìnyòngkǎ
credit card

支票簿
zhīpiàobù
checkbook

支票
zhīpiào
check

词汇 cíhuì · vocabulary

储蓄 chǔxù savings	抵押贷款 dǐyā dàikuǎn mortgage	付款 fùkuǎn payment	存入 cúnrù deposit (v)	活期存款账户 huóqīcúnkuǎn zhànghù checking account
税 shuì tax	透支 tòuzhī line of credit	直接借记 zhíjiē jièjì automatic payment	银行手续费 yínháng shǒuxùfèi fee	储蓄账户 chǔxù zhànghù savings account
贷款 dàikuǎn loan	利率 lìlǜ interest rate	取款单 qǔkuǎndān withdrawal slip	银行转账 yínháng zhuǎnzhàng electronic transfer	密码 mìmǎ PIN

硬币
yìngbì
coin

纸币
zhǐbì
bill

屏幕
píngmù
screen

插卡口
chākǎkǒu
card slot

按键区
ànjiànqū
keypad

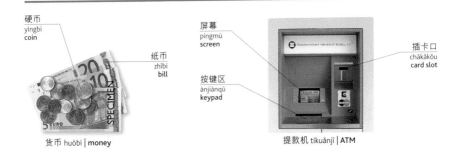

货币 huòbì | money

提款机 tíkuǎnjī | ATM

外币 wàibì • foreign currency

旅行支票
lǚxíng zhīpiào
traveler's check

外币兑换处
wàibì duìhuànchù
currency exchange bureau

汇率
huìlǜ
exchange rate

词汇 cíhuì • vocabulary

兑现
duìxiàn
cash (v)

股份
gǔfèn
shares

货币面额
huòbì miàné
denomination

股息
gǔxī
dividends

佣金
yòngjīn
commission

会计师
kuàijìshī
accountant

投资
tóuzī
investment

有价证券组合
yǒujià zhèngquàn zǔhé
portfolio

证券
zhèngquàn
stocks

股权
gǔquán
equity

我能兑换吗？
wǒ néng duìhuàn ma?
Can I change this, please?

今天的汇率是多少？
jīntiān de huìlǜ shì duōshǎo?
What's today's exchange rate?

金融 jīnróng • finance

股票价格
gǔpiào jiàgé
share price

股票经纪人
gǔpiào jīngjìrén
stockbroker

投资顾问
tóuzī gùwèn
financial advisor

证券交易所 zhèngquàn jiāoyìsuǒ
stock exchange

通讯 tōngxùn • communications

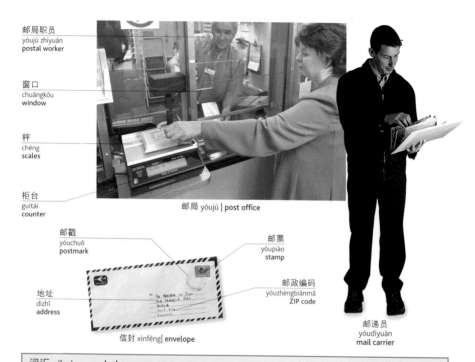

邮局职员
yóujú zhíyuán
postal worker

窗口
chuāngkǒu
window

秤
chèng
scales

柜台
guìtái
counter

邮局 yóujú | post office

邮戳
yóuchuō
postmark

邮票
yóupiào
stamp

地址
dìzhǐ
address

邮政编码
yóuzhèngbiānmǎ
ZIP code

信封 xìnfēng| envelope

邮递员
yóudìyuán
mail carrier

词汇 cíhuì • vocabulary

信 xìn letter	寄信人地址 jìxìnrén dìzhǐ return address	递送 dìsòng delivery	易损坏 yìsǔnhuài fragile	勿折 wùzhé do not bend (v)
航空邮件 hángkōng yóujiàn by airmail	签名 qiānmíng signature	汇票 huìpiào money order	邮袋 yóudài mailbag	此面向上 cǐmiàn xiàngshàng this way up
挂号邮件 guàhào yóujiàn registered mail	(从邮筒中)取信 (cóng yóutǒng zhōng) qǔxìn pickup	邮资 yóuzī postage	电报 diànbào telegram	传真 chuánzhēn fax

邮筒
yóutǒng
mailbox

信箱
xìnxiāng
letter slot

包裹
bāoguǒ
package

速递
sùdì
delivery service

电话 diànhuà • telephone

话机
huàjī
handset

机座
jīzuò
base station

无绳电话
wúshéng diànhuà
cordless phone

答录机
dálùjī
answering machine

可视电话
kěshìdiànhuà
video phone

电话亭
diànhuàtíng
phone booth

按键区
ànjiànqū
keypad

移动电话
yídòng diànhuà
cell phone

听筒
tīngtǒng
receiver

退币口
tuìbìkǒu
coin return

投币电话
tóubìdiànhuà
coin phone

磁卡电话
cíkǎdiànhuà
card phone

词汇 cíhuì • vocabulary

电话号码查询台
diànhuàhào mǎcháxúntái
directory assistance

接听电话
jiētīng diànhuà
answer (v)

接线员
jiēxiànyuán
operator

你能告诉我...的号码吗？
nǐ néng gàosù wǒ...de hàomǎ ma?
Can you give me the number for...?

对方付费电话
duìfāng fùfèi diànhuà
collect call

文字讯息
wénzì xùnxī
text message

占线
zhànxiàn
busy

...的拨叫号码是多少？
...de bōjiào hàomǎ shì duōshǎo?
What is the area code for...?

拨号
bōhào
dial (v)

语音讯息
yǔyīn xùnxī
voice message

断线
duànxiàn
disconnected

旅馆 lǚguǎn • hotel

大厅 dàtīng • lobby

客人
kèrén
guest

房间钥匙
fángjiān yàoshi
room key

留言
liúyán
messages

分类架
fēnlèijià
pigeonhole

接待员
jiēdàiyuán
receptionist

登记簿
dēngjìbù
register

柜台
guìtái
counter

接待总台 jiēdài zǒngtái | reception

行李
xíngli
luggage

行李车
xínglichē
cart

搬运工 bānyùngōng | porter

电梯 diàntī | elevator

房间号码
fángjiān hàomǎ
room number

房间 fángjiān • rooms

单人间
dānrénjiān
single room

双人间
shuāngrénjiān
double room

标准间
biāozhǔnjiān
twin room

专用浴室
zhuān yòngyùshì
private bathroom

服务 fúwù • services

客房清洁服务
kèfáng qīngjié fúwù
maid service

洗衣服务
xǐyī fúwù
laundry service

早餐盘
zǎocānpán
breakfast tray

房间送餐服务 fángjiān sòngcān fúwù | **room service**

小冰箱
xiǎobīngxiāng
minibar

餐厅
cāntīng
restaurant

健身房
jiànshēnfáng
gym

游泳池
yóuyǒngchí
swimming pool

词汇 cíhuì • vocabulary

提供住宿和早餐 tígōng zhùsù hé zǎocān **bed and breakfast**	有空房间吗？ yǒu kōng fángjiān ma? **Do you have any vacancies?**	我要一个房间，住三天。 wǒ yào yīgè fángjiān, zhù sāntiān. **I'd like a room for three nights.**
供应三餐 gōngyìng sāncān **all meals included**	我预定了房间。 wǒ yùdìngle fángjiān. **I have a reservation.**	住一晚多少钱？ zhù yīwǎn duōshǎoqián? **What is the charge per night?**
半食宿 bànshísù **some meals included**	我想要一个单人间。 wǒ xiǎngyào yīgè dānrénjiān. **I'd like a single room.**	我什么时候得腾房？ wǒ shénme shíhòu děi téng fáng? **When do I have to check out?**

购物 gòuwù
shopping

购物中心 gòuwùzhōngxīn • shopping center

大厅
dàtīng
atrium

招牌
zhāopái
sign

电梯
diàntī
elevator

三层
sāncéng
third floor

二层
èrcéng
second floor

自动扶梯
zìdòng fútī
escalator

一层
yīcéng
ground floor

顾客
gùkè
customer

词汇 cíhuì • vocabulary

儿童用品部 értóng yòngpǐnbù **children's department**	购物指南 gòuwù zhǐnán **store directory**	更衣室 gēngyīshì **fitting rooms**	这个多少钱？ zhège duōshǎo qián? **How much is this?**
箱包部 xiāngbāobù **luggage department**	售货员 shòuhuòyuán **sales clerk**	婴儿间 yīng'érjiān **baby changing facilities**	我可以换一件吗？ wǒ kěyǐ huàn yíjiàn ma? **May I exchange this?**
鞋靴部 xiéxuēbù **shoe department**	客户服务 kèhù fúwù **customer services**	卫生间 wèishēngjiān **restrooms**	

百货商店 bǎihuò shāngdiàn · department store

男装
nánzhuāng
menswear

女装
nǚzhuāng
women's wear

女用内衣
nǚyòng nèiyī
lingerie

香水
xiāngshuǐ
perfume

美容用品
měiróng yòngpǐn
beauty

家用纺织品
jiāyòng fǎngzhīpǐn
bed and bath

家具
jiājù
home furnishings

缝纫用品
féngrèn yòngpǐn
notions

厨房用品
chúfáng yòngpǐn
kitchenware

瓷器
cíqì
china

电子产品
diànzǐ chǎnpǐn
electronics

灯具
dēngjù
lighting

体育用品
tǐyù yòngpǐn
sporting goods

玩具
wánjù
toys

文具
wénjù
stationery

食品
shípǐn
groceries

超级市场 chāojí shìchǎng · supermarket

过道
guòdào
aisle

货架
huòjià
shelf

传送带
chuánsòngdài
conveyor belt

收银员
shōuyínyuán
checker

促销海报
cùxiāo hǎibào
specials

收款台 shōukuǎntái | checkout

顾客
gùkè
customer

收款机
shōukuǎnjī
cash register

购物袋
gòuwùdài
shopping bag

食品杂货
shípǐn záhuò
groceries

提手
tíshǒu
handle

条形码
tiáoxíngmǎ
bar code

购物车 gòuwùchē | cart

购物篮 gòuwùlán | basket

条形码扫描器 tiáoxíngmǎ
sǎomiáoqì | scanner

中文 zhōngwén · english

烘烤食品
hōngkǎo shípǐn
bakery

乳制品
rǔzhìpǐn
dairy

早餐麦片
zǎocān màipiàn
breakfast cereals

罐装食品
guànzhuāng shípǐn
canned food

甜食
tiánshí
confectionery

蔬菜
shūcài
vegetables

水果
shuǐguǒ
fruit

肉禽
ròuqín
meat and poultry

鱼
yú
fish

熟食
shúshí
deli

冷冻食品
lěngdòng shípǐn
frozen food

方便食品
fāngbiàn shípǐn
convenience food

饮料
yǐnliào
drinks

家庭日用品
jiātíng rìyòngpǐn
household products

化妆品
huàzhuāngpǐn
toiletries

婴儿用品
yīngér yòngpǐn
baby products

家用电器
jiāyòng diànqì
electrical goods

宠物饲料
chǒngwù sìliào
pet food

杂志 zázhì | **magazines**

药店 yàodiàn • drugstore

牙齿护理
yáchǐ hùlǐ
dental care

妇女保健
fùnǚ bǎojiàn
feminine hygiene

除臭剂
chúchòujì
deodorants

维生素
wéishēngsù
vitamins

药剂室
yàojìshì
pharmacy

药剂师
yàojìshī
pharmacist

止咳药
zhǐkéyào
cough medicine

草药
cǎoyào
herbal remedies

皮肤护理
pífū hùlǐ
skin care

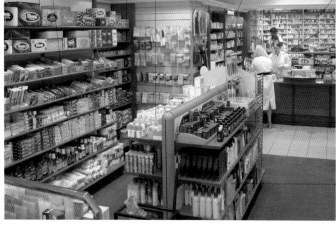

晒后护肤液
shàihòu hùfūyè
after-sun lotion

防晒霜
fángshàishuāng
sunscreen

防晒液
fángshàiyè
sunblock

驱虫剂
qūchóngjì
insect repellent

湿纸巾
shīzhǐjīn
wet wipe

纸巾
zhǐjīn
tissue

卫生巾
wèishēngjīn
sanitary napkin

卫生棉条
wèishēng miántiáo
tampon

卫生护垫
wèishēng hùdiàn
panty liner

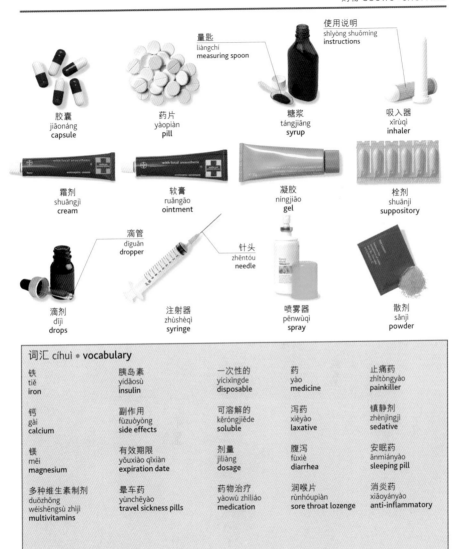

量匙
liàngchí
measuring spoon

使用说明
shǐyòng shuōmíng
instructions

胶囊
jiāonáng
capsule

药片
yàopiàn
pill

糖浆
tángjiāng
syrup

吸入器
xīrùqì
inhaler

霜剂
shuāngjì
cream

软膏
ruǎngāo
ointment

凝胶
níngjiāo
gel

栓剂
shuānjì
suppository

滴管
dīguǎn
dropper

针头
zhēntóu
needle

滴剂
dījì
drops

注射器
zhùshèqì
syringe

喷雾器
pēnwùqì
spray

散剂
sǎnjì
powder

词汇 cíhuì • vocabulary

铁 tiě **iron**	胰岛素 yídǎosù **insulin**	一次性的 yícixìngde **disposable**	药 yào **medicine**	止痛药 zhǐtòngyào **painkiller**
钙 gài **calcium**	副作用 fùzuòyòng **side effects**	可溶解的 kěróngjiěde **soluble**	泻药 xièyào **laxative**	镇静剂 zhènjìngjì **sedative**
镁 měi **magnesium**	有效期限 yǒuxiào qíxiàn **expiration date**	剂量 jìliàng **dosage**	腹泻 fùxiè **diarrhea**	安眠药 ānmiányào **sleeping pill**
多种维生素制剂 duōzhǒng wéishēngsù zhìjì **multivitamins**	晕车药 yùnchēyào **travel sickness pills**	药物治疗 yàowù zhìliáo **medication**	润喉片 rùnhóupiàn **sore throat lozenge**	消炎药 xiāoyányào **anti-inflammatory**

花店 huādiàn • florist

花
huā
flowers

百合
bǎihé
lily

洋槐
yánghuái
acacia

康乃馨
kāngnǎixīn
carnation

盆栽植物
pénzāi zhíwù
potted plant

剑兰
jiànlán
gladiolus

鸢尾
yuānwěi
iris

雏菊
chújú
daisy

菊花
júhuā
chrysanthemum

满天星
mǎntiānxīng
gypsophila

紫罗兰
zǐluólán
stocks

非洲菊
fēizhōujú
gerbera

叶簇
yècù
foliage

玫瑰
méiguī
rose

小苍兰
xiǎocānglán
freesia

花瓶
huāpíng
vase

兰花
lánhuā
orchid

牡丹
mǔdān
peony

花束
huāshù
bunch

茎
jīng
stem

黄水仙
huángshuǐxiān
daffodil

花苞
huābāo
bud

包装纸
bāozhuāngzhǐ
wrapping

郁金香 yùjīnxiāng | tulip

插花 chāhuā • arabrgements

插花 chāhuā • **arrangements**

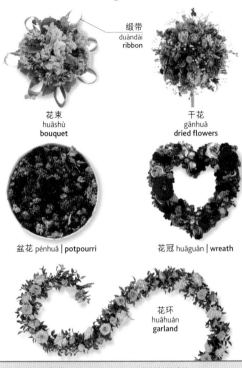

缎带
duàndài
ribbon

花束
huāshù
bouquet

干花
gānhuā
dried flowers

盆花 pénhuā | potpourri

花冠 huāguān | wreath

花环
huāhuán
garland

我能附上留言吗？
wǒ néng fùshàng liúyán ma?
Can I attach a message?

能帮我包一下吗？
néng bāng wǒ bāo yíxià ma?
Can I have them wrapped?

能不能将它们送到...？
néngbùnéng jiāng tāmen
sòngdào...?
Can you send them to....?

这些花能开多久？
zhèxiē huā néng kāi duōjiǔ?
How long will these last?

这些花香吗？
zhèxiē huā xiāng ma?
Are they fragrant?

我想买一束...
wǒ xiǎng mǎi yìshù...
**May I have a bunch of...,
please?**

报刊亭 bàokāntíng • newsstand

香烟
xiāngyān
cigarettes

烟盒
yānhé
pack of cigarettes

火柴
huǒchái
matches

彩票，奖券
cǎipiào, jiǎngquàn
lottery tickets

邮票
yóupiào
stamps

明信片
míngxìnpiàn
postcard

连环画
liánhuánhuà
comic book

杂志
zázhì
magazine

报纸
bàozhǐ
newspaper

吸烟 xīyān • smoking

烟嘴
yānzuǐ
stem

烟锅
yānguō
bowl

烟草
yāncǎo
tobacco

打火机
dǎhuǒjī
lighter

烟斗
yāndǒu
pipe

雪茄
xuějiā
cigar

糖果店 tángguǒdiàn • confectionery

巧克力盒
qiǎokèlihé
box of chocolates

零食
língshí
snack bar

薯片
shǔpiàn
chips

甜食店 tiánshídiàn | candy store

词汇 cíhuì • vocabulary

牛奶巧克力 niúnǎiqiǎokèlì milk chocolate	**焦糖** jiāotáng caramel
黑巧克力 hēiqiǎokèlì dark chocolate	**巧克力球** qiǎokèliqiú truffle
白巧克力 báiqiǎokèlì white chocolate	**饼干** bǐnggān cookie
杂拌糖果 zábàntángguǒ pick-and-mix	**硬糖** yìngtáng hard candy

糖果 tángguǒ • candy

巧克力
qiǎokèlì
chocolate

块状巧克力板
kuàizhuàng qiǎokèlìbǎn
chocolate bar

糖果
tángguǒ
candies

棒棒糖
bàngbàngtáng
lollipop

太妃糖 tàifēitáng | toffee

奶油杏仁糖 nǎiyóuxìngréntáng | nougat

棉花软糖
miánhuāruǎntáng
marshmallow

薄荷糖
bòhétáng
mint

口香糖
kǒuxiāngtáng
chewing gum

软心豆粒糖
ruǎnxīndòulìtáng
jellybean

果味橡皮糖
guǒwèixiàngpítáng
jelly candy

甘草糖
gāncǎotáng
licorice

其他店铺 qítā diànpù • other stores

面包店
miànbāodiàn
bakery

糕点店
gāodiǎndiàn
pastry shop

肉铺
ròupù
butcher shop

水产店
shuǐchǎndiàn
fishmonger

蔬菜水果店
shūcàishuǐguǒdiàn
greengrocer

食品杂货店
shípǐnzáhuòdiàn
grocery store

鞋店
xiédiàn
shoe store

五金店
wǔjīndiàn
hardware store

古董店
gǔdǒngdiàn
antique shop

礼品店
lǐpǐndiàn
gift shop

旅行社
lǚxíngshè
travel agent

首饰店
shǒushìdiàn
jeweler

书店
shūdiàn
bookstore

音像店
yīnxiàngdiàn
record store

酒类专卖店
jiǔlèizhuānmàidiàn
liquor store

宠物商店
chǒngwùshāngdiàn
pet store

家具店
jiājùdiàn
furniture store

时装店
shízhuāngdiàn
boutique

词汇 cíhuì • vocabulary

房地产商
fángdìchǎnshāng
real estate agent

园艺用品店
yuányì yòngpǐndiàn
garden center

干洗店
gānxǐdiàn
dry cleaner

投币式自动洗衣店
tóubìshì zìdòngxǐyīdiàn
laundromat

照相器材店
zhàoxiàng qìcáidiàn
camera store

绿色食品店
lǜsèshípǐndiàn
health food store

艺术品店
yìshùpǐndiàn
art supply store

旧货商店
jiùhuò shāngdiàn
second-hand store

裁缝店
cáifengdiàn
tailor

美发厅
měifàtīng
salon

市场 shìchǎng | **market**

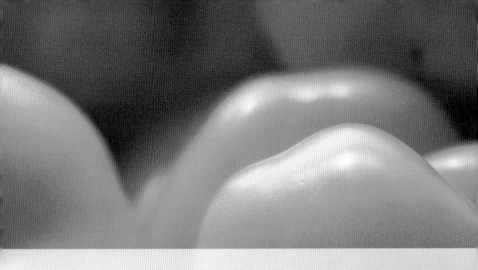

食物 shíwù
food

肉 ròu · meat

羌羊肉
gāoyángròu
lamb

肉店老板
ròudiànlǎobǎn
butcher

吊肉钩
diàoròugōu
meat hook

秤
chèng
scales

磨刀器
módāoqì
knife sharpener

熏肉
xūnròu
bacon

香肠
xiāngcháng
sausages

肝脏
gānzàng
liver

词汇 cíhuì · vocabulary

猪肉 zhūròu pork	野味肉 yěwèiròu venison	下水 xiàshuǐ variety meat	放养的 fàngyǎngde free range	熟肉 shúròu cooked meat
牛肉 niúròu beef	兔肉 tùròu rabbit	腌制的 yānzhìde cured	有机(饲养)的 yǒujī(sìyǎng)de organic	白肉 (指家禽肉、鱼肉等) báiròu (zhǐjiāqínròu, yúròuděng) white meat
小牛肉 xiǎoniúròu veal	牛舌 niúshé tongue	熏制的 xūnzhìde smoked	瘦肉 shòuròu lean meat	红肉(指牛肉、猪肉和羊肉) hóngròu (zhǐniúròu, zhūròuhéyángròu) red meat

切块 qiēkuài • cuts

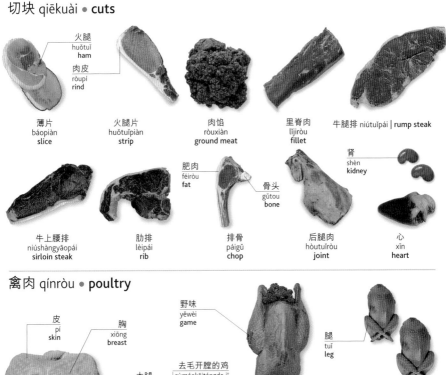

火腿
huǒtuǐ
ham

肉皮
ròupí
rind

薄片
báopiàn
slice

火腿片
huǒtuǐpiàn
strip

肉馅
ròuxiàn
ground meat

里脊肉
lǐjǐròu
fillet

牛腿排 niútuǐpái | rump steak

肥肉
féiròu
fat

骨头
gǔtou
bone

肾
shèn
kidney

牛上腰排
niúshàngyāopái
sirloin steak

肋排
lèipái
rib

排骨
páigǔ
chop

后腿肉
hòutuǐròu
joint

心
xīn
heart

禽肉 qínròu • poultry

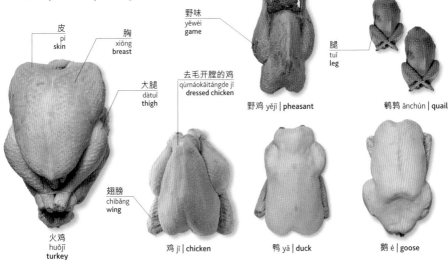

皮
pí
skin

胸
xiōng
breast

野味
yěwèi
game

腿
tuǐ
leg

大腿
dàtuǐ
thigh

去毛开膛的鸡
qùmáokāitángde jī
dressed chicken

野鸡 yějī | pheasant

鹌鹑 ānchún | quail

翅膀
chìbǎng
wing

火鸡
huǒjī
turkey

鸡 jī | chicken

鸭 yā | duck

鹅 é | goose

鱼 yú • fish

去皮虾
qùpíxiā
peeled shrimp

羊鱼
yángyú
red mullet

大比目鱼片
dàbǐmùyúpiàn
halibut fillets

虹鳟鱼
hóngzūnyú
rainbow trout

冰
bīng
ice

鳐鱼翅
yáoyúchì
skate wings

水产店
shuǐchǎndiàn
fish counter

鮟鱇鱼
ānkāngyú
monkfish

鲭鱼
qīngyú
mackerel

鳟鱼
zūnyú
trout

剑鱼
jiànyú
swordfish

鳎鱼
tǎyú
Dover sole

黄盖鲽
huánggàidié
lemon sole

黑线鳕
hēixiànxuě
haddock

沙丁鱼
shādīngyú
sardine

鳐鱼
yáoyú
skate

牙鳕
yáxuě
whiting

海鲈
hǎilú
sea bass

鲑鱼 guīyú | salmon

鳕鱼
xuěyú
cod

鲷鱼
diāoyú
sea bream

金枪鱼
jīnqiāngyú
tuna

海鲜 hǎixiān • seafood

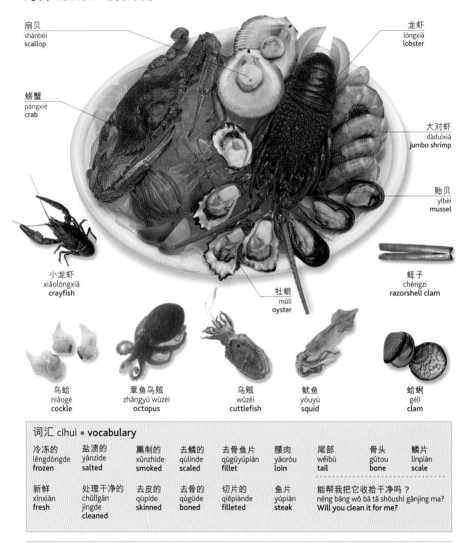

扇贝
shànbèi
scallop

龙虾
lóngxiā
lobster

螃蟹
pángxiè
crab

大对虾
dàduìxiā
jumbo shrimp

贻贝
yíbèi
mussel

小龙虾
xiǎolóngxiā
crayfish

牡蛎
mǔlì
oyster

蛏子
chēngzi
razorshell clam

鸟蛤
niǎogé
cockle

章鱼乌贼
zhāngyú wūzéi
octopus

乌贼
wūzéi
cuttlefish

鱿鱼
yóuyú
squid

蛤蜊
gélí
clam

词汇 cíhuì • vocabulary

冷冻的 lěngdòngde frozen	盐渍的 yánzìde salted	熏制的 xūnzhìde smoked	去鳞的 qùlínde scaled	去骨鱼片 qùgǔyúpiàn fillet	腰肉 yāoròu loin	尾部 wěibù tail	骨头 gǔtou bone	鳞片 línpiàn scale
新鲜 xīnxiān fresh	处理干净的 chǔlǐgān jìngde cleaned	去皮的 qùpíde skinned	去骨的 qùgǔde boned	切片的 qiēpiànde filleted	鱼片 yúpiàn steak	能帮我把它收拾干净吗？ néng bāng wǒ bǎ tā shōushi gānjìng ma? Will you clean it for me?		

蔬菜1 shūcàiyī • vegetables 1

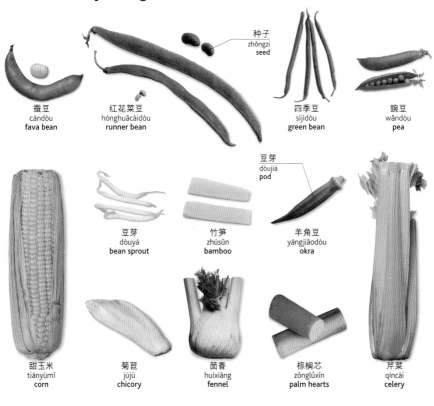

种子
zhǒngzi
seed

蚕豆
cándòu
fava bean

红花菜豆
hónghuācàidòu
runner bean

四季豆
sìjìdòu
green bean

豌豆
wāndòu
pea

豆芽
dòujiá
pod

豆芽
dòuyá
bean sprout

竹笋
zhúsǔn
bamboo

羊角豆
yángjiǎodòu
okra

甜玉米
tiányùmǐ
corn

菊苣
júiù
chicory

茴香
huíxiāng
fennel

棕榈芯
zōnglǘxīn
palm hearts

芹菜
qíncài
celery

词汇 cíhuì • vocabulary

叶 yè leaf	小花 xiǎohuā floret	尖 jiān tip	有机(栽培)的 yǒujī(zāipéi)de organic	这儿卖有机蔬菜吗？ zhè'er mài yǒujīshūcài ma? **Do you sell organic vegetables?**
菜梗 càigěng stalk	果仁 guǒrén kernel	芯 xīn heart	塑料袋 sùliàodài plastic bag	这些是当地产的吗？ zhèxiē shì dāngdìchǎnde ma? **Are these grown locally?**

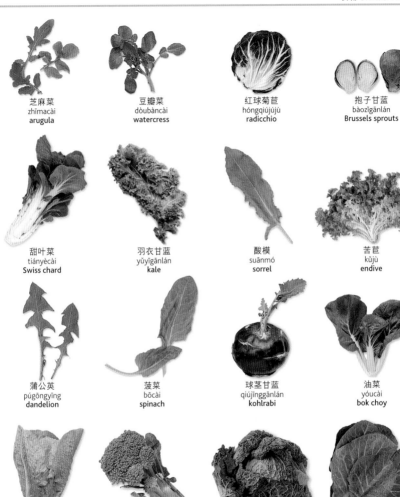

芝麻菜
zhīmacài
arugula

豆瓣菜
dòubàncài
watercress

红球菊苣
hóngqiújújù
radicchio

抱子甘蓝
bàozǐgānlán
Brussels sprouts

甜叶菜
tiányècài
Swiss chard

羽衣甘蓝
yǔyīgānlán
kale

酸模
suānmó
sorrel

苦苣
kǔjù
endive

蒲公英
púgōngyīng
dandelion

菠菜
bōcài
spinach

球茎甘蓝
qiújīnggānlán
kohlrabi

油菜
yóucài
bok choy

莴苣
wōjù
lettuce

西兰花
xīlánhuā
broccoli

卷心菜
juǎnxīncài
cabbage

嫩圆白菜
nènyuánbáicài
greens

蔬菜2 shūcài'èr • vegetables 2

朝鲜蓟
cháoxiǎnjì
artichoke

小红萝卜
xiǎohóngluóbo
radish

花椰菜，菜花
huāyēcài, càihuā
cauliflower

萝卜，芜菁
luóbo, wújīng
turnip

马铃薯
mǎlíngshǔ
potato

洋葱
yángcōng
onion

甜椒
tiánjiāo
sweet pepper

辣椒
làjiāo
chili pepper

西葫芦
xīhúlu
summer squash

词汇 cíhuì • vocabulary

樱桃番茄 yīngtáofānqié **cherry tomato**	块根芹 kuàigēnqín **celeriac**	冷冻的 lěngdòngde **frozen**	苦 kǔ **bitter**	请给我一公斤马铃薯。 qǐng gěi wǒ yì gōngjīn mǎlíngshǔ. **Can I have one kilo of potatoes, please?**
胡萝卜 húluóbo **carrot**	芋头 yùtou **taro root**	生 shēng **raw**	硬 yìng **firm**	每公斤多少钱？ měi gōngjīn duōshǎo qián? **What's the price per kilo?**
面包果 miànbāoguǒ **breadfruit**	木薯 mùshǔ **cassava**	辣 là **hot (spicy)**	果肉 guǒròu **flesh**	那些叫什么？ nàxiē jiào shénme? **What are those called?**
嫩马铃薯 nènmǎlíngshǔ **new potato**	荸荠 bíqí **water chestnut**	甜 tián **sweet**	根 gēn **root**	

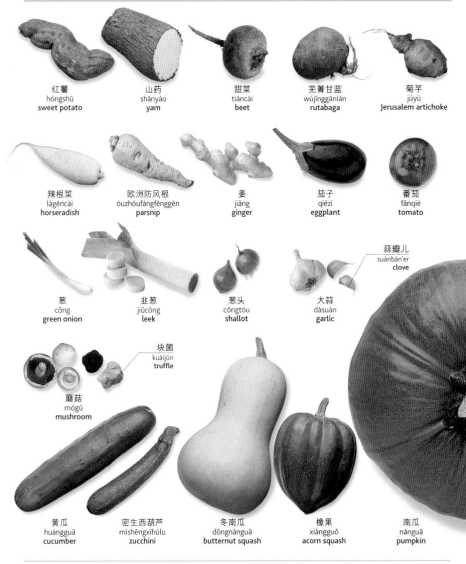

红薯
hóngshǔ
sweet potato

山药
shānyào
yam

甜菜
tiáncài
beet

芜菁甘蓝
wújīnggānlán
rutabaga

菊芋
júyù
Jerusalem artichoke

辣根菜
làgēncài
horseradish

欧洲防风根
ōuzhōufángfēnggēn
parsnip

姜
jiāng
ginger

茄子
qiézi
eggplant

番茄
fānqié
tomato

葱
cōng
green onion

韭葱
jiǔcōng
leek

葱头
cōngtóu
shallot

大蒜
dàsuàn
garlic

蒜瓣儿
suànbàn'er
clove

块菌
kuàijūn
truffle

蘑菇
mógū
mushroom

黄瓜
huángguā
cucumber

密生西葫芦
mìshēngxīhúlu
zucchini

冬南瓜
dōngnánguā
butternut squash

橡果
xiàngguǒ
acorn squash

南瓜
nánguā
pumpkin

水果1 shuǐguǒyī • fruit 1

柑橘类水果 gānjúlèishuǐguǒ • citrus fruit

橙子
chéngzi
orange

细皮小柑橘
xìpíxiǎogānjú
clementine

牙买加丑橘
yámǎijiāchǒujú
ugli fruit

海绵层
hǎimiáncéng
pith

葡萄柚
pútáoyòu
grapefruit

橘瓣儿
júbànér
segment

无核蜜橘
wúhémíjú
satsuma

橘子
júzi
tangerine

外皮
wàipí
zest

酸橙
suānchéng
lime

柠檬
níngméng
lemon

金橘
jīnjú
kumquat

有核水果 yǒuhéshuǐguǒ • stone fruit

桃
táo
peach

油桃
yóutáo
nectarine

杏
xìng
apricot

李子
lǐzi
plum

樱桃
yīngtáo
cherry

梨
lí
pear

苹果
píngguǒ
apple

果篮 guǒlán | basket of fruit

浆果和甜瓜 jiāngguǒ hé tiánguā · berries and melons

草莓
cǎoméi
strawberry

覆盆子
fùpénzǐ
raspberry

黑莓
hēiméi
blackberry

红醋栗
hóngcùlì
red currant

蔓越橘
mànyuèjú
cranberry

黑醋栗
hēicùlì
black currant

蓝莓
lánméi
blueberry

白醋栗
báicùlì
white currant

罗甘莓
luógānméi
loganberry

醋栗
cùlì
gooseberry

甜瓜
tiánguā
melon

葡萄
pútáo
grapes

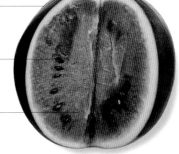

瓜皮
guāpí
rind

瓜籽
guāzǐ
seed

瓜瓤
guāráng
flesh

西瓜
xīguā
watermelon

词汇 cíhuì · vocabulary

大黄 dàihuáng rhubarb	酸 suān sour	脆 cuì crisp	汁液 zhīyè juice	它们熟吗？ tāmen shú ma? Are they ripe?
纤维 xiānwéi fiber	新鲜 xīnxiān fresh	烂 làn rotten	核 hé core	我可以尝一个吗？ wǒ kěyǐ cháng yígè ma? Can I try one?
甜 tián sweet	多汁 duōzhī juicy	果肉 guǒròu pulp	无核 wúhé seedless	它们能放多久？ tāmen néng fàng duōjiǔ? How long will they keep?

水果2 shuǐguǒ 2 · fruit 2

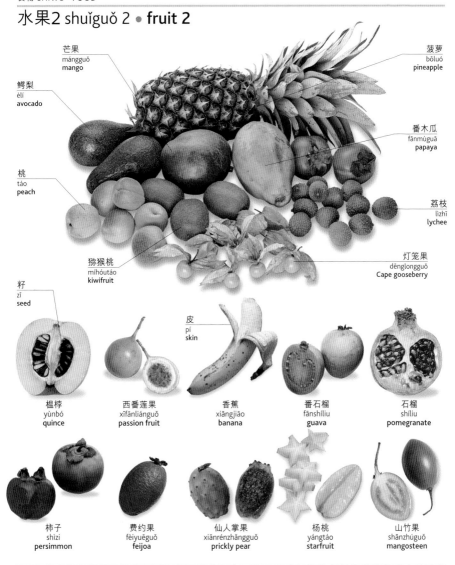

芒果
mángguǒ
mango

菠萝
bōluó
pineapple

鳄梨
èlí
avocado

番木瓜
fānmùguā
papaya

桃
táo
peach

荔枝
lìzhī
lychee

猕猴桃
míhóutáo
kiwifruit

灯笼果
dēnglóngguǒ
Cape gooseberry

籽
zǐ
seed

皮
pí
skin

榅桲
yùnbó
quince

西番莲果
xīfānliánguǒ
passion fruit

香蕉
xiāngjiāo
banana

番石榴
fānshíliu
guava

石榴
shíliu
pomegranate

柿子
shìzi
persimmon

费约果
fèiyuēguǒ
feijoa

仙人掌果
xiānrénzhǎngguǒ
prickly pear

杨桃
yángtáo
starfruit

山竹果
shānzhúguǒ
mangosteen

坚果和干果 jiānguǒ hé gānguǒ · **nuts and dried fruit**

松子
sōngzǐ
pine nut

开心果
kāixīnguǒ
pistachio

腰果
yāoguǒ
cashew

花生
huāshēng
peanut

榛子
zhēnzi
hazelnut

巴西果
bāxīguǒ
Brazil nut

美洲山核桃
měizhōushānhétao
pecan

杏仁
xìngrén
almond

核桃
hétao
walnut

栗子
lìzi
chestnut

澳洲坚果
àozhōujiānguǒ
macadamia

无花果
wúhuāguǒ
fig

椰枣
yēzǎo
date

梅干
méigān
prune

壳
ké
shell

果肉
guǒròu
flesh

椰子
yēzi
coconut

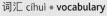
无核葡萄干
wúhépútáogān
seedless raisin

葡萄干
pútáogān
raisin

无核小葡萄干
wúhéxiǎopútáogān
currant

词汇 cíhuì · **vocabulary**

未熟的 wèishúde **green**	硬 yìng **hard**	果仁 guǒrén **kernel**	盐渍的 yánzìde **salted**	烘烤的 hōngkǎode **roasted**	去壳的 qùkéde **shelled**	蜜饯 mìjiàn **candied fruit**
成熟的 chéngshúde **ripe**	软 ruǎn **soft**	脱水的 tuōshuǐde **desiccated**	生 shēng **raw**	应季的 yìngjìde **seasonal**	完整 wánzhěng **whole**	热带水果 rèdàishuǐguǒ **tropical fruit**

谷物及豆类 gǔwùjídòulèi · grains and legumes

谷物 gǔwù · grains

小麦
xiǎomài
wheat

燕麦
yànmài
oats

大麦
dàmài
barley

小米
xiǎomǐ
millet

玉米
yùmǐ
corn

奎奴亚藜
kuínúyàlí
quinoa

米 mǐ · rice

白米
báimǐ
white rice

糙米
cāomǐ
brown rice

菰米
gūmǐ
wild rice

布丁米
bùdīngmǐ
arborio rice

加工过的谷物 jiāgōngguòde gǔwù · processed grains

蒸粗麦粉
zhēngcūmàifěn
couscous

碎粒小麦
suìlìxiǎomài
cracked wheat

粗粒小麦粉
cūlìxiǎomàifěn
semolina

麦麸
màifū
bran

豆类 dòulèi • beans and peas

棉豆
miándòu
butter beans

菜豆
càidòu
haricot beans

红芸豆
hóngyúndòu
red kidney beans

赤豆
chìdòu
adzuki beans

蚕豆
cándòu
fava beans

大豆
dàdòu
soybeans

黑眼豆
hēiyǎndòu
black-eyed peas

斑豆
bāndòu
pinto beans

绿豆
lǜdòu
mung beans

小(粒)菜豆
xiǎo(li)càidòu
flageolet beans

褐色小扁豆
hèsèxiǎobiǎndòu
brown lentils

红豆
hóngdòu
red lentils

青豆
qīngdòu
green peas

鹰嘴豆
yīngzuǐdòu
garbanzos

半粒豆
bànlìdòu
split peas

种子 zhǒngzi • seeds

南瓜籽
nánguāzǐ
pumpkin seed

芥菜籽
jiècàizǐ
mustard seed

葛缕子籽
gélǚzǐzǐ
caraway

芝麻籽
zhīmazǐ
sesame seed

向日葵籽
xiàngrìkuízǐ
sunflower seed

香草和香辛料 xiāngcǎo hé xiāngxīnliào · herbs and spices

香辛料 xiāngxīnliào · spices

香子兰 xiāngzǐlán | vanilla

肉豆蔻
ròudòukòu
nutmeg

肉豆蔻衣
ròudòukòuyī
mace

姜黄根
jiānghuánggēn
turmeric

枯茗，小茴香
kūmíng, xiǎohuíxiāng
cumin

香料包
xiāngliàobāo
bouquet garni

多香果
duōxiāngguǒ
allspice

胡椒粒
hújiāolì
peppercorn

葫芦巴
húlúbā
fenugreek

辣椒末
làjiāomò
chili pepper

颗粒状
kēlìzhuàng
whole

压碎的
yāsuìde
crushed

藏红花
zànghónghuā
saffron

小豆蔻
xiǎodòukòu
cardamom

咖喱粉
gālífěn
curry powder

磨碎的
mósuìde
ground

辣椒粉
làjiāofěn
paprika

片状
piànzhuàng
flakes

大蒜
dàsuàn
garlic

香草 xiāngcǎo • herbs

桂皮
guìpí
sticks

肉桂
ròuguì
cinnamon

柠檬草
níngméngcǎo
lemon grass

丁香
dīngxiāng
cloves

八角，大料
bājiǎo, dàliào
star anise

姜
jiāng
ginger

茴香
huíxiāng
fennel

茴香籽
huíxiāngzǐ
fennel seeds

细香葱
xìxiāngcōng
chives

龙蒿
lónghāo
tarragon

牛至
niúzhì
oregano

薄荷
bòhe
mint

墨角兰
mòjiǎolán
marjoram

香菜
xiāngcài
cilantro

月桂叶
yuèguìyè
bay leaf

百里香
bǎilǐxiāng
thyme

罗勒
luólè
basil

莳萝
shíluó
dill

欧芹
ōuqín
parsley

鼠尾草
shǔwěicǎo
sage

迷迭香
mídiéxiāng
rosemary

瓶装食品 píngzhuāngshípǐn • bottled foods

核桃油
hétaoyóu
walnut oil

杏仁油
xìngrényóu
almond oil

葡萄籽油
pútáozǐyóu
grapeseed oil

软木塞
ruǎnmùsāi
cork

葵花籽油
kuíhuāzǐyóu
sunflower oil

芝麻油
zhīmayóu
sesame seed
oil

榛仁油
zhēnrényóu
hazelnut oil

橄榄油
gǎnlǎnyóu
olive oil

香草
xiāngcǎo
herbs

香油
xiāngyóu
flavored oil

油
yóu
oils

甜酱 tiánjiàng • sweet spreads

广口瓶
guǎngkǒupíng
jar

蜜脾
mìpí
honeycomb

固体蜂蜜
gùtǐfēngmì
set honey

柠檬酱
níngméngjiàng
lemon curd

覆盆子酱
fùpénzǐjiàng
raspberry jam

橘子酱
júzijiàng
marmalade

液体蜂蜜
yètǐfēngmì
clear honey

枫糖浆
fēngtángjiāng
maple syrup

调味品 tiáowèipǐn • condiments and spreads

苹果醋
píngguǒcù
cider vinegar

香脂醋
xiāngzhīcù
balsamic vinegar

瓶
píng
bottle

蛋黄酱
dànhuángjiàng
mayonnaise

英式芥末酱
yīngshì jièmojiàng
English mustard

番茄酱
fānqiéjiàng
ketchup

法式芥末酱
fǎshì jièmojiàng
French mustard

酸辣酱
suānlàjiàng
chutney

麦芽醋
màiyácù
malt vinegar

酒醋
jiǔcù
wine vinegar

醋
cù
vinegar

调味汁
tiáowèizhī
sauce

颗粒芥末酱
kēlì jièmojiàng
whole-grain mustard

密封瓶
mìfēngpíng
canning jar

花生酱
huāshēngjiàng
peanut butter

巧克力酱
qiǎokèlìjiàng
chocolate spread

罐装水果
guànzhuāngshuǐguǒ
preserved fruit

词汇 cíhuì • vocabulary

玉米油
yùmǐyóu
corn oil

菜籽油
càizǐyóu
canola oil

花生油
huāshēngyóu
peanut oil

冷榨油
lěngzhàyóu
cold-pressed oil

植物油
zhíwùyóu
vegetable oil

乳制品 rǔzhìpǐn • dairy products

奶酪 nǎilào • cheese

奶酪皮
nǎilàopí
rind

半硬奶酪
bànyìngnǎilào
semihard cheese

碎奶酪
suìnǎilào
grated cheese

硬奶酪
yìngnǎilào
hard cheese

半软奶酪
bànruǎnnǎilào
semisoft cheese

白干酪
báigānlào
cottage cheese

奶油干酪
nǎiyóugānlào
cream cheese

蓝纹奶酪
lánwénnǎilào
blue cheese

软奶酪
ruǎnnǎilào
soft cheese

鲜奶酪 xiānnǎilào I fresh cheese

奶 nǎi • milk

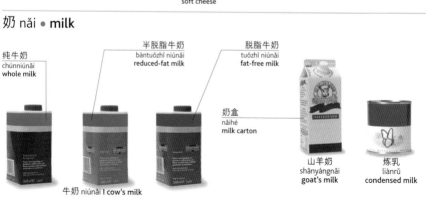

纯牛奶
chúnniúnǎi
whole milk

半脱脂牛奶
bàntuōzhī niúnǎi
reduced-fat milk

脱脂牛奶
tuōzhī niúnǎi
fat-free milk

奶盒
nǎihé
milk carton

牛奶 niúnǎi I cow's milk

山羊奶
shānyángnǎi
goat's milk

炼乳
liànrǔ
condensed milk

黄油
huángyóu
butter

人造黄油
rénzàohuángyóu
margarine

奶油
nǎiyóu
cream

脱脂奶油
tuōzhīnǎiyóu
light cream

高脂肪奶油
gāozhīfángnǎiyóu
heavy cream

掼奶油
guànnǎiyóu
whipped cream

酸奶油
suānnǎiyóu
sour cream

酸奶
suānnǎi
yogurt

冰激凌
bīngjīlíng
ice cream

蛋 dàn • eggs

蛋黄
dànhuáng
yolk

蛋白
dànbái
egg white

蛋壳
dànké
shell

蛋杯
dànbēi
egg cup

煮鸡蛋 zhǔjīdàn **I boiled egg**

鸡蛋
jīdàn
hen's egg

鸭蛋
yādàn
duck egg

鹅蛋
édàn
goose egg

鹌鹑蛋
ānchúndàn
quail egg

词汇 cíhuì • vocabulary

已经过巴氏消毒的 yǐ jīngguò bāshìxiāodúde **pasteurized**	奶昔 nǎixī **milkshake**	盐渍的 yánzìde **salted**	绵羊奶 miányángnǎi **sheep's milk**	乳糖 rǔtáng **lactose**	均质 jūnzhì **homogenized**
未经过巴氏消毒的 wèi jīngguò bāshìxiāodúde **unpasteurized**	冻酸奶 dòngsuānnǎi **frozen yogurt**	无盐的 wúyánde **unsalted**	酪乳 làorǔ **buttermilk**	不含脂肪的 bùhánzhīfángde **fat-free**	奶粉 nǎifěn **powdered milk**

面包和面粉 miànbāo hé miànfěn • **breads and flours**

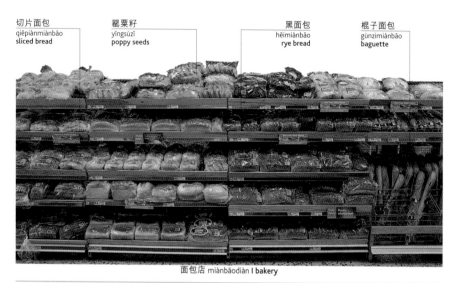

切片面包
qiēpiànmiànbāo
sliced bread

罂粟籽
yīngsùzǐ
poppy seeds

黑面包
hēimiànbāo
rye bread

棍子面包
gùnzimiànbāo
baguette

面包店 miànbāodiàn **I bakery**

制作面包 zhìzuò miànbāo • **making bread**

精白面粉
jīngbáimiànfěn
white flour

黑麦面粉
hēimàimiànfěn
brown flour

全麦面粉
quánmàimiànfěn
whole-wheat flour

酵母
jiàomǔ
yeast

筛撒 shāisǎ **I sift (v)**

生面团
shēng
miàntuán
dough

搅拌 jiǎobàn **I mix (v)**

和面 huómiàn **I knead (v)**

烘制 hōngzhì **I bake (v)**

面包皮
miànbāopí
crust

面包块
miànbāokuài
loaf

切片
qiēpiàn
slice

白面包
báimiànbāo
white bread

黑面包
hēimiànbāo
brown bread

全麦面包
quánmàimiànbāo
whole-wheat bread

麸皮面包
fūpímiànbāo
multigrain bread

玉米面包
yùmǐmiànbāo
corn bread

苏打面包
sūdámiànbāo
soda bread

酸面包
suānmiànbāo
sourdough bread

薄干脆饼
báogāncuìbǐng
flatbread

硬面包圈，百吉饼
yìngmiànbāoquān, bǎijíbǐng
bagel

软面包片
ruǎnmiànbāopiàn I **bun**

小面包
xiǎomiànbāo I **roll**

葡萄干面包
pútáogānmiànbāo
fruit bread

撒籽面包
sāzǐmiànbāo
seeded bread

印度式面包
yìndùshìmiànbāo
naan bread

皮塔饼
pítábǐng
pita bread

薄脆饼干
báocuìbǐnggān
crispbread

词汇 cíhuì • vocabulary

高筋面粉 gāojīnmiànfěn **bread flour**	发起 fāqǐ **rise (v)**	发酵 fājiào **prove (v)**	面包屑 miànbāoxiè **breadcrumbs**	切片机 qiēpiànjī **slicer**
自发粉 zìfāfěn **self-rising flour**	中筋面粉 zhōngjīnmiànfěn **all-purpose flour**	浇糖 jiāotáng **glaze (v)**	细长形面包 xìchángxíngmiànbāo **flute**	面包师 miànbāoshī **baker**

糕点 gāodiǎn • cakes and desserts

长条奶油夹心点心
chángtiáo nǎiyóu jiāxīn diǎnxīn
éclair

奶油
nǎiyóu
cream

夹心
jiāxīn
filling

油酥点心
yóusūdiǎnxīn
choux pastry

奶油泡芙
nǎiyóupàofú
puff pastry

夹心酥
jiāxīnsū
phyllo pastry

水果蛋糕
shuǐguǒ dàngāo
fruit cake

水果馅饼
shuǐguǒ xiànbǐng
fruit tart

蛋白甜饼
dànbái tiánbǐng
meringue

外覆巧克力
wàifù qiǎokèlì
chocolate-covered

松饼
sōngbǐng
muffin

松糕
sōnggāo
sponge cake

蛋糕 dàngāo I cakes

词汇 cíhuì • vocabulary

奶油蛋糕 nǎiyóu dàngāo crème pâtissière	小圆蛋糕 xiǎoyuán dàngāo bun	面团 miàntuán pastry	米饭布丁 mǐfàn bùdīng rice pudding	我可以吃一片吗？ wǒ kěyǐ chī yīpiàn ma? May I have a slice, please?
巧克力蛋糕 qiǎokèlì dàngāo chocolate cake	蛋奶糕 dànnǎigāo custard	切片 qiēpiàn slice	庆祝会 qìngzhùhuì celebration	

巧克力脆片
qiǎokèlì cuìpiàn
chocolate chip

指形饼干
zhǐxíng bǐnggān
ladyfinger

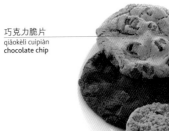

果仁巧克力脆饼
guǒrén qiǎokèlì cuìbǐng
Florentine

蜜饯布丁
mìjiàn bùdīng
trifle

饼干 bǐnggān I cookies

奶油冻，慕思
nǎiyóudòng, mùsī
mousse

果汁冰糕
guǒzhī bīnggāo
sherbet

奶油馅饼
nǎiyóu xiànbǐng
cream pie

焦糖蛋奶
jiāotáng dànnǎi
crème caramel

庆祝蛋糕 qìngzhù dàngāo • celebration cakes

顶层
dǐngcéng
top tier

缎带
duàndài
ribbon

底层
dǐcéng
bottom tier

糖霜
tángshuāng
icing

杏仁糊
xìngrénhú
marzipan

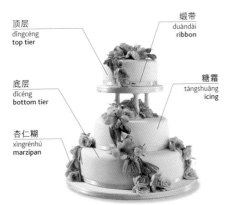

婚礼蛋糕 hūnlǐ dàngāo I wedding cake

装饰
zhuāngshì
decoration

生日蜡烛
shēngrì làzhú
birthday candles

吹熄
chuīxī
blow out (v)

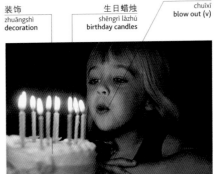

生日蛋糕 shēngrì dàngāo I birthday cake

熟食店 shúshídiàn • delicatessen

辣香肠
làxiāngcháng
spicy sausage

果酱饼
guǒjiàngbǐng
flan

醋
cù
vinegar

油
yóu
oil

生肉
shēngròu
uncooked meat

柜台
guìtái
counter

肉酱
ròujiàng
pâté

萨拉米香肠
sàlāmǐ
xiāngcháng
salami

意大利辣香肠
yìdàlìlà
xiāngcháng
pepperoni

莫泽雷勒干酪
mòzéléilè gānlào
mozzarella

布里干酪
bùlǐ gānlào
Brie

山羊奶酪
shānyáng nǎilào
goat cheese

切达干酪
qiēdá gānlào
cheddar

帕尔马干酪
pà'ěrmǎ gānlào
Parmesan

卡门贝干酪
kǎménbèi gānlào
Camembert

外皮
wàipí
rind

伊丹奶酪
yīdānnǎilào
Edam

蒙切各干酪
méngqiēgè gānlào
Manchego

西式馅饼，派
xīshì xiànbǐng, pài
potpies

小圆面包
xiǎoyuán miànbāo
dinner roll

熟肉
shúròu
cooked meat

绿橄榄
lǜgǎnlǎn
green olive

黑橄榄
hēigǎnlǎn
black olive

辣椒
làjiāo
chili pepper

酱
jiàng
sauce

三明治柜台 sānmíngzhì guìtái | **sandwich counter**

火腿
huǒtuǐ
ham

熏鱼
xūnyú
smoked fish

马槟榔
mǎbīngláng
capers

蒜味腊肠
suànwèilàcháng
chorizo

意大利熏火腿
yìdàlì xūnhuǒtuǐ
prosciutto

填馅橄榄
tiánxiàn gǎnlǎn
stuffed olive

词汇 cíhuì • vocabulary

油渍 yóuzì **in oil**	醋渍的 cùzìde **marinated**	熏制的 xūnzhìde **smoked**
卤制 lǔzhì **in brine**	盐渍的 yánzìde **salted**	风干的 fēnggānde **cured**

请拿一个号。
qǐng ná yīgè hào.
Take a number, please.

我能尝尝吗？
wǒ néng chángcháng ma?
Can I try some of that, please?

请来6片。
qǐng lái liùpiàn.
May I have six slices of that, please?

饮料 yǐnliào • drinks

水 shuǐ • water

瓶装水
píngzhuāng shuǐ
bottled water

碳酸(饮料)
tànsuān (yǐnliào)
sparkling

非碳酸(饮料)
fēitànsuān(yǐnliào)
still

自来水
zìlái shuǐ
tap water

奎宁水
kuíníng shuǐ
tonic water

苏打水
sūdá shuǐ
soda water

矿泉水 kuàngquán shuǐ | **mineral water**

热饮 rèyǐn • hot drinks

茶包
chábāo
teabag

茶叶
cháyè
loose tea

茶
chá
tea

咖啡豆
kāfēidòu
beans

咖啡末
kāfēimò
ground coffee

咖啡
kāfēi
coffee

热巧克力
rèqiǎokèlì
hot chocolate

麦芽饮料
màiyáyǐnliào
malted drink

软(不含酒精的)饮料 ruǎn (bùhán jiǔjīngde) yǐnliào • soft drinks

吸管
xīguǎn
straw

番茄汁
fānqiézhī
tomato juice

葡萄汁
pútáozhī
grape juice

柠檬水
níngméng shuǐ
lemonade

橘子水
júzi shuǐ
orange soda

可乐
kělè
cola

含酒精饮料 hán jiǔjīng yǐnliào • alcoholic drinks

罐
guàn
can

啤酒
píjiǔ
beer

苹果酒
píngguǒjiǔ
hard cider

苦啤酒
kǔpíjiǔ
bitter

浓烈黑啤酒
nóngliè hēipíjiǔ
stout

杜松子酒
dùsōngzǐjiǔ | gin

伏特加酒
fútèjiājiǔ | vodka

威士忌 wēishìjì | whisky

朗姆酒
lǎngmǔjiǔ
rum

白兰地
báilándì
brandy

波尔图葡萄酒
bōěrtú pútáojiǔ
port

雪利酒
xuělìjiǔ
sherry

无糖份的
wútángfènde
dry

堪培利酒
kānpéilìjiǔ
bitters

玫瑰红(葡萄酒)
méiguīhóng
(pútáojiǔ)
rosé (wine)

白(葡萄酒)
bái (pútáojiǔ)
white (wine)

红(葡萄酒)
hóng
(pútáojiǔ)
red (wine)

利口酒
likǒujiǔ
liqueur

龙舌兰酒
lóngshélánjiǔ
tequila

香槟酒
xiāngbīnjiǔ
champagne

葡萄酒 pútáojiǔ | wine

外出就餐 wàichū jiùcān
eating out

咖啡馆 kāfēiguǎn · café

菜单
càidān
menu

遮阳篷
zhēyángpéng
awning

遮阳伞
zhēyángsǎn
umbrella

露天咖啡座
lùtiān kāfēizuò
patio café

侍者
shìzhě
server

咖啡机
kāfēijī
coffee machine

桌子
zhuōzi
table

路边咖啡座 lùbiān kāfēizuò I **sidewalk café**

快餐店 kuàicāndiàn I **snack bar**

咖啡 kāfēi · coffee

牛奶咖啡
niúnǎi kāfēi
coffee with
milk

黑咖啡
hēikāfēi
black coffee

可可粉
kěkěfěn
cocoa powder

泡沫
pàomò
froth

过滤式咖啡
guòlǜshì kāfēi
filter coffee

意式浓缩咖啡
yìshìnóngsuō kāfēi
espresso

卡布奇诺咖啡
kǎbùqínuò kāfēi
cappuccino

冰咖啡
bīngkāfēi
iced coffee

茶 chá • tea

草药茶
cǎoyàochá
herbal tea

菊花茶
júhuāchá
chamomile tea

绿茶
lǜchá
green tea

奶茶
nǎichá
tea with milk

红茶
hóngchá
black tea

柠檬茶
níngméngchá
tea with lemon

薄荷茶
bòhéchá
mint tea

冰茶
bīngchá
iced tea

果汁和奶昔 guǒzhī hé nǎixī • juices and milkshakes

巧克力奶昔
qiǎokèlì nǎixī
chocolate milkshake

草莓奶昔
cǎoméi nǎixī
strawberry
milkshake

咖啡奶昔
kāfēi nǎixī
coffee milkshake

橘子汁
júzizhī
orange juice

苹果汁
píngguǒzhī
apple juice

菠萝汁
bōluózhī
pineapple juice

番茄汁
fānqiézhī
tomato juice

食物 shíwù • food

黑面包
hēimiànbāo
brown bread

一勺量
yìsháoliàng
scoop

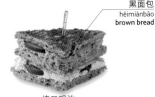

烤三明治
kǎosānmíngzhì
toasted sandwich

沙拉
shālā
salad

冰激凌
bīngjīlíng
ice cream

油酥点心
yóusūdiǎnxīn
pastry

酒吧 jiǔbā • bar

玻璃杯
bōlibēi
glasses

量杯
liángbēi
dispenser

收款机
shōukuǎnjī
cash
register

酒保
jiǔbǎo
bartender

啤酒龙头
píjiǔ lóngtóu
beer tap

咖啡机
kāfēijī
coffee machine

冰桶
bīngtǒng
ice bucket

酒吧椅
jiǔbāyǐ
bar stool

烟灰缸
yānhuīgāng
ashtray

杯垫
bēidiàn
coaster

吧台
bātái
bar counter

开瓶器
kāipíngqì
bottle opener

摇杆
yáogǎn
lever

拔塞钻 básāizuàn I corkscrew

夹钳
jiáqián
tongs

搅拌棒
jiǎobànbàng
stirrer

量杯
liángbēi
measure

鸡尾酒调制器 jīwěijiǔ tiáozhìqì
cocktail shaker

水罐
shuǐguàn
pitcher

冰块
bīngkuài
ice cube

奎宁杜松子酒
kuíníng dùsōngzǐjiǔ
gin and tonic

加水威士忌
jiāshuǐ wēishìjì
Scotch and water

加可乐朗姆酒
jiākělè lǎngmǔjiǔ
rum and Coke

加橙汁伏特加酒
jiāchéngzhī fútèjiājiǔ
screwdriver

马提尼酒
mǎtíníjiǔ
martini

鸡尾酒
jīwěijiǔ
cocktail

葡萄酒
pútáojiǔ
wine

啤酒 píjiǔ I beer

双份
shuāngfèn
double

单份
dānfèn
single

一小杯
yì xiǎobēi
a shot

量杯
liángbēi
measure

不加冰
bù jiābīng
without ice

冰和柠檬
bīng hé níngméng
ice and lemon

加冰
jiābīng
with ice

酒吧小吃 jiǔbā xiǎochī • **bar snacks**

腰果
yāoguǒ
cashews

花生
huāshēng
peanuts

杏仁
xìngrén
almonds

炸薯片 zhàshǔpiàn I potato chips

坚果 jiānguǒ I nuts

橄榄 gǎnlǎn I olives

餐馆 cānguǎn • restaurant

禁烟区
jìnyānqū
nonsmoking
section

餐巾
cānjīn
napkin

助厨
zhùchú
commis chef

餐具摆放
cānjù bǎifàng
table setting

玻璃杯
bōlibēi
glass

主厨
zhǔchú
chef

托盘
tuōpán
tray

厨房 chúfáng | kitchen

侍者 shìzhě | server

词汇 cíhuì • vocabulary

晚餐菜单 wǎncān càidān evening menu	特色菜 tèsècài specials	价格 jiàgé price	小费 xiǎofèi tip	自助餐 zìzhùcān buffet	客人 kèrén customer
酒单 jiǔdān wine list	按菜单点菜 àn càidān diǎncài à la carte	账单 zhàngdān check	含服务费 hán fúwùfèi service included	酒吧 jiǔbā bar	盐 yán salt
午餐菜单 wǔcān càidān lunch menu	甜食小车 tiánshí xiǎochē dessert cart	收据 shōujù receipt	不含服务费 bùhán fúwùfèi service not included	吸烟区 xīyānqū smoking section	胡椒粉 hújiāofěn pepper

菜单
càidān
menu

儿童套餐
értóng tàocān
child's meal

点菜 diǎncài | order (v)

付账 fùzhàng | pay (v)

菜肴 càiyáo • courses

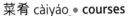

开胃酒
kāiwèijiǔ
apéritif

开胃酒
kāiwèijiǔ
appetizer

汤
tāng
soup

主菜
zhǔcài
entrée

配菜
pèicài
side order

餐叉
cānchā
fork

咖啡匙
kāfēichí
coffee spoon

餐后甜点 cānhòu tiándiǎn
dessert

咖啡 kāfēi | coffee

要一张两人桌。
yào yìzhāng liǎngrénzhuō.
A table for two, please.

能让我看看菜单/酒单吗？
néng ràng wǒ kànkan càidān/jiǔdān ma?
Can I see the menu/winelist, please?

有固定价格菜单吗？
yǒu gùdìng jiàgé càidān ma?
Is there a fixed-price menu?

有素食吗？
yǒu sùshí ma?
Do you have any vegetarian dishes?

请给我账单/收据。
qǐng gěi wǒ zhàngdān/shōujù.
May I have the check/a receipt, please?

我们能分开结账吗？
wǒmen néng fēnkāi jiézhàng ma?
Can we have separate checks?

请问卫生间在哪儿？
qǐngwèn wèishēngjiān zàinǎ'er?
Where are the restrooms, please?

快餐 kuàicān • fast food

汉堡包
hànbǎobāo
burger

吸管
xīguǎn
straw

软饮料
ruǎn yǐnliào
soft drink

薯条
shǔtiáo
french fries

餐巾纸
cānjīnzhǐ
paper napkin

托盘
tuōpán
tray

汉堡套餐 hànbǎotàocān | burger meal

词汇 cíhuì • vocabulary

比萨饼店
bǐsàbǐngdiàn
pizzeria

快餐店
kuàicāndiàn
burger bar

菜单
càidān
menu

店内用餐
diànnèi yòngcān
eat-in

外带
wàidài
carry-out

重新加热
chóngxīn jiārè
reheat (v)

番茄酱
fānqiéjiàng
ketchup

我带走吃。
wǒ dàizǒu chī.
Can I have that to go, please?

你们提供送餐服务吗？
nǐmen tígōng sòngcānfúwù ma?
Do you deliver?

比萨饼
bǐsàbǐng
pizza

价目表
jiàmùbiǎo
price list

罐装饮料
guànzhuāng yǐnliào
canned beverage

送餐 sòngcān | home delivery

食品摊 shípǐntān | street stand

小圆面包
xiǎoyuán
miànbāo
bun

芥末
jièmo
mustard

香肠
xiāngcháng
sausage

汉堡包
hànbǎobāo
hamburger

鸡肉汉堡
jīròu hànbǎo
chicken patty

蔬菜汉堡
shūcài hànbǎo
veggie burger

热狗 règǒu | hot dog

馅
xiàn
filling

三明治
sānmíngzhì
sandwich

总汇三明治
zǒnghuì sānmíngzhì
club sandwich

单片三明治
dānpiàn sānmíngzhì
open-face sandwich

菜卷
càijuǎn
wrap

酱
jiàng
sauce

开胃的
kāiwèide
savory

甜味的
tiánwèide
sweet

装饰配料
zhuāngshìpèiliào
topping

烤肉串
kǎoròuchuàn
kebab

鸡块
jīkuài
chicken nuggets

薄饼卷 báobǐngjuǎn | crepes

鱼和薯条
yú hé shǔtiáo
fish and chips

肋排
lèipái
ribs

炸鸡
zhájī
fried chicken

比萨饼
bǐsàbǐng
pizza

早餐 zǎocān • breakfast

牛奶
niúnǎi
milk

谷类食品
gǔlèishípǐn
cereal

果酱
guǒjiàng
jam

干果
gānguǒ
dried fruit

火腿
huǒtuǐ
ham

奶酪
nǎilào
cheese

薄脆饼干
báocuìbǐnggān
crispbread

自助早餐
zìzhùzǎocān
breakfast buffet

橘子酱
júzijiàng
marmalade

肉酱
ròujiàng
pâté

黄油
huángyóu
butter

果汁
guǒzhī
fruit juice

咖啡
kāfēi
coffee

热巧克力
rèqiǎokèlì
hot chocolate

羊角面包
yángjiǎo miànbāo
croissant

茶
chá
tea

早餐桌 zǎocānzhuō | breakfast table

饮料 yǐnliào | drinks

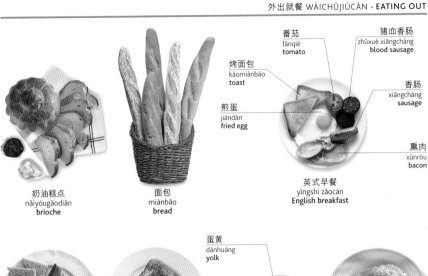

番茄
fānqié
tomato

猪血香肠
zhūxuè xiāngcháng
blood sausage

烤面包
kǎomiànbāo
toast

香肠
xiāngcháng
sausage

煎蛋
jiāndàn
fried egg

熏肉
xūnròu
bacon

英式早餐
yīngshì zǎocān
English breakfast

奶油糕点
nǎiyóugāodiǎn
brioche

面包
miànbāo
bread

蛋黄
dànhuáng
yolk

熏鲱鱼
xūnfēiyú
kippers

法式吐司
fǎshìtǔsī
French toast

煮鸡蛋
zhǔjīdàn
soft-boiled egg

炒鸡蛋
chǎojīdàn
scrambled eggs

奶油
nǎiyóu
cream

果味酸奶
guǒwèisuānnǎi
fruit yogurt

薄煎饼
báojiānbǐng
pancakes

华夫饼
huáfūbǐng
waffles

麦片粥
màipiànzhōu
oatmeal

鲜果
xiānguǒ
fresh fruit

正餐 zhèngcān · **dinner**

汤 tāng | soup

肉汤 ròutāng | broth

炖菜 dùncài | stew

咖喱 gālí | curry

烤肉 kǎoròu | roast

馅饼 xiànbǐng | potpie

蛋奶酥 dànnǎisū | soufflé

烤肉串 kǎoròuchuàn | kebab

肉丸 ròuwán | meatballs

煎蛋饼 jiāndànbǐng | omelet

炒菜 chǎocài | stir-fry

面条
miàntiáo
noodles

意大利面食 yìdàlì miànshí
pasta

米饭 mǐfàn | rice

什锦沙拉 shíjǐnshālā
tossed salad

蔬菜沙拉 shūcàishālā
green salad

酸醋调味汁 suāncù
tiáowèizhī | dressing

中文 zhōngwén · **english**

烹调手法 pēngtiáo shǒufǎ · **techniques**

装馅 zhuāngxiàn | stuffed

浇汁 jiāozhī | **in sauce**

烤制 kǎozhì | grilled

醋渍 cùzì | marinated

水煮 shuǐzhǔ | poached

捣成糊状
dǎochénghúzhuàng | mashed

烘制 hōngzhì | baked

煎制 jiānzhì | pan-fried

炒制 chǎozhì | fried

腌渍 yānzì | pickled

熏制 xūnzhì | smoked

油炸 yóuzhá | deep-fried

枫糖浸泡 fēngtángjìnpào
in syrup

调味 tiáowèi | dressed

清蒸 qīngzhēng | steamed

风干 fēnggān | cured

学习 xuéxí
study

学校 xuéxiào • school

老师
lǎoshī
teacher

黑板
hēibǎn
blackboard

男生 nánshēng I schoolboy

学生
xuéshēng
pupil

校服
xiàofú
school uniform

课桌
kèzhuō
desk

书包
shūbāo
school bag

粉笔
fěnbǐ
chalk

教室 jiàoshì | classroom

女生
nǚshēng
schoolgirl

词汇 cíhuì • vocabulary

历史 lìshǐ history	自然科学 zìránkēxué science	物理 wùlǐ physics
语言 yǔyán languages	艺术 yìshù art	化学 huàxué chemistry
文学 wénxué literature	音乐 yīnyuè music	生物学 shēngwùxué biology
地理 dìlǐ geography	数学 shùxué math	体育 tǐyù physical education

学习活动 xuéxí huódòng • activities

读 dú | read (v)

写 xiě | write (v)

拼写 pīnxiě | spell (v)

画 huà | draw (v)

中文 zhōngwén • english

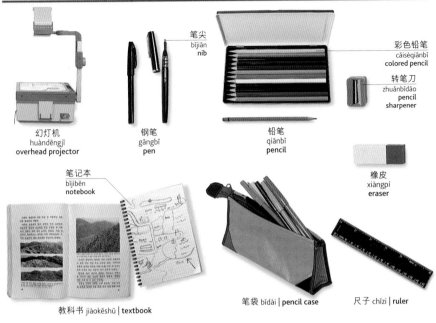

笔尖 bǐjiān nib

彩色铅笔 cǎisèqiānbǐ colored pencil

转笔刀 zhuǎnbǐdāo pencil sharpener

幻灯机 huàndēngjī overhead projector

钢笔 gāngbǐ pen

铅笔 qiānbǐ pencil

橡皮 xiàngpí eraser

笔记本 bǐjìběn notebook

教科书 jiàokēshū | textbook

笔袋 bǐdài | pencil case

尺子 chǐzi | ruler

词汇 cíhuì • vocabulary

校长 xiàozhǎng principal

答案 dáàn answer

评分 píngfēn grade

课 kè lesson

作业 zuòyè homework

年级 niánjí year

问题 wèntí question

考试 kǎoshì test

字典 zìdiǎn dictionary

记笔记 jìbǐjì take notes (v)

作文 zuòwén essay

百科全书 bǎikēquánshū encyclopedia

提问 tíwèn | question (v)

回答 huídá | answer (v)

讨论 tǎolùn | discuss (v)

学习 xuéxí | learn (v)

数学 shùxué · math

平面图形 píngmiàntúxíng · shapes

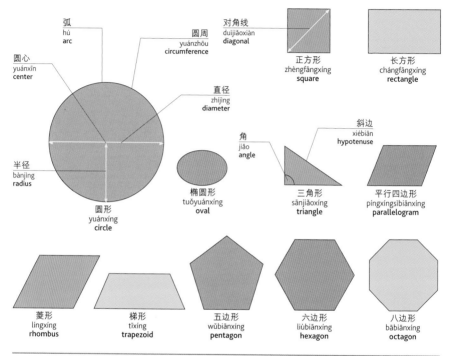

弧
hú
arc

圆周
yuánzhōu
circumference

对角线
duìjiǎoxiàn
diagonal

圆心
yuánxīn
center

直径
zhíjìng
diameter

正方形
zhèngfāngxíng
square

长方形
chángfāngxíng
rectangle

斜边
xiébiān
hypotenuse

角
jiǎo
angle

半径
bànjìng
radius

圆形
yuánxíng
circle

椭圆形
tuǒyuánxíng
oval

三角形
sānjiǎoxíng
triangle

平行四边形
píngxíngsìbiānxíng
parallelogram

菱形
língxíng
rhombus

梯形
tīxíng
trapezoid

五边形
wǔbiānxíng
pentagon

六边形
liùbiānxíng
hexagon

八边形
bābiānxíng
octagon

立体 lìtǐ · solids

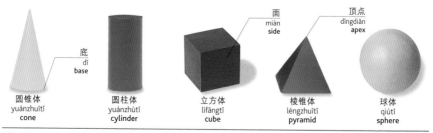

面
miàn
side

顶点
dǐngdiǎn
apex

底
dǐ
base

圆锥体
yuánzhuītǐ
cone

圆柱体
yuánzhùtǐ
cylinder

立方体
lìfāngtǐ
cube

棱锥体
léngzhuītǐ
pyramid

球体
qiútǐ
sphere

线 xiàn • **lines**

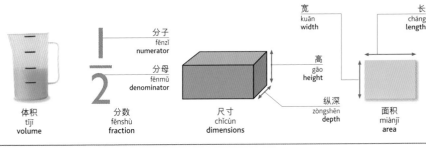

平直	平行	垂直	弯曲
píngzhí	píngxíng	chuízhí	wānqū
straight	**parallel**	**perpendicular**	**curved**

度量 dùliàng • **measurements**

分子
fēnzǐ
numerator

分母
fēnmǔ
denominator

宽
kuān
width

长
cháng
length

高
gāo
height

纵深
zòngshēn
depth

体积	分数	尺寸	面积
tǐjī	fēnshù	chǐcùn	miànjī
volume	**fraction**	**dimensions**	**area**

学习用具 xuéxíyòngjù • **equipment**

三角板	量角器	直尺	圆规	计算器
sānjiǎobǎn	liángjiǎoqì	zhíchǐ	yuánguī	jìsuànqì
triangle	**protractor**	**ruler**	**compass**	**calculator**

词汇 cíhuì • **vocabulary**

几何	正	倍	等于	加	乘	等式
jīhé	zhèng	bèi	děngyú	jiā	chéng	děngshì
geometry	**plus**	**times**	**equals**	**add (v)**	**multiply (v)**	**equation**
算术	负	除以	计数	减	除	百分比
suànshù	fù	chúyǐ	jìshù	jiǎn	chú	bǎifēnbǐ
arithmetic	**minus**	**divided by**	**count (v)**	**subtract (v)**	**divide (v)**	**percentage**

科学 kēxué • science

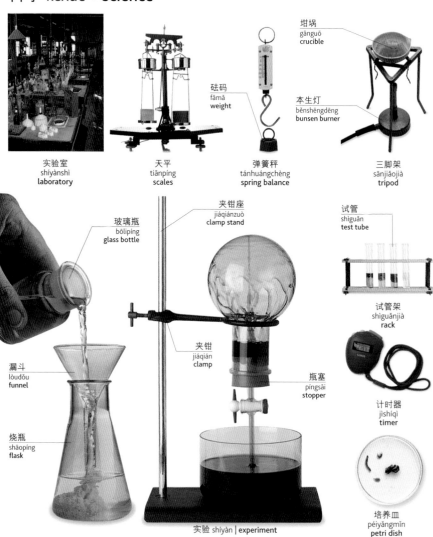

实验室
shíyànshì
laboratory

天平
tiānpíng
scales

砝码
fǎmǎ
weight

弹簧秤
tánhuángchèng
spring balance

坩埚
gānguō
crucible

本生灯
běnshēngdēng
bunsen burner

三脚架
sānjiǎojià
tripod

玻璃瓶
bōlípíng
glass bottle

夹钳座
jiáqiánzuò
clamp stand

试管
shìguǎn
test tube

试管架
shìguǎnjià
rack

夹钳
jiáqián
clamp

漏斗
lòudǒu
funnel

瓶塞
píngsāi
stopper

计时器
jìshíqì
timer

烧瓶
shāopíng
flask

实验 shíyàn | experiment

培养皿
péiyǎngmǐn
petri dish

中文 zhōngwén • english

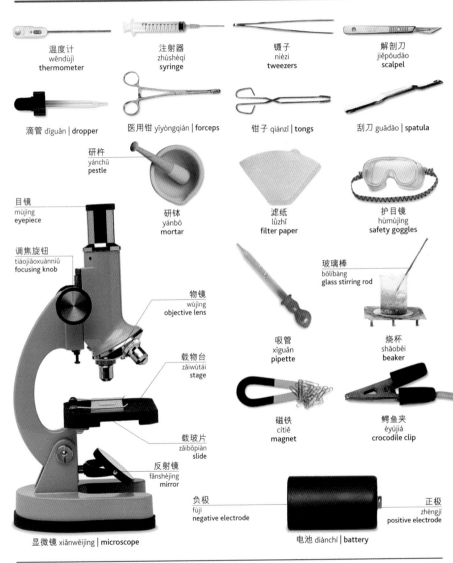

温度计
wēndùjì
thermometer

注射器
zhùshèqì
syringe

镊子
nièzi
tweezers

解剖刀
jiěpōudāo
scalpel

滴管 dīguǎn | dropper

医用钳 yīyòngqián | forceps

钳子 qiánzi | tongs

刮刀 guādāo | spatula

研杵
yánchǔ
pestle

目镜
mùjìng
eyepiece

研钵
yánbō
mortar

滤纸
lǜzhǐ
filter paper

护目镜
hùmùjìng
safety goggles

调焦旋钮
tiáojiāoxuánniǔ
focusing knob

玻璃棒
bōlíbàng
glass stirring rod

物镜
wùjìng
objective lens

载物台
zǎiwùtái
stage

吸管
xīguǎn
pipette

烧杯
shāobēi
beaker

载玻片
zǎibōpiàn
slide

反射镜
fǎnshèjìng
mirror

磁铁
cítiě
magnet

鳄鱼夹
èyújiá
crocodile clip

显微镜 xiǎnwēijìng | microscope

负极
fùjí
negative electrode

正极
zhèngjí
positive electrode

电池 diànchí | battery

高等院校 gāoděngyuànxiào · college

招生办
zhāoshēngbàn
admissions

学生食堂
xuéshēngshítáng
cafeteria

健康中心
jiànkāngzhōngxīn
health center

校园 xiàoyuán | campus

运动场
yùndòngchǎng
playing field

学生宿舍
xuéshēngsùshè
residence hall

书目
shūmù
card catalog

图书管理员
túshūguǎnlǐyuán
librarian

借书处
jièshūchù
circulation desk

书架
shūjià
bookshelf

期刊
qīkān
periodical

杂志
zázhì
journal

词汇 cíhuì · vocabulary

借书证 jièshūzhèng **library card**	**问询处** wènxúnchù **help desk**	**借出** jièchū **loan**
阅览室 yuèlǎnshì **reading room**	**借入** jièrù **borrow (v)**	**书** shū **book**
推荐书目 tuījiànshūmù **reading list**	**预订** yùdìng **reserve (v)**	**书名** shūmíng **title**
还书日期 huánshūrìqī **due date**	**续借** xùjiè **renew (v)**	**走廊** zǒuláng **aisle**

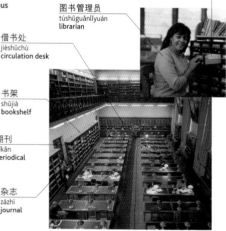

图书馆 túshūguǎn | library

大学生
dàxuéshēng
undergraduate

讲师
jiǎngshī
lecturer

毕业生
bìyèshēng
graduate

学位袍
xuéwèipáo
robe

阶梯教室 jiētījiàoshì | lecture hall

毕业典礼 bìyèdiǎnlǐ | graduation ceremony

高等专科学校 gāoděngzhuānkē xuéxiào • schools

模特
mótè
model

美术学院 měishùxuéyuàn
art college

音乐学院 yīnyuèxuéyuàn
music school

舞蹈学院 wǔdǎoxuéyuàn
dance academy

词汇 cíhuì • vocabulary

奖学金 jiǎngxuéjīn **scholarship**	研究 yánjiū **research**	(学位) 论文 (xuéwèi) lùnwén **dissertation**	医学 yīxué **medicine**	哲学 zhéxué **philosophy**
文凭 wénpíng **diploma**	硕士学位 shuòshìxuéwèi **master's**	系 xì **department**	动物学 dòngwùxué **zoology**	文学 wénxué **literature**
学位 xuéwèi **degree**	博士学位 bóshìxuéwèi **doctorate**	法律 fǎlǜ **law**	物理学 wùlǐxué **physics**	艺术史 yìshùshǐ **art history**
研究生阶段的 yánjiūshēng jiēduànde **postgraduate**	论文 lùnwén **thesis**	工程学 gōngchéngxué **engineering**	政治学 zhèngzhìxué **politics**	经济学 jīngjìxué **economics**

工作 gōngzuò
work

办公室1 bàngōngshìyī · office 1
办公室 bàngōngshì · office

显示器
xiǎnshìqì
monitor

笔筒
bǐtǒng
desktop organizer

文件夹
wénjiànjiā
file

收件篮
shōujiànlán
in-tray

计算机
jìsuànjī
computer

发件篮
fājiànlán
out-tray

键盘
jiànpán
keyboard

电话
diànhuà
telephone

笔记本
bǐjìběn
notebook

标签
biāoqiān
label

办公桌
bàngōngzhuō
desk

废纸篓
fèizhǐlǒu
wastebasket

转椅
zhuànyǐ
swivel chair

组合抽屉
zǔhéchōutì
drawer unit

抽屉
chōutì
drawer

文件柜
wénjiànguì
filing cabinet

办公设备 bàngōngshèbèi · office equipment

纸盒
zhǐhé
paper tray

送纸器
sòngzhǐqì
paper guide

传真
chuánzhēn
fax

打印机 dǎyìnjī | printer

传真机 chuánzhēnjī | fax machine

词汇 cíhuì · vocabulary

打印
dǎyìn
print (v)

放大
fàngdà
enlarge (v)

复印
fùyìn
copy (v)

缩小
suōxiǎo
reduce (v)

我要复印。
wǒ yào fùyìn.
I need to make some copies.

办公用品 bàngōngyòngpǐn · office supplies

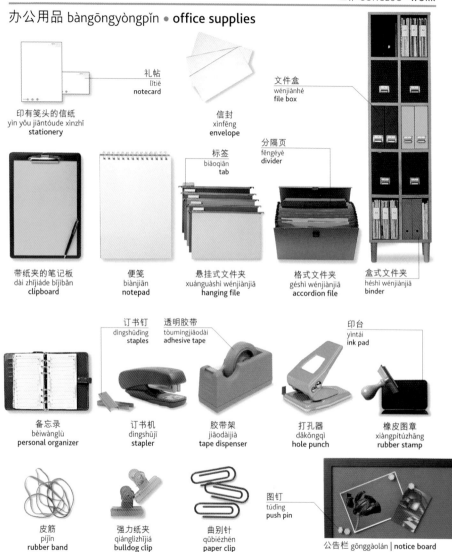

礼帖
lǐtiē
notecard

文件盒
wénjiànhé
file box

印有笺头的信纸
yìn yǒu jiāntóude xìnzhǐ
stationery

信封
xìnfēng
envelope

分隔页
fēngéyè
divider

标签
biāoqiān
tab

带纸夹的笔记板
dài zhǐjiáde bǐjìbǎn
clipboard

便笺
biànjiān
notepad

悬挂式文件夹
xuánguàshì wénjiànjiā
hanging file

格式文件夹
géshì wénjiànjiā
accordion file

盒式文件夹
héshì wénjiànjiā
binder

订书钉
dìngshūdīng
staples

透明胶带
tòumíngjiāodài
adhesive tape

印台
yìntái
ink pad

备忘录
bèiwànglù
personal organizer

订书机
dìngshūjī
stapler

胶带架
jiāodàijià
tape dispenser

打孔器
dǎkǒngqì
hole punch

橡皮图章
xiàngpítúzhāng
rubber stamp

皮筋
píjīn
rubber band

强力纸夹
qiánglìzhǐjiá
bulldog clip

曲别针
qūbiézhēn
paper clip

图钉
túdīng
push pin

公告栏 gōnggàolán | notice board

办公室2 bàngōngshì'èr · office 2

活动挂图
huódòngguàtú
flipchart

挂图架
guàtújià
easel

会议记录
huìyìjìlù
minutes

报告
bàogào
report

经理
jīnglǐ
manager

提案
tí'àn
proposal

主管
zhǔguǎn
executive

会议 huìyì | meeting

词汇 cíhuì · vocabulary

会议室
huìyìshì
meeting room

参加
cānjiā
attend (v)

议程
yìchéng
agenda

主持
zhǔchí
chair (v)

什么时候开会？
shénme shíhòu kāihuì?
What time is the meeting?

您几点上下班？
nín jǐdiǎn shàngxiàbān?
What are your office hours?

讲解人
jiǎngjiěrén
speaker

幻灯机
huàndēngjī
projector

介绍 jièshào | presentation

商务 shāngwù · business

笔记本电脑
bǐjìběn diànnǎo
laptop

笔记
bǐjì
notes

商人
shāngrén
businessman

女商人
nǚshāngrén
businesswoman

工作午餐 gōngzuòwǔcān | business lunch

商务旅行 shāngwùlǚxíng | business trip

客户
kèhù
client

约会
yuēhuì
appointment

掌上电脑
zhǎngshàng diànnǎo
palmtop

总经理
zǒngjīnglǐ
CEO

客户 kèhù | calendar

商业交易 shāngyèjiāoyì | business deal

词汇 cíhuì · vocabulary

公司 gōngsī company	员工 yuángōng staff	会计部 kuàijìbù accounts department	法律事务部 fǎlǜshìwùbù legal department
总部，总公司 zǒngbù, zǒnggōngsī headquarters	薪水 xīnshuǐ salary	市场部 shìchǎngbù marketing department	客户服务部 kèhùfúwùbù customer service department
分部，分公司 fēnbù, fēngōngsī regional office	工资单 gōngzīdān payroll	销售部 xiāoshòubù sales department	人力资源部 rénlìzīyuánbù human resources department

计算机 jìsuànjī · computer

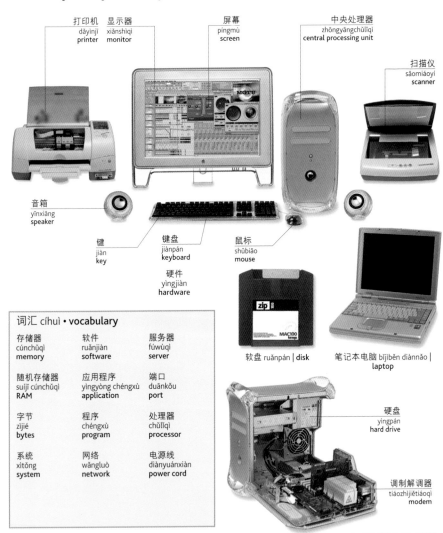

打印机
dǎyìnjī
printer

显示器
xiǎnshìqì
monitor

屏幕
píngmù
screen

中央处理器
zhōngyāngchǔlǐqì
central processing unit

扫描仪
sǎomiáoyí
scanner

音箱
yīnxiāng
speaker

键
jiàn
key

键盘
jiànpán
keyboard

鼠标
shǔbiāo
mouse

硬件
yìngjiàn
hardware

词汇 cíhuì · vocabulary

存储器 cúnchǔqì **memory**	软件 ruǎnjiàn **software**	服务器 fúwùqì **server**
随机存储器 suíjī cúnchǔqì **RAM**	应用程序 yìngyòng chéngxù **application**	端口 duānkǒu **port**
字节 zìjié **bytes**	程序 chéngxù **program**	处理器 chǔlǐqì **processor**
系统 xìtǒng **system**	网络 wǎngluò **network**	电源线 diànyuánxiàn **power cord**

软盘 ruǎnpán | **disk**

笔记本电脑 bǐjìběn diànnǎo |
laptop

硬盘
yìngpán
hard drive

调制解调器
tiáozhìjiětiáoqì
modem

桌面 zhuōmiàn • desktop

菜单栏
càidānlán
menu bar

字体
zìtǐ
font

图标
túbiāo
icon

工具栏
gōngjùlán
toolbar

滚动条
gǔndòngtiáo
scrollbar

桌面背景
zhuōmiànbèijīng
wallpaper

视窗
shìchuāng
window

AF008.psd
文件
wénjiàn
file

AF008
文件夹
wénjiànjiā
folder

Trash
回收站
huíshōuzhàn
trash

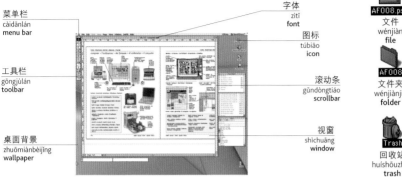

互联网 hùliánwǎng • Internet

浏览器
liúlǎnqì
browser

收件箱
shōujiànxiāng
inbox

网站
wǎngzhàn
website

浏览 liúlǎn | browse (v)

电子邮件 diànzǐyóujiàn • email

电子邮件地址
diànzǐyóujiàn dìzhǐ
email address

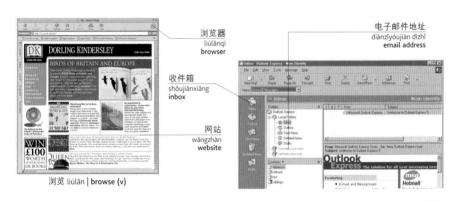

词汇 cíhuì • vocabulary

连接
liánjiē
connect (v)

服务商
fúwùshāng
service provider

登录
dēnglù
log on (v)

下载
xiàzǎi
download (v)

发送
fāsòng
send (v)

保存
bǎocún
save (v)

安装
ānzhuāng
install (v)

电子邮件账户
diànzǐyóujiàn zhànghù
email account

在线
zàixiàn
online

附件
fùjiàn
attachment

接收
jiēshōu
receive (v)

搜索
sōusuǒ
search (v)

媒体 méitǐ · media

电视演播室 diànshì yǎnbōshì · television studio

节目主持人
jiémùzhǔchírén
presenter

照明
zhàomíng
light

布景
bùjǐng
set

摄像机
shèxiàngjī
camera

摄像机升降器
shèxiàngjī shēngjiàngqì
camera crane

摄像师
shèxiàngshī
camera operator

词汇 cíhuì · vocabulary

频道 píndào channel	新闻 xīnwén news	新闻媒体 xīnwénméitǐ press	肥皂剧 féizàojù soap	动画片 dònghuàpiān cartoon	直播 zhíbō live
节目编排 jiémùbiānpái programming	纪录片 jìlùpijìlùpiānn documentary	电视连续剧 diànshì liánxùjù television series	游戏节目 yóuxìjiémù game show	录播 lùbō prerecorded	播放 bōfàng broadcast (v)

采访记者 cǎifǎngjìzhě
interviewer

记者 jìzhě | reporter

自动提示机 zìdòngtíshìjī
teleprompter

新闻播音员 xīnwénbōyīnyuán
news anchor

演员 yǎnyuán | actors

录音吊杆 lùyīndiàogǎn
sound boom

场记板 chǎngjìbǎn
clapper board

电影布景 diànyǐngbùjǐng
movie set

无线电广播 wúxiàndiànguǎngbō · radio

混音台
húnyīntái
mixing desk

话筒
huàtǒng
microphone

录音师
lùyīnshī
sound technician

录音室 lùyīnshì | recording studio

词汇 cíhuì · vocabulary

广播电台
guǎngbōdiàntái
radio station

中波
zhōngbō
medium wave

广播
guǎngbō
broadcast

频率
pínlǜ
frequency

波长
bōcháng
wavelength

音量
yīnliàng
volume

长波
chángbō
long wave

调音
tiáoyīn
tune (v)

短波
duǎnbō
short wave

流行音乐节目主持人
liúxíngyīnyuè jiémù
zhǔchírén
DJ

法律 fǎlǜ • law

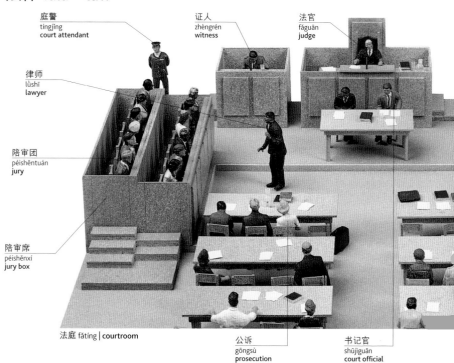

庭警
tíngjǐng
court attendant

证人
zhèngrén
witness

法官
fǎguān
judge

律师
lǜshī
lawyer

陪审团
péishěntuán
jury

陪审席
péishěnxí
jury box

法庭 fǎtíng | courtroom

公诉
gōngsù
prosecution

书记官
shūjìguān
court official

词汇 cíhuì • vocabulary

律师事务所 lǜshīshìwùsuǒ **lawyer's office**	**传讯** chuánxùn **summons**	**传票** chuánpiào **writ**	**诉讼案件** sùsòng ànjiàn **court case**
法律咨询 fǎlǜzīxún **legal advice**	**陈辞** chéncí **statement**	**开庭日** kāitíngrì **court date**	**控告** kònggào **charge**
诉讼委托人 sùsòngwěituōrén **client**	**逮捕令** dàibǔlìng **warrant**	**抗辩** kàngbiàn **plea**	**被告** bèigào **accused**

速记员
sùjìyuán
stenographer

嫌疑犯
xiányífàn
suspect

被告人
bèigàorén
defendant

应诉方
yìngsùfāng
defense

罪犯
zuìfàn
criminal

拼凑人像 pīncòurénxiàng | **composite**

犯罪记录 fànzuìjìlù | **criminal record**

狱警 yùjǐng | **prison guard**

单人牢房 dānrénláofáng **cell**

监狱 jiānyù | **prison**

词汇 cíhuì • vocabulary

证据 zhèngjù **evidence**	有罪 yǒuzuì **guilty**	保释金 bǎoshìjīn **bail**	我要见律师。 wǒ yào jiàn lǜshī. **I want to see a lawyer.**
判决 pànjué **verdict**	无罪释放 wúzuìshìfàng **acquitted**	上诉 shàngsù **appeal**	法院在哪儿? fǎyuàn zàinǎ'er? **Where is the courthouse?**
无罪 wúzuì **innocent**	判刑 pànxíng **sentence**	假释 jiǎshì **parole**	我可以保释吗? wǒ kěyǐ bǎoshì ma? **Can I post bail?**

农场1 nóngchǎngyī · farm 1

农田
nóngtián
farmland

农家场院
nóngjiā chǎngyuàn
farmyard

附属建筑物
fùshǔ jiànzhùwù
outbuilding

农舍
nóngshè
farmhouse

田地
tiándì
field

农民
nóngmín
farmer

谷仓
gǔcāng
barn

菜地
càidì
vegetable
garden

树篱
shùlí
fencerow

大门
dàmén
gate

围栏
wéilán
fence

牧场
mùchǎng
pasture

家畜
jiāchù
livestock

中耕机
zhōnggēngjī
cultivator

拖拉机 tuōlājī | tractor

联合收割机　　liánhéshōugējī | combine

农场类型 nóngchǎng lèixíng · types of farms

庄稼
zhuāngjia
crop

种植园
zhòngzhíyuán
crop farm

乳牛场
rǔniúchǎng
dairy farm

牧羊场
mùyángchǎng
sheep farm

羊群
yángqún
flock

养鸡场 yǎngjīchǎng
poultry farm

养猪场
yǎngzhūchǎng
pig farm

养鱼场
yǎngyúchǎng
fish farm

果园
guǒyuán
fruit farm

葡萄树
pútáoshù
vine

葡萄园
pútáoyuán
vineyard

农活 nónghuó · actions

犁
lí
furrow

犁地
lídì
plow (v)

播种
bōzhǒng
sow (v)

挤奶
jǐ'nǎi
milk (v)

饲养
sìyǎng
feed (v)

灌溉 guàngài | **water (v)**

收获 shōuhuò | **harvest (v)**

词汇 cíhuì · vocabulary

除草剂 chúcǎojì **herbicide**	牧群 mùqún **herd**	饲料槽 sìliàocáo **trough**
杀虫剂 shāchóngjì **pesticide**	地窖 dìjiào **silo**	种植 zhòngzhí **plant (v)**

农场2 nóngchǎng'èr • farm 2

农作物 nóngzuòwù • crops

小麦
xiǎomài
wheat

玉米
yùmǐ
corn

大麦
dàmài
barley

油菜籽
yóucàizǐ
rapeseed

向日葵
xiàngrìkuí
sunflower

捆包
kǔnbāo
bale

干草
gāncǎo
hay

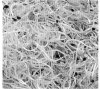

紫花苜蓿
zǐhuāmùxu
alfalfa

烟草
yāncǎo
tobacco

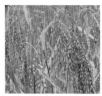

水稻
shuǐdào
rice

茶
chá
tea

咖啡
kāfēi
coffee

亚麻
yàmá
flax

甘蔗
gānzhè
sugarcane

棉花
miánhuā
cotton

稻草人
dàocǎorén
scarecrow

家畜 jiāchù • livestock

小猪
xiǎozhū
piglet

牛犊
niúdú
calf

猪
zhū
pig

母牛
mǔniú
cow

公牛
gōngniú
bull

绵羊
miányáng
sheep

小山羊
xiǎoshānyáng
kid

马驹
mǎjū
foal

羊羔
yánggāo
lamb

山羊
shānyáng
goat

马
mǎ
horse

驴
lú
donkey

小鸡
xiǎojī
chick

小鸭
xiǎoyā
duckling

鸡
jī
chicken

公鸡
gōngjī
rooster

火鸡
huǒjī
turkey

鸭
yā
duck

马厩
mǎjiù
stable

家畜圈
jiāchùquān
pen

鸡舍
jīshè
chicken coop

猪圈
zhūjuàn
pigsty

建筑 jiànzhù • construction

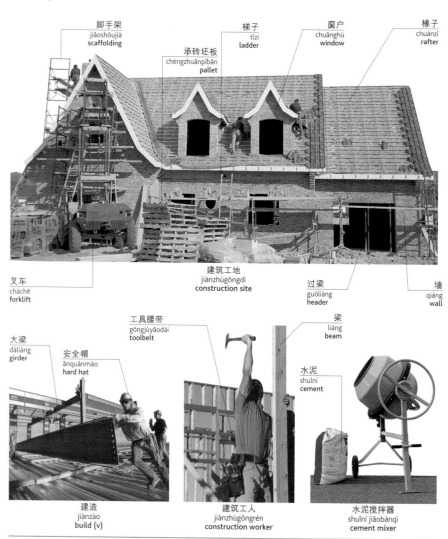

脚手架
jiǎoshǒujià
scaffolding

承砖坯板
chéngzhuānpībǎn
pallet

梯子
tīzi
ladder

窗户
chuānghù
window

椽子
chuánzǐ
rafter

叉车
chāchē
forklift

建筑工地
jiànzhùgōngdì
construction site

过梁
guòliáng
header

墙
qiáng
wall

大梁
dàliáng
girder

安全帽
ānquánmào
hard hat

工具腰带
gōngjùyāodài
toolbelt

梁
liáng
beam

水泥
shuǐní
cement

建造
jiànzào
build (v)

建筑工人
jiànzhùgōngrén
construction worker

水泥搅拌器
shuǐní jiǎobànqì
cement mixer

建筑材料 jiànzhù cáiliào • materials

砖
zhuān
brick

木材
mùcái
lumber

瓦片
wǎpiàn
roof tile

混凝土块
hùnníngtǔkuài
concrete block

工具 gōngjù • tools

灰浆
huījiāng
mortar

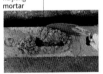

抹刀
mǒdāo
trowel

水准仪
shuǐzhǔnyí
level

柄
bǐng
handle

大锤
dàchuí
sledgehammer

丁字镐
dīngzigǎo
pickax

铁锹
tiěqiāo
shovel

(工程)机械 (gōngchéng) jīxiè • machinery

压路机
yālùjī
roller

翻斗卡车
fāndǒukǎchē
dump truck

支座
zhīzuò
support

吊钩
diàogōu
hook

起重机 qǐzhòngjī l crane

道路施工 dàolùshīgōng • roadwork

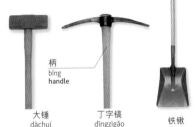

柏油路面
bǎiyóulùmiàn
asphalt

锥形隔离墩
zhuīxínggélídūn
cone

风钻
fēngzuàn
jackhammer

重铺路面
zhòngpū lùmiàn
resurfacing

挖掘机
wājuéjī
excavator

职业1 zhíyèyī · occupations 1

木匠
mùjiàng
carpenter

电工
diàngōng
electrician

水暖工
shuǐnuǎngōng
plumber

建筑工人
jiànzhùgōngrén
construction worker

园丁
yuándīng
gardener

吸尘器
xīchénqì
vacuum cleaner

清洁工
qīngjiégōng
cleaner

机械师
jīxièshī
mechanic

屠户
túhù
butcher

剪刀
jiǎndāo
scissors

鱼贩
yúfàn
fishmonger

蔬菜水果商
shūcài shuǐguǒshāng
greengrocer

花商
huāshāng
florist

美发师
měifàshī
hair stylist

理发师
lǐfàshī
barber

珠宝匠
zhūbǎojiàng
jeweler

售货员
shòuhuòyuán
store clerk

口罩
kǒuzhào
mask

房地产商
fángdìchǎnshāng
real estate agent

配镜师
pèijìngshī
optician

牙医
yáyī
dentist

医生
yīshēng
doctor

药剂师
yàojìshī
pharmacist

护士
hùshi
nurse

兽医
shòuyī
veterinarian

农民
nóngmín
farmer

渔民
yúmín
fisher

徽章
huīzhāng
identity badge

保安
bǎoān
security guard

机枪
jīqiāng
machine gun

制服
zhìfú
uniform

水手
shuǐshǒu
sailor

士兵
shìbīng
soldier

警察
jǐngchá
police officer

消防队员
xiāofángduìyuán
firefighter

职业2 zhíyè'èr • occupations 2

律师
lǜshī
lawyer

会计师
kuàijìshī
accountant

模型
móxíng
model

建筑师 jiànzhùshī I architect

科学家
kēxuéjiā
scientist

老师
lǎoshī
teacher

图书管理员
túshūguǎnlǐyuán
librarian

接待员
jiēdàiyuán
receptionist

邮袋
yóudài
mailbag

邮递员
yóudìyuán
mail carrier

公共汽车司机
gōnggòngqìchē sījī
bus driver

卡车司机
kǎchē sījī
truck driver

出租车司机
chūzūchē sījī
cab driver

飞行员
fēixíngyuán
pilot

空中小姐
kōngzhōngxiǎojiě
flight attendant

旅行代理
lǚxíngdàilǐ
travel agent

厨师帽
chúshīmào
chef's hat

厨师
chúshī
chef

芭蕾舞裙
bālěiwǔqún
tutu

音乐家
yīnyuèjiā
musician

舞蹈演员
wǔdǎoyǎnyuán
dancer

演员
yǎnyuán
actor

歌手
gēshǒu
singer

女侍者
nǚshìzhě
food server

酒保
jiǔbǎo
bartender

运动员
yùndòngyuán
athlete

雕塑家
diāosùjiā
sculptor

笔记
bǐjì
notes

画家
huàjiā
painter

摄影师
shèyǐngshī
photographer

新闻播音员
xīnwén bōyīnyuán
news anchor

新闻记者
xīnwén jìzhě
journalist

编辑
biānjí
editor

制图员
zhìtúyuán
designer

女缝纫师
nǚféngrènshī
textile worker

裁缝
cáiféng
tailor

交通运输 jiāotōngyùnshū
transportation

道路 dàolù • **roads**

高速公路
gāosùgōnglù
freeway

收费站
shōufèizhàn
toll booth

路面标志
lùmiànbiāozhì
road markings

主路入口
zhǔlùrùkǒu
on-ramp

单行
dānxíng
one-way

隔离带
gélídài
divider

交汇处
jiāohuìchù
intersection

交通信号灯
jiāotōng
xìnhàodēng
traffic light

内车道
nèichēdào
inside lane

中央车道
zhōngyāngchēdào
middle lane

外车道
wàichēdào
outside lane

出口
chūkǒu
exit ramp

交通
jiāotōng
traffic

立交桥
lìjiāoqiáo
overpass

硬质路肩
yìngzhìlùjiān
hard shoulder

载重汽车
zàizhòngqìchē
truck

中央分车带
zhōngyāng fēnchēdài
median

高架桥下通道
gāojià qiáoxià tōngdào
underpass

人行横道
rénxínghéngdào
pedestrian crossing

求救电话
qiújiù diànhuà
emergency phone

残疾人停车处
cánjírén tíngchēchù
disabled parking

人行横道
rénxínghéngdào
traffic jam

地图
dìtú
map

停车计时收费器
tíngchē jìshí shōufèiqì
parking meter

交通警察
jiāotōng jǐngchá
traffic police officer

词汇 cíhuì • vocabulary

道路交叉处的环行路 dàolù jiāochāchùde huánxínglù **roundabout**	(有中央分隔带的) 复式车道 (yǒu zhōngyāng fēngédàide) fùshì chēdào **divided highway**	超车 chāochē **pass (v)**
绕行道路 ràoxíngdàolù **detour**	停车 tíngchē **park (v)**	拖走 tuōzǒu **tow away (v)**
道路施工 dàolùshīgōng **roadwork**	驾驶 jiàshǐ **drive (v)**	这是去... 的路吗？ zhèshìqù... de lù ma? **Is this the road to...?**
防撞护栏 fángzhuànghùlán **crash barrier**	倒车 dàochē **back up (v)**	哪里可以停车？ nǎlǐ kěyǐ tíngchē? **Where can I park?**

交通标志 jiāotōng biāozhì • road signs

禁行
jìnxíng
do not enter

限速
xiànsù
speed limit

危险
wēixiǎn
hazard

禁止停车
jìnzhǐ tíngchē
no stopping

禁止右转
jìnzhǐ yòuzhuǎn
no right turn

公共汽车 gōnggòngqìchē • bus

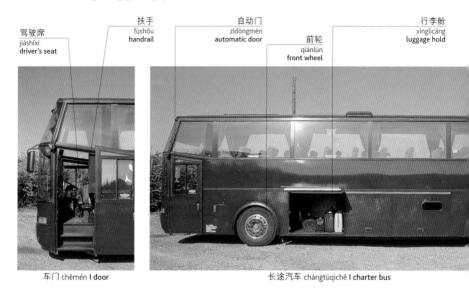

驾驶席
jiàshǐxí
driver's seat

扶手
fúshǒu
handrail

自动门
zìdòngmén
automatic door

前轮
qiánlún
front wheel

行李舱
xínglǐcāng
luggage hold

车门 chēmén **I door**

长途汽车 chángtúqìchē **I charter bus**

公共汽车种类 gōnggòngqìchē zhǒnglèi • types of buses

公交线路号
gōngjiāoxiànlùhào
route number

司机
sījī
driver

双层公共汽车
shuāngcéng gōnggòngqìchē
double-decker bus

有轨电车
yǒuguǐdiànchē
tram

无轨电车
wúguǐdiànchē
trolley bus

校车 xiàochē **I school bus**

后轮
hòulún
rear wheel

窗户
chuānghù
window

停车按钮
tíngchē ànniǔ
stop button

公共汽车票
gōnggòngqìchēpiào
bus ticket

铃
líng
bell

公共汽车总站
gōnggòngqìchē zǒngzhàn
bus station

公共汽车站
gōnggòngqìchēzhàn
bus stop

词汇 cíhuì • vocabulary

车费
chēfèi
fare

时刻表
shíkèbiǎo
schedule

您在... 停吗？
nín zài... tíng ma?
Do you stop at...?

轮椅通道
lúnyǐ tōngdào
wheelchair access

公共汽车候车亭
gōngqìchē hòuchētíng
bus shelter

哪路车去... ？
nǎlù chē qù...?
Which bus goes to...?

游览车 yóulǎnchē I tourist bus

小型公共汽车
xiǎoxíng gōnggòngqìchē
minibus

班车 bānchē I shuttle bus

汽车1 qìchēyī · **car 1**

外部 wàibù · **exterior**

外后视镜
wàihòushìjìng
side mirror

风挡
fēngdǎng
windshield

内后视镜
nèihòushìjìng
rearview mirror

雨刷
yǔshuā
windshield wiper

车门
chēmén
door

引擎盖
yǐnqínggài
hood

行李箱
xínglǐxiāng
trunk

转向灯
zhuǎnxiàngdēng
turn signal

保险杠
bǎoxiǎngàng
bumper

前灯
qiándēng
headlight

车轮
chēlún
wheel

轮胎
lúntāi
tire

车牌
chēpái
license plate

行李
xíngli
luggage

车顶行李架
chēdǐng xínglǐjià
roof rack

尾部车门
wěibùchēmén
tailgate

安全带
ānquándài
seat belt

儿童座椅
értóngzuòyǐ
child's car seat

种类 zhǒnglèi · types

微型车
wēixíngchē
compact

揭背式轿车
jiēbèishì jiàochē
hatchback

家庭轿车，三厢车
jiātíng jiàochē, sānxiāngchē
sedan

客货两用车
kèhuò liǎngyòngchē
station wagon

敞篷车
chǎngpéngchē
convertible

跑车
pǎochē
sports car

六座厢式车
liùzuò xiāngshìchē
minivan

四轮驱动(车)
sìlúnqūdòng(chē)
four-wheel drive

老式汽车
lǎoshìqìchē
vintage

大型高级轿车
dàxínggāojí jiàochē
limousine

加油站 jiāyóuzhàn · gas station

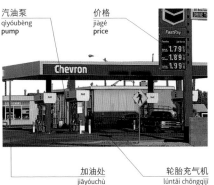

汽油泵
qìyóubèng
pump

价格
jiàgé
price

加油处
jiāyóuchù
forecourt

轮胎充气机
lúntāi chōngqìjī
air supply

词汇 cíhuì · vocabulary

油 yóu **oil**	含铅 hánqiān **leaded**	自动洗车站 zìdòngxǐ chēzhàn **car wash**
汽油 qìyóu **gasoline**	柴油 cháiyóu **diesel**	防冻液 fángdòngyè **antifreeze**
无铅 wúqiān **unleaded**	汽车修理站 qìchē xiūlǐzhàn **garage**	喷水器 pēnshuǐqì **windshield wash**

请加满油。
qǐng jiāmǎn yóu.
Fill it up, please.

汽车 2 qìchē'èr · car 2

内部 nèibù · interior

		座椅头枕		门锁		车门把手
后座	扶手	zuòyǐ tóuzhěn		ménsuǒ		chēmén
hòuzuò	fúshǒu	**headrest**		**door lock**		bǎshou
backseat	**armrest**					**handle**

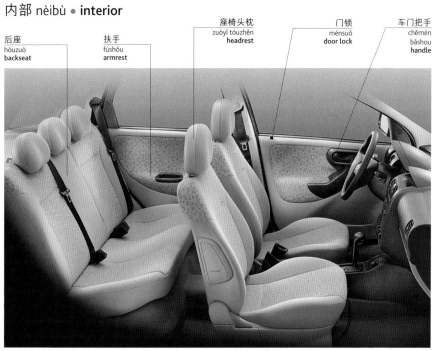

词汇 cíhuì · vocabulary

双门	四门	自动	刹车	加速器，油门
shuāngmén	sìmén	zìdòng	shāchē	jiāsùqì, yóumén
two-door	**four-door**	**automatic**	**brake**	**accelerator**
三门	手动	点火	离合器	空调
sānmén	shǒudòng	diǎnhuǒ	líhéqì	kōngtiáo
three-door	**manual**	**ignition**	**clutch**	**air conditioning**

您能告诉我去...的路吗？
nín néng gàosù wǒ qù...de lù ma?
Can you tell me the way to...?

停车场在哪里？
tíngchēchǎng zàinǎli?
Where is the parking lot?

这儿可以停车吗？
zhè'er kěyǐ tíngchē ma?
Can I park here?

操作装置 cāozuòzhuāngzhì · **controls**

方向盘
fāngxiàngpán
steering
wheel

喇叭
lǎba
horn

仪表盘
yíbiǎopán
dashboard

警示灯
jǐngshìdēng
hazard lights

卫星导航仪
wèixīng dǎohángyí
satellite navigation

左侧驾驶 zuǒcèjiàshǐ I **left-hand drive**

温度计
wēndùjì
temperature gauge

转速表
zhuànsùbiǎo
tachometer

车速表
chēsùbiǎo
speedometer

油量表
yóuliàngbiǎo
fuel gauge

汽车音响
qìchē
yīnxiǎng
car stereo

车灯开关
chēdēng kāiguān
light switch

暖风开关
nuǎnfēng kāiguān
heater controls

里程表
lǐchéngbiǎo
odometer

安全气囊
ānquánqìnáng
air bag

变速杆
biànsùgǎn
gearshift

右侧驾驶 yòucèjiàshǐ I **right-hand drive**

汽车 3 qìchēsān • car 3

机械构造 jīxiègòuzào • mechanics

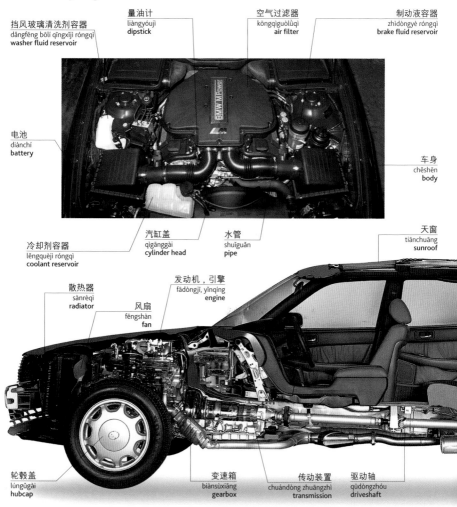

挡风玻璃清洗剂容器
dǎngfēng bōlí qīngxǐjì róngqì
washer fluid reservoir

量油计
liàngyóujì
dipstick

空气过滤器
kōngqìguòlǜqì
air filter

制动液容器
zhìdòngyè róngqì
brake fluid reservoir

电池
diànchí
battery

车身
chēshēn
body

冷却剂容器
lěngquèjì róngqì
coolant reservoir

汽缸盖
qìgānggài
cylinder head

水管
shuǐguǎn
pipe

天窗
tiānchuāng
sunroof

散热器
sànrèqì
radiator

发动机，引擎
fādòngjī, yǐnqíng
engine

风扇
fēngshàn
fan

轮毂盖
lúngǔgài
hubcap

变速箱
biànsùxiāng
gearbox

传动装置
chuándòng zhuāngzhì
transmission

驱动轴
qūdòngzhóu
driveshaft

爆胎 bàotāi • flat tire

备用轮胎
bèiyòng lúntāi
spare tire

曲柄
qūbǐng
tire iron

固定螺母
gùdìngluómǔ
lug nuts

千斤顶
qiānjīndǐng
jack

更换轮胎
gēnghuàn lúntāi
change a tire (v)

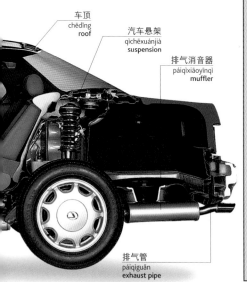

车顶
chēdǐng
roof

汽车悬架
qìchēxuánjià
suspension

排气消音器
páiqìxiāoyīnqì
muffler

油箱
yóuxiāng
gas tank

排气管
páiqìguǎn
exhaust pipe

词汇 cíhuì • vocabulary

车祸 chēhuò **car accident**	涡轮增压器 wōlúnzēngyāqì **turbocharger**
故障 gùzhàng **breakdown**	配电器 pèidiànqì **distributor**
保险 bǎoxiǎn **insurance**	底盘 dǐpán **chassis**
拖车 tuōchē **tow truck**	手刹车 shǒushāchē **parking brake**
机械师 jīxièshī **mechanic**	交流发电机 jiāoliúfādiànjī **alternator**
胎压 tāiyā **tire pressure**	轮轴皮带 lúnzhóupídài **cam belt**
保险盒 bǎoxiǎnhé **fuse box**	我的车坏了。 wǒ de chē huàile. **I've had a breakdown.**
火花塞 huǒhuāsāi **spark plug**	我的车发动不起来。 wǒ de chē fādòng bù qǐlái. **My car won't start.**
风扇皮带 fēngshànpídài **fan belt**	您修车吗？ nín xiūchē ma **Do you do repairs?**
油箱 yóuxiāng **gas tank**	发动机过热。 fādòngjī guòrè **The engine is overheating**
点火定时 diǎnhuǒdìngshí **timing**	

摩托车 mótuōchē · **motorcycle**

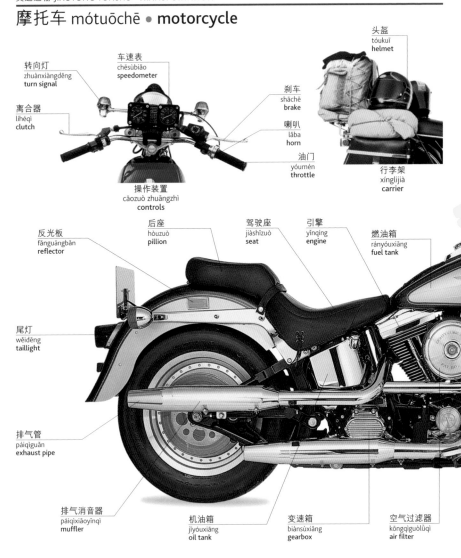

头盔
tóukuī
helmet

转向灯
zhuǎnxiàngdēng
turn signal

车速表
chēsúbiǎo
speedometer

刹车
shāchē
brake

离合器
líhéqì
clutch

喇叭
lǎba
horn

油门
yóumén
throttle

操作装置
cāozuò zhuāngzhì
controls

行李架
xínglǐjià
carrier

反光板
fǎnguāngbǎn
reflector

后座
hòuzuò
pillion

驾驶座
jiàshǐzuò
seat

引擎
yǐnqíng
engine

燃油箱
rányóuxiāng
fuel tank

尾灯
wěidēng
taillight

排气管
páiqìguǎn
exhaust pipe

排气消音器
páiqìxiāoyīnqì
muffler

机油箱
jīyóuxiāng
oil tank

变速箱
biànsùxiāng
gearbox

空气过滤器
kōngqìguòlǜqì
air filter

种类 zhǒnglèi • types

头盔面罩
tóukuīmiànzhào
visor

皮衣
píyī
leathers

反光肩带
fǎnguāng jiāndài
reflector strap

护膝
hùxī
knee pad

服装 fúzhuāng I clothing

赛车 sàichē I racing bike

前灯
qiándēng
headlight

减震器
jiǎnzhènqì
suspension

挡泥板
dǎngníbǎn
mudguard

风挡
fēngdǎng
windshield

旅行摩托 lǚxíngmótuō I tourer

越野摩托 yuèyěmótuō I dirt bike

支架
zhījià
stand

刹车踏板
shāchētàbǎn
brake pedal

轮轴
lúnzhóu
axle

轮胎
lúntāi
tire

小轮摩托 xiǎolúnmótuō I scooter

自行车 zìxíngchē • bicycle

双座自行车 shuāngzuò zìxíngchē
tandem

赛车 sàichē
racing bike

山地车 shāndìchē
mountain bike

旅行车 lǚxíngchē
touring bike

公路车 gōnglùchē
road bike

车座 chēzuò
saddle

座杆 zuògǎn
seat post

水瓶 shuǐpíng
water bottle

车架 chējià
frame

刹车 shāchē
brake

轮毂 lúngǔ
hub

齿轮 chǐlún
gears

轮圈 lúnquān
rim

轮胎 lúntāi
tire

车链 chēliàn
chain

脚蹬 jiǎodēng
pedal

链盘 liànpán
cog

头盔 tóukuī
helmet

自行车道 zìxíngchēdào **l cycle lane**

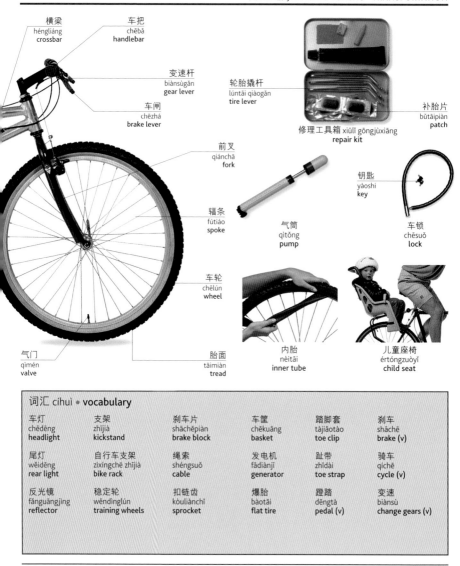

横梁
héngliáng
crossbar

车把
chēbǎ
handlebar

变速杆
biànsùgǎn
gear lever

车闸
chēzhá
brake lever

轮胎撬杆
lúntāi qiàogǎn
tire lever

补胎片
bǔtāipiàn
patch

修理工具箱 xiūlǐ gōngjùxiāng
repair kit

前叉
qiánchā
fork

钥匙
yàoshi
key

车锁
chēsuǒ
lock

辐条
fútiáo
spoke

气筒
qìtǒng
pump

车轮
chēlún
wheel

气门
qìmén
valve

胎面
tāimiàn
tread

内胎
nèitāi
inner tube

儿童座椅
értóngzuòyǐ
child seat

词汇 cíhuì · vocabulary

车灯 chēdēng headlight	支架 zhījià kickstand	刹车片 shāchēpiàn brake block	车筐 chēkuāng basket	踏脚套 tàjiǎotào toe clip	刹车 shāchē brake (v)
尾灯 wěidēng rear light	自行车支架 zìxíngchē zhījià bike rack	绳索 shéngsuǒ cable	发电机 fādiànjī generator	趾带 zhǐdài toe strap	骑车 qíchē cycle (v)
反光镜 fǎnguāngjìng reflector	稳定轮 wěndìnglún training wheels	扣链齿 kòuliànchǐ sprocket	爆胎 bàotāi flat tire	蹬踏 dēngtà pedal (v)	变速 biànsù change gears (v)

列车 lièchē • train

客车厢
kèchēxiāng
car

站台
zhàntái
platform

手推车
shǒutuīchē
cart

站台号
zhàntáihào
platform number

旅客
lǚkè
commuter

火车站 huǒchēzhàn | train station

列车种类 lièchē zhǒnglèi • types of train

火车头
huǒchētóu
engine

驾驶室
jiàshǐshì
engineer's cab

铁轨
tiěguǐ
rail

蒸汽机车
zhēngqìjīchē
steam train

柴油机车 cháiyóujīchē | diesel train

电力机车
diànlìjīchē
electric train

高速列车
gāosùlièchē
high-speed train

单轨列车
dānguǐlièchē
monorail

地铁
dìtiě
subway

有轨电车
yǒuguǐdiànchē
tram

货车
huòchē
freight train

行李架
xínglijià
luggage rack

车窗
chēchuāng
window

轨道
guǐdào
track

门
mén
door

座位
zuòwèi
seat

检票口 jiǎnpiàokou | **ticket gates**

车厢隔间
chēxiānggéjiān
compartment

扩音器
kuòyīnqì
public address system

列车时刻表
lièchē shíkèbiǎo
schedule

41213
KUPONG 7.00 kr

车票
chēpiào
ticket

餐车 cānchē | **dining car**

车站大厅 chēzhàndàtīng | **concourse**

卧铺车厢
wòpùchēxiāng
sleeping compartment

词汇 cíhuì • vocabulary

铁路网 tiělùwǎng **rail network**	地铁线路图 dìtiě xiànlùtú **subway map**	售票处 shòupiàochù **ticket office**	接触轨 jiēchùguǐ **third rail**
城际列车 chéngjì lièchē **intercity train**	晚点 wǎndiǎn **delay**	检票员 jiǎnpiàoyuán **conductor**	信号 xìnhào **signal**
上下班高峰期 shàngxiàbān gāofēngqī **rush hour**	车费 chēfèi **fare**	换乘 huànchéng **change trains**	紧急刹车闸 jǐnjí shāchēzhá **emergency handle**

飞机 fēijī • aircraft

班机 bānjī • airliner

机头
jītóu
nose

驾驶舱
jiàshǐcāng
cockpit

引擎
yǐnqíng
engine

机身
jīshēn
fuselage

机翼
jīyì
wing

尾翼
wěiyì
tail

方向舵
fāngxiàngduò
rudder

舱门
cāngmén
exit

前起落架
qiánqǐluòjià
nosewheel

起落架
qǐluòjià
landing gear

副翼
fùyì
aileron

垂直尾翼
chuízhíwěiyì
fin

水平尾翼
shuǐpíngwěiyì
tailplane

机舱 jīcāng • cabin

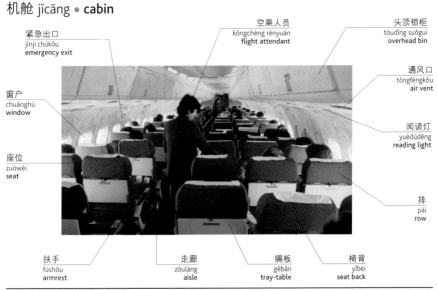

紧急出口
jǐnjí chūkǒu
emergency exit

空乘人员
kōngchèng rényuán
flight attendant

头顶锁柜
tóudǐng suǒguì
overhead bin

窗户
chuānghù
window

通风口
tōngfēngkǒu
air vent

阅读灯
yuèdúdēng
reading light

座位
zuòwèi
seat

排
pái
row

扶手
fúshǒu
armrest

走廊
zǒuláng
aisle

搁板
gēbǎn
tray-table

椅背
yǐbèi
seat back

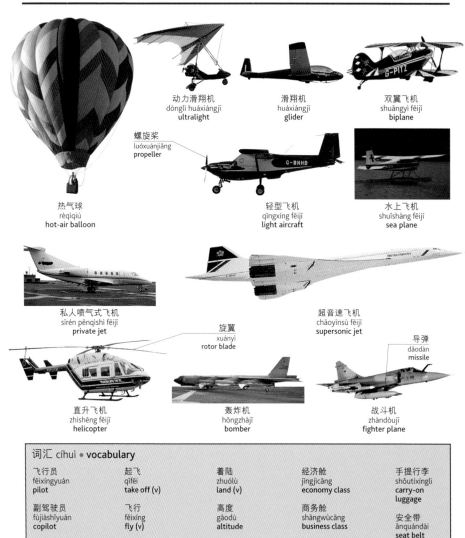

动力滑翔机
dònglì huáxiángjī
ultralight

滑翔机
huáxiángjī
glider

双翼飞机
shuāngyì fēijī
biplane

螺旋桨
luóxuánjiǎng
propeller

热气球
rèqìqiú
hot-air balloon

轻型飞机
qīngxíng fēijī
light aircraft

水上飞机
shuǐshàng fēijī
sea plane

私人喷气式飞机
sīrén pēnqìshì fēijī
private jet

超音速飞机
chāoyīnsù fēijī
supersonic jet

旋翼
xuányì
rotor blade

导弹
dǎodàn
missile

直升飞机
zhíshēng fēijī
helicopter

轰炸机
hōngzhàjī
bomber

战斗机
zhàndòujī
fighter plane

词汇 cíhuì • **vocabulary**

飞行员 fēixíngyuán **pilot**	起飞 qǐfēi **take off (v)**	着陆 zhuólù **land (v)**	经济舱 jīngjìcāng **economy class**	手提行李 shǒutíxínglǐ **carry-on luggage**
副驾驶员 fùjiàshǐyuán **copilot**	飞行 fēixíng **fly (v)**	高度 gāodù **altitude**	商务舱 shāngwùcāng **business class**	安全带 ānquándài **seat belt**

机场 jīchǎng · **airport**

停机坪
tíngjīpíng
apron

行李拖车
xínglituōchē
baggage trailer

候机楼
hòujīlóu
terminal

服务车
fúwùchē
service vehicle

登机通道
dēngjītōngdào
walkway

班机 bānjī I **airliner**

词汇 cíhuì · **vocabulary**

跑道 pǎodào **runway**	航班号 hángbānhào **flight number**	行李传送带 xíngli chuánsòngdài **carousel**	假日 jiàrì **vacation**
国际航线 guójì hángxiàn **international flight**	入境检查 rùjìngjiǎnchá **immigration**	安全 ānquán **security**	办理登机手续 bànlǐ dēngjī shǒuxù **check in (v)**
国内航线 guónèi hángxiàn **domestic flight**	海关 hǎiguān **customs**	X光行李检查机 Xguāng xíngli jiǎnchájī **X-ray machine**	控制塔 kòngzhìtǎ **control tower**
联运 liányùn **connection**	超重行李 chāozhòng xíngli **excess baggage**	假日指南 jiàrì zhǐnán **travel brochure**	订机票 dìngjīpiào **book a flight (v)**

签证
qiānzhèng
visa

手提行李
shǒutí xíngli
carry-on luggage

护照 hùzhào | passport

登机牌
dēngjīpái
boarding pass

(大件)行李
(dàjiàn) xíngli
luggage

行李推车
xíngli tuīchē
cart

办理登机手续处
bànlǐ dēngjī shǒuxùchù
check-in desk

护照检查处
hùzhào jiǎncháchù
passport control

机票
jīpiào
ticket

登机门号
dēngjīménhào
gate number

出发
chūfā
departures

目的地
mùdìdì
destination

抵达
dǐdá
arrivals

候机大厅
hòujīdàtīng
departure lounge

信息屏
xìnxīpíng
information screen

免税商店
miǎnshuì shāngdiàn
duty-free shop

领取行李处
lǐngqǔ xínglichù
baggage claim

出租车站
chūzūchēzhàn
cab stand

租车处
zūchēchù
car rental

船 chuán • ship

雷达
léidá
radar

无线电天线
wúxiàndiàn tiānxiàn
radio antenna

甲板
jiǎbǎn
deck

烟囱
yāncōng
funnel

后甲板
hòujiǎbǎn
quarterdeck

船首
chuánshǒu
prow

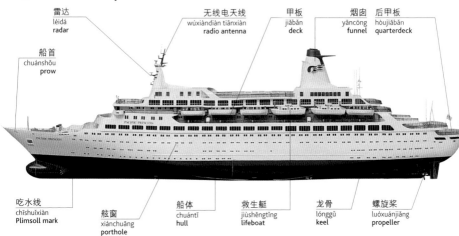

吃水线
chīshuǐxiàn
Plimsoll mark

舷窗
xiánchuāng
porthole

船体
chuántǐ
hull

救生艇
jiùshēngtǐng
lifeboat

龙骨
lónggǔ
keel

螺旋桨
luóxuánjiǎng
propeller

远洋客轮 yuǎnyángkèlún I ocean liner

驾驶台
jiàshǐtái
bridge

轮机舱
lúnjīcāng
engine room

客舱
kècāng
cabin

船上厨房
chuánshàng chúfáng
galley

词汇 cíhuì • vocabulary

船坞
chuánwù
dock

港口
gǎngkǒu
port

舷梯
xiántī
gangway

锚
máo
anchor

岸边缆桩
ànbiānlǎnzhuāng
bollard

卷扬机
juǎnyángjī
windlass

船长
chuánzhǎng
captain

快艇
kuàitǐng
speedboat

划桨船
huájiǎngchuán
rowboat

独木舟
dúmùzhōu
canoe

其他船型 qítāchuánxíng · other ships

舷外马达
xiánwàimǎdá
outboard motor

渡船
dùchuán
ferry

充气式橡皮艇
chōngqìshì xiàngpítǐng
inflatable dinghy

水翼艇
shuǐyìtǐng
hydrofoil

游艇
yóutǐng
yacht

双体船
shuāngtǐchuán
catamaran

拖船
tuōchuán
tugboat

气垫船
qìdiànchuán
hovercraft

帆缆
fānlǎn
rigging

货舱
huòcāng
hold

集装箱船
jízhuāngxiāng chuán
container ship

帆船
fānchuán
sailboat

货船
huòchuán
freighter

指挥塔
zhǐhuītǎ
conning tower

油轮
yóulún
oil tanker

航空母舰
hángkōng mǔjiàn
aircraft carrier

战舰
zhànjiàn
battleship

潜水艇
qiánshuǐtǐng
submarine

港口 gǎngkǒu • port

仓库
cāngkù
warehouse

起重机
qǐzhòngjī
crane

叉车
chāchē
forklift

出入港通道
chūrùgǎng tōngdào
access road

海关
hǎiguān
customs house

船坞
chuánwù
dock

集装箱
jízhuāngxiāng
container

码头
mǎtóu
quay

货物
huòwù
cargo

渡船码头
dùchuán mǎtóu
ferry terminal

渡船
dùchuán
ferry

售票处
shòupiàochù
ticket office

乘客
chéngkè
passenger

集装箱港口 jízhuāngxiāng gǎngkǒu I container port

客运码头 kèyùn mǎtóu I passenger port

渔网
yúwǎng
net

渔船
yúchuán
fishing boat

缆绳
lǎnshéng
mooring

小船停靠区 xiǎochuántíngkàoqū I marina

渔港 yúgǎng I fishing port

港口 gǎngkǒu I harbor

栈桥 zhànqiáo I pier

防波堤
fángbōdī
jetty

船厂
chuánchǎng
shipyard

塔灯
tǎdēng
beacon

灯塔
dēngtǎ
lighthouse

浮标
fúbiāo
buoy

词汇 cíhuì • vocabulary

海岸警卫队
hǎi'àn jǐngwèiduì
coastguard

港务局长
gǎngwù júzhǎng
harbor master

抛锚
pāomáo
drop anchor (v)

干船坞
gānchuánwù
dry dock

停泊
tíngbó
moor (v)

进入船坞
jìnrùchuánwù
dock (v)

上船
shàngchuán
board (v)

离船登岸
líchuándēngàn
disembark (v)

起航
qǐháng
set sail (v)

体育运动 tǐyùyùndòng
sports

美式橄榄球 měishì gǎnlǎnqiú • football

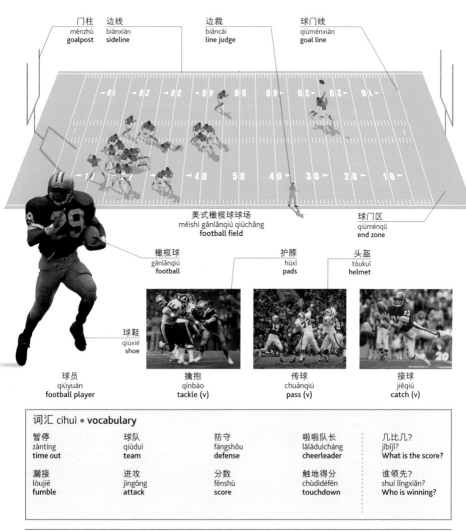

门柱 ménzhù goalpost	边线 biānxiàn sideline	边裁 biāncái line judge	球门线 qiúménxiàn goal line

美式橄榄球球场
měishì gǎnlǎnqiú qiúchǎng
football field

球门区
qiúménqū
end zone

橄榄球
gǎnlǎnqiú
football

护膝
hùxī
pads

头盔
tóukuī
helmet

球鞋
qiúxié
shoe

球员
qiúyuán
football player

擒抱
qínbào
tackle (v)

传球
chuánqiú
pass (v)

接球
jiēqiú
catch (v)

词汇 cíhuì • vocabulary

暂停 zàntíng time out	球队 qiúduì team	防守 fángshǒu defense	啦啦队长 lālāduìcháng cheerleader	几比几? jǐbǐjǐ? What is the score?
漏接 lòujiē fumble	进攻 jìngōng attack	分数 fēnshù score	触地得分 chùdìdéfēn touchdown	谁领先? shuí lǐngxiān? Who is winning?

英式橄榄球 yīngshì gǎnlǎnqiú • rugby

球门
qiúmén
goal

得分区
défēnqū
in-goal area

边线
biānxiàn
touch line

旗
qí
flag

死球线
sǐqiúxiàn
dead ball line

英式橄榄球球场 yīngshì gǎnlǎnqiú qiúchǎng | rugby field

球
qiú
ball

抛球
pāoqiú
throw (v)

(英式)橄榄球球衣
(yīngshi) gǎnlǎnqiú qiúyī
rugby uniform

踢球
tīqiú
kick (v)

传球
chuánqiú
pass (v)

擒抱
qínbào
tackle (v)

持球触地得分
chíqiú chùdìdéfēn
try

球员
qiúyuán
player

密集争球 mìjí zhēngqiú | ruck

并列争球 bìngliè zhēngqiú | scrum

足球 zúqiú • soccer

足球
zúqiú
soccer ball

守门员
shǒuményuán
goalkeeper

前锋
qiánfēng
forward

主裁判
zhǔcáipàn
referee

中圈
zhōngquān
center circle

足球球衣
zúqiú qiúyī
soccer uniform

足球球员
zúqiú qiúyuán
soccer player

足球场
zúqiúchǎng
soccer field

门柱
ménzhù
goalpost

球网
qiúwǎng
net

球门横梁
qiúmén héngliáng
crossbar

带球 dàiqiú I **dribble (v)**

头球
tóuqiú
head (v)

人墙
rénqiáng
wall

球门 qiúmén I **goal**

任意球 rènyìqiú I **free kick**

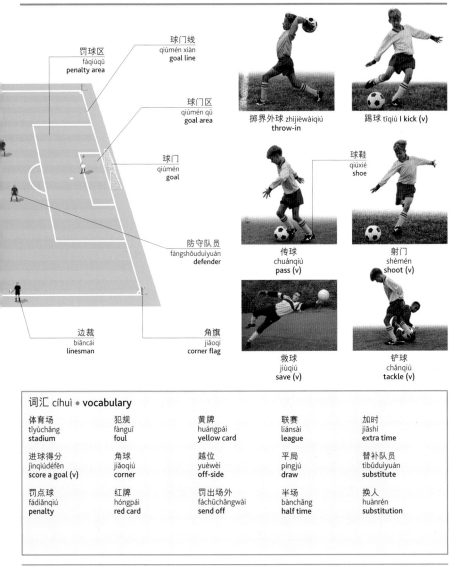

罚球区
fáqiúqū
penalty area

球门线
qiúmén xiàn
goal line

球门区
qiúmén qū
goal area

球门
qiúmén
goal

防守队员
fángshǒuduìyuán
defender

边裁
biāncái
linesman

角旗
jiǎoqí
corner flag

掷界外球 zhìjièwàiqiú
throw-in

踢球 tīqiú I kick (v)

球鞋
qiúxié
shoe

传球
chuánqiú
pass (v)

射门
shèmén
shoot (v)

救球
jiùqiú
save (v)

铲球
chǎnqiú
tackle (v)

词汇 cíhuì • vocabulary

体育场 tǐyùchǎng **stadium**	犯规 fànguī **foul**	黄牌 huángpái **yellow card**	联赛 liánsài **league**	加时 jiāshí **extra time**
进球得分 jìnqiúdéfēn **score a goal (v)**	角球 jiǎoqiú **corner**	越位 yuèwèi **off-side**	平局 píngjú **draw**	替补队员 tìbǔduìyuán **substitute**
罚点球 fádiǎnqiú **penalty**	红牌 hóngpái **red card**	罚出场外 fáchūchǎngwài **send off**	半场 bànchǎng **half time**	换人 huànrén **substitution**

曲棍类运动 qūgùnlèi yùndòng • hockey

冰球 bīngqiú • ice hockey

防守区
fángshǒuqū
defending zone

球门线
qiúmén xiàn
goal line

进攻区
jìngōngqū
attack zone

中场
zhōngchǎng
neutral zone

守门员
shǒuményuán
goalkeeper

球门
qiúmén
goal

开球区
kāiqiúqū
face-off circle

中圈
zhōngquān
center circle

手套
shǒutào
glove

护肩
hùjiān
pad

冰球场
bīngqiú chǎng
hockey rink

球杆
qiúgān
stick

冰鞋
bīngxié
ice skate

曲棍球 qūgùnqiú • field hockey

曲棍球棒
qūgùnqiú bàng
hockey stick

冰球
bīngqiú
puck

冰球球员 bīngqiú qiúyuán
hockey player

曲棍球
qūgùnqiú
ball

滑行
huáxíng
skate (v)

击球
jīqiú
hit (v)

板球 bǎnqiú • cricket

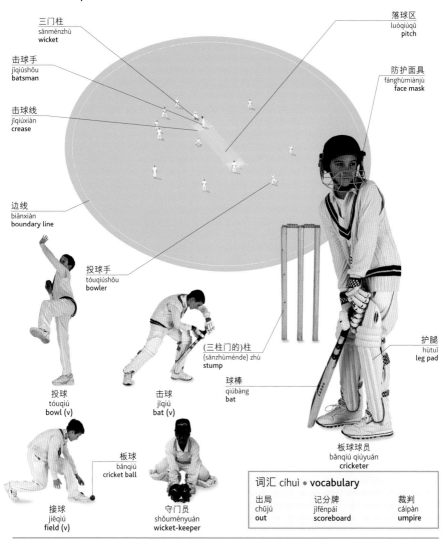

三门柱
sānménzhù
wicket

击球手
jīqiúshǒu
batsman

击球线
jīqiúxiàn
crease

边线
biānxiàn
boundary line

落球区
luòqiúqū
pitch

防护面具
fánghùmiànjù
face mask

投球手
tóuqiúshǒu
bowler

(三柱门的)柱
(sānzhùménde) zhù
stump

护腿
hùtuǐ
leg pad

球棒
qiúbàng
bat

投球
tóuqiú
bowl (v)

击球
jīqiú
bat (v)

板球球员
bǎnqiú qiúyuán
cricketer

接球
jiēqiú
field (v)

板球
bǎnqiú
cricket ball

守门员
shǒuményuán
wicket-keeper

词汇 cíhuì • vocabulary

出局 chūjú **out**	记分牌 jìfēnpái **scoreboard**	裁判 cáipàn **umpire**

篮球 lánqiú • basketball

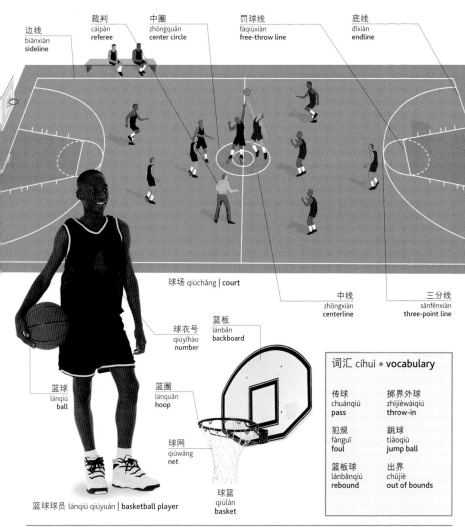

边线
biānxiàn
sideline

裁判
cáipàn
referee

中圈
zhōngquān
center circle

罚球线
fáqiúxiàn
free-throw line

底线
dǐxiàn
endline

球场 qiúchǎng | court

中线
zhōngxiàn
centerline

三分线
sānfēnxiàn
three-point line

球衣号
qiúyīhào
number

篮板
lánbǎn
backboard

篮球
lánqiú
ball

篮圈
lánquān
hoop

球网
qiúwǎng
net

球篮
qiúlán
basket

篮球球员 lánqiú qiúyuán | basketball player

词汇 cíhuì • vocabulary

传球 chuánqiú pass	掷界外球 zhìjièwàiqiú throw-in
犯规 fànguī foul	跳球 tiàoqiú jump ball
篮板球 lánbǎnqiú rebound	出界 chūjiè out of bounds

动作 dòngzuò ● actions

掷球 zhìqiú **throw (v)**	接球 jiēqiú **catch (v)**	投篮 tóulán **shoot (v)**	跳投 tiàotóu **jump (v)**	

盯人 dīngrén **mark (v)**	阻挡 zǔdǎng **block (v)**	运球 yùnqiú **bounce (v)**	灌篮 guànlán **dunk (v)**

排球 páiqiú ● volleyball

拦网
lánwǎng
block (v)

球网
qiúwǎng
net

垫球
diànqiú
dig (v)

裁判
cáipàn
referee

护膝
hùxī
knee support

球场 qiúchǎng | court

棒球 bàngqiú • baseball

球场 qiúchǎng • field

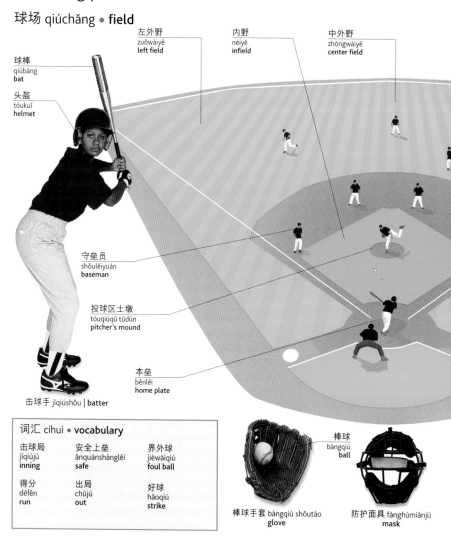

左外野
zuǒwàiyě
left field

内野
nèiyě
infield

中外野
zhōngwàiyě
center field

球棒
qiúbàng
bat

头盔
tóukuī
helmet

守垒员
shǒulěiyuán
baseman

投球区土墩
tóuqiúqū tǔdūn
pitcher's mound

本垒
běnlěi
home plate

击球手 jīqiúshǒu | **batter**

词汇 cíhuì • vocabulary

击球局 jīqiújú **inning**	安全上垒 ānquánshànglěi **safe**	界外球 jièwàiqiú **foul ball**
得分 défēn **run**	出局 chūjú **out**	好球 hǎoqiú **strike**

棒球
bàngqiú
ball

棒球手套 bàngqiú shǒutào
glove

防护面具 fánghùmiànjù
mask

动作 dòngzuò • actions

外野
wàiyě
outfield

右外野
yòuwàiyě
right field

边线
biānxiàn
foul line

球队
qiúduì
team

队员席
duìyuánxí
dugout

投球 tóuqiú | throw (v)

接球 jiēqiú | catch (v)

跑垒
pǎolěi
run (v)

守球 shǒuqiú | field (v)

滑垒
huálěi
slide (v)

触杀
chùshā
tag (v)

投球
tóuqiú
pitch (v)

击球
jīqiú
bat (v)

裁判
cáipàn
umpire

比赛 bǐsài | play (v)

接球手 jiēqiúshǒu | catcher

投球手 tóuqiúshǒu | pitcher

网球 wǎngqiú • tennis

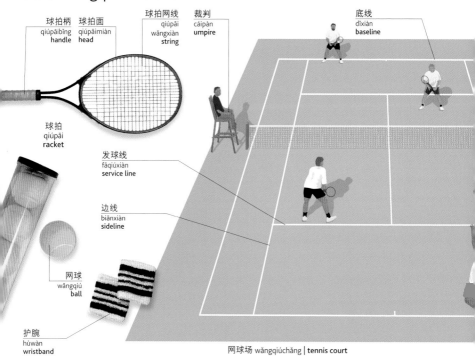

球拍柄
qiúpāibǐng
handle

球拍面
qiúpāimiàn
head

球拍网线
qiúpāi
wǎngxiàn
string

裁判
cáipàn
umpire

底线
dǐxiàn
baseline

球拍
qiúpāi
racket

发球线
fāqiúxiàn
service line

边线
biānxiàn
sideline

网球
wǎngqiú
ball

护腕
hùwàn
wristband

网球场 wǎngqiúchǎng | tennis court

词汇 cíhuì • vocabulary

单打 dāndǎ singles	盘, 局 pán, jú set	零分 língfēn love	发球失误 fāqiúshīwù fault	削球 xiāoqiú slice	边裁 biāncái linesman
双打 shuāngdǎ doubles	比赛 bǐsài match	评分 píngfēn deuce	发球得分 fāqiúdéfēn ace	回合 huíhé rally	锦标赛 jǐnbiāosài championship
比赛 bǐsài game	抢七局 qiǎngqījú tiebreak	发球方占先 fāqiúfāng zhànxiān advantage	近网短球 jìnwǎng duǎnqiú dropshot	触网! chùwǎng! let!	(球在空中)旋转 (qiúzàikōngzhōng) xuánzhuǎn spin

中文 zhōngwén • english

击球动作 jīqiúdòngzuò • strokes

球网
qiúwǎng
net

扣球
kòuqiú
smash

球童
qiútóng
ballboy

发球
fāqiú
serve (v)

网球鞋
wǎngqiúxié
tennis shoes

网球手 wǎngqiúshǒu | player

发球
fāqiú
serve

拦击球
lánjīqiú
volley

回球
huíqiú
return

吊高球
diàogāoqiú
lob

正手
zhèngshǒu
forehand

反手
fǎnshǒu
backhand

拍类运动 pāilèi yùndòng • racquet games

羽毛球
yǔmáoqiú
shuttlecock

乒乓球拍
pīngpāngqiúpāi
paddle

羽毛球(运动)
yǔmáoqiú (yùndòng)
badminton

乒乓球
pīngpāngqiú
table tennis

壁球
bìqiú
squash

短拍壁球
duǎnpāibìqiú
racquetball

高尔夫球 gāo'ěrfūqiú • golf

球洞
qiúdòng
hole

挥杆
huīgān
swing (v)

发球区
fāqiúqū
teeing ground

果岭
guǒlǐng
green

沙坑
shākēng
bunker

旗
qí
flag

球道
qiúdào
fairway

长草区
chángcǎoqū
rough

水障碍
shuǐzhàng'ài
water hazard

高尔夫球场
gāo'ěrfū qiúchǎng
golf course

短途小车
duǎntú xiǎochē
golf cart

击球姿势
jīqiúzīshì
stance

高尔夫球员 gāo'ěrfū qiúyuán | golfer

会所 huìsuǒ | clubhouse

球具 qiújù • equipment

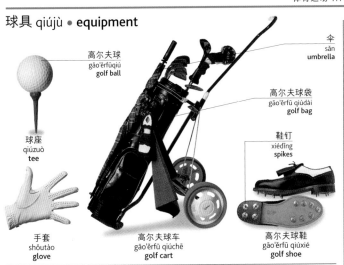

高尔夫球
gāo'ěrfūqiú
golf ball

球座
qiúzuò
tee

伞
sǎn
umbrella

高尔夫球袋
gāo'ěrfū qiúdài
golf bag

鞋钉
xiédīng
spikes

手套
shǒutào
glove

高尔夫球车
gāo'ěrfū qiúchē
golf cart

高尔夫球鞋
gāo'ěrfū qiúxié
golf shoe

高尔夫球杆
gāo'ěrfū qiúgān • golf clubs

木杆
mùgān
wood

推杆
tuīgān
putter

铁杆
tiěgān
iron

挖起杆
wāqǐgān
wedge

动作 dòngzuò • actions

开球
kāiqiú
tee-off (v)

远打
yuǎndǎ
drive (v)

轻击
qīngjī
putt (v)

切击
qiējī
chip (v)

词汇 cíhuì • vocabulary

一杆入洞 yīgān rùdòng **hole in one**	标准杆数 biāozhǔn gānshù **par**	差点 chàdiǎn **handicap**	球童 qiútóng **caddy**	向后挥杆 xiàng hòu huīgān **backswing**	击球 jīqiú **stroke**
低于标准杆数 dīyú biāozhǔn gānshù **under par**	高于标准杆数 gāoyú biāozhǔn gānshù **over par**	巡回赛 xúnhuísài **tournament**	观众 guānzhòng **spectators**	练习挥杆 liànxí huīgān **practice swing**	打球线 dǎqiúxiàn **line of play**

田径运动 tiánjìng yùndòng • track and field

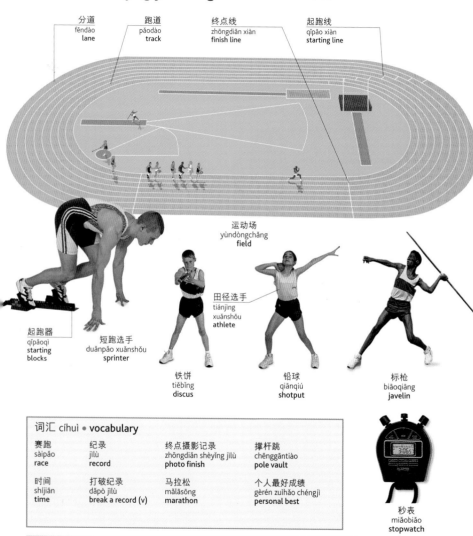

分道
fēndào
lane

跑道
pǎodào
track

终点线
zhōngdiǎn xiàn
finish line

起跑线
qǐpǎo xiàn
starting line

运动场
yùndòngchǎng
field

田径选手
tiánjìng
xuǎnshǒu
athlete

起跑器
qǐpǎoqì
starting
blocks

短跑选手
duǎnpǎo xuǎnshǒu
sprinter

铁饼
tiěbǐng
discus

铅球
qiānqiú
shotput

标枪
biāoqiāng
javelin

词汇 cíhuì • vocabulary

赛跑 sàipǎo race	**纪录** jìlù record	**终点摄影记录** zhōngdiǎn shèyǐng jìlù photo finish	**撑杆跳** chēnggǎntiào pole vault
时间 shíjiān time	**打破纪录** dǎpò jìlù break a record (v)	**马拉松** mǎlāsōng marathon	**个人最好成绩** gèrén zuìhǎo chéngjì personal best

秒表
miǎobiǎo
stopwatch

接力棒
jiēlìbàng
baton

横杆
hénggān
crossbar

接力
jiēlì
relay race

跳高
tiàogāo
high jump

跳远
tiàoyuǎn
long jump

跨栏
kuàlán
hurdles

体操 tǐcāo • gymnastics

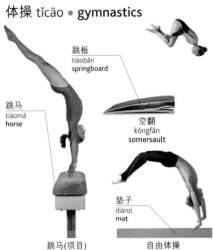

跳板
tiàobǎn
springboard

跳马
tiàomǎ
horse

空翻
kōngfān
somersault

垫子
diànzi
mat

体操选手
tǐcāo xuǎnshǒu
gymnast

平衡木 pínghéngmù | beam

丝带
sīdài
ribbon

跳马(项目)
tiàomǎ (xiàngmù)
vault

自由体操
zìyóutǐcāo
floor exercises

翻筋斗
fānjīndǒu
tumble

艺术体操
yìshù tǐcāo
rhythmic gymnastics

词汇 cíhuì • vocabulary

单杠 dāngàng **horizontal bar**	鞍马 ānmǎ **pommel horse**	吊环 diàohuán **rings**	奖牌 jiǎngpái **medals**	银牌 yínpái **silver**
双杠 shuānggàng **parallel bars**	高低杠 gāodīgàng **asymmetric bars**	领奖台 lǐngjiǎngtái **podium**	金牌 jīnpái **gold**	铜牌 tóngpái **bronze**

格斗运动 gédòuyùndòng ● **combat sports**

对手
duìshǒu
opponent

护盔
hùkuī
guard

手套
shǒutào
glove

腰带
yāodài
belt

空手道 kōngshǒudào | **karate**

跆拳道 táiquándào | **tae kwon do**

防护面具
fánghùmiànjù
mask

竹剑
zhújiàn
sword

柔道 róudào | **judo**

合气道 héqìdào | **aikido**

剑道 jiàndào | **kendo**

中国武术 zhōngguówǔshù
kung fu

泰拳 tàiquán | **kickboxing**

摔跤 shuāijiāo | **wrestling**

拳击 quánjī | **boxing**

动作 dòngzuò • **actions**

摔倒 shuāidǎo | fall

抓握 zhuāwò | **hold**

摔 shuāi | **throw**

压倒 yādǎo | **pin**

侧踢 cètī | **kick**

出拳 chūquán | **punch**

击打 jīdǎ | **strike**

跳踢 tiàotī | **jump**

挡 dǎng | **block**

劈 pī | **chop**

词汇 cíhuì • **vocabulary**

拳击台 quánjī tái **boxing ring**	回合 huíhé **round**	拳头 quántóu **fist**	黑带 hēidài **black belt**	卡波卫勒舞 kǎbōwèilèwǔ **capoeira**
拳击手套 quánjī shǒutào **boxing gloves**	拳击比赛 quánjī bǐsài **bout**	击倒 (对手) jīdǎo (duìshǒu) **knockout**	自卫 zìwèi **self-defense**	相扑 xiàngpū **sumo wrestling**
护齿 hùchǐ **mouth guard**	拳击练习 quánjī liànxí **sparring**	沙袋 shādài **punching bag**	武术 wǔshù **martial arts**	太极拳 tàijíquán **tai chi**

游泳 yóuyǒng ● swimming
泳具 yǒngjù ● equipment

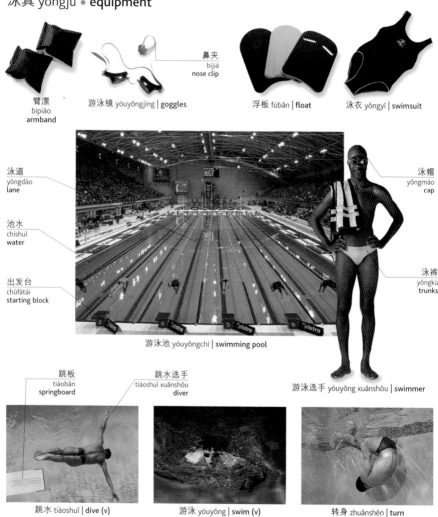

臂漂
bìpiāo
armband

游泳镜 yóuyǒngjìng | goggles

鼻夹
bíjiá
nose clip

浮板 fúbǎn | float

泳衣 yǒngyī | swimsuit

泳道
yǒngdào
lane

池水
chíshuǐ
water

出发台
chūfātái
starting block

泳帽
yǒngmào
cap

泳裤
yǒngkù
trunks

游泳池 yóuyǒngchí | swimming pool

跳板
tiàobǎn
springboard

跳水选手
tiàoshuǐ xuǎnshǒu
diver

游泳选手 yóuyǒng xuǎnshǒu | swimmer

跳水 tiàoshuǐ | dive (v)

游泳 yóuyǒng | swim (v)

转身 zhuǎnshēn | turn

泳姿 yǒngzī • styles

自由泳 zìyóuyǒng | front crawl

蛙泳 wāyǒng | breaststroke

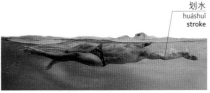

划水
huáshuǐ
stroke

仰泳 yǎngyǒng | backstroke

打水
dǎshuǐ
kick

蝶泳 diéyǒng | butterfly

水肺潜水 shuǐfèi qiánshuǐ • scuba diving

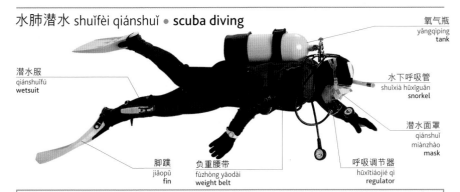

氧气瓶
yǎngqìpíng
tank

潜水服
qiánshuǐfú
wetsuit

水下呼吸管
shuǐxià hūxīguǎn
snorkel

潜水面罩
qiánshuǐ
miànzhào
mask

脚蹼
jiǎopǔ
fin

负重腰带
fùzhòng yāodài
weight belt

呼吸调节器
hūxītiáojié qì
regulator

词汇 cíhuì • vocabulary

跳水 tiàoshuǐ **dive**	踩水 cǎishuǐ **tread water (v)**	锁柜 suǒguì **lockers**	水球 shuǐqiú **water polo**	浅水区 qiǎnshuǐqū **shallow end**	抽筋 chōujīn **cramp**
高台跳水 gāotái tiàoshuǐ **high dive**	出发跳水 chūfā tiàoshuǐ **racing dive**	救生员 jiùshēngyuán **lifeguard**	深水区 shēnshuǐqū **deep end**	花样游泳 huāyàng yóuyǒng **synchronized swimming**	溺水 nìshuǐ . **drown (v)**

帆船运动 fānchuán yùndòng • sailing

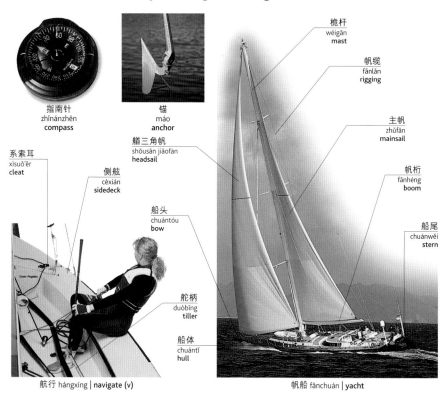

指南针
zhǐnánzhēn
compass

锚
máo
anchor

桅杆
wéigān
mast

帆缆
fānlǎn
rigging

舳三角帆
shǒusān jiǎofān
headsail

系索耳
xìsuǒ'ěr
cleat

侧舷
cèxián
sidedeck

主帆
zhǔfān
mainsail

船头
chuántóu
bow

帆桁
fānhéng
boom

船尾
chuánwěi
stern

舵柄
duòbǐng
tiller

船体
chuántǐ
hull

航行 hángxíng | **navigate (v)**

帆船 fānchuán | **yacht**

救生器具 jiùshēngqìjù • safety

照明弹
zhàomíngdàn
flare

救生圈
jiùshēngquān
lifebuoy

救生衣
jiùshēngyī
life jacket

救生筏
jiùshēngfá
life raft

水上运动 shuǐshàng yùndòng · **watersports**

桨手
jiǎngshǒu
rower

桨
jiǎng
oar

皮筏
pífá
kayak

双叶桨
shuāngyèjiǎng
paddle

划船 huáchuán | **row (v)**

独木舟
dúmùzhōu
canoeing

帆
fān
sail

冲浪板
chōnglàngbǎn
surfboard

滑水橇
huáshuǐqiāo
ski

帆板运动员
fānbǎn
yùndòngyuán
windsurfer

冲浪
chōnglàng
surfing

滑水
huáshuǐ
waterskiing

快艇
kuàitǐng
speedboating

帆板
fānbǎn
board

套脚带
tàojiǎodài
footstrap

帆板运动 fānbǎn yùndòng | **windsurfing**

皮划艇
píhuátǐng
rafting

水上摩托
shuǐshàng mótuō
jet-skiing

词汇 cíhuì · **vocabulary**

滑水者 huáshuǐzhě **waterskier**	艇员 tǐngyuán **crew**	风 fēng **wind**	浪花 lànghuā **surf**	帆脚索 fānjiǎosuǒ **sheet**	稳向板 wěnxiàngbǎn **centerboard**
冲浪运动员 chōnglàng yùndòngyuán **surfer**	抢风航行 qiǎngfēng hángxíng **tack (v)**	波浪 bōlàng **wave**	激流 jīliú **rapids**	舵 duò **rudder**	(船)倾覆 (chuán) qīngfù **capsize (v)**

马上运动 mǎshàng yùndòng • horseback riding

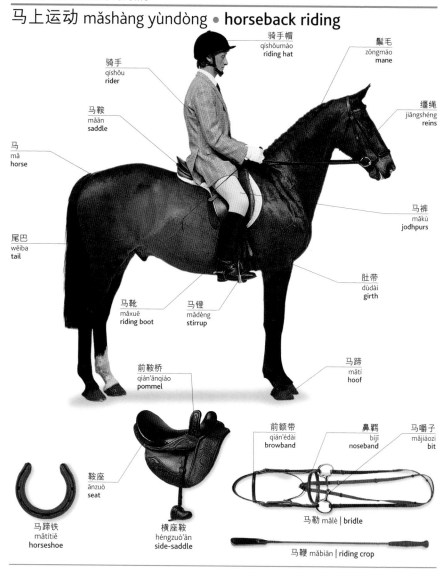

骑手帽
qíshǒumào
riding hat

鬃毛
zōngmáo
mane

骑手
qíshǒu
rider

缰绳
jiāngshéng
reins

马鞍
mǎān
saddle

马
mǎ
horse

马裤
mǎkù
jodhpurs

尾巴
wěiba
tail

肚带
dùdài
girth

马靴
mǎxuē
riding boot

马镫
mǎdèng
stirrup

马蹄
mǎtí
hoof

前鞍桥
qián'ānqiáo
pommel

前额带
qián'édài
browband

鼻羁
bíjī
noseband

马嚼子
mǎjiáozi
bit

鞍座
ānzuò
seat

马蹄铁
mǎtítiě
horseshoe

横座鞍
héngzuò'ān
side-saddle

马勒 mǎlè | bridle

马鞭 mǎbiān | riding crop

赛事 sàishì • events

赛马
sàimǎ
racehorse

障碍
zhàng'ài
fence

赛马(比赛)
sàimǎ (bǐsài)
horse race

障碍赛
zhàng'àisài
steeplechase

轻驾车赛
qīngjiàchēsài
harness race

牛仔竞技表演
niúzǎijìngjì biǎoyǎn
rodeo

越障碍赛
yuèzhàng'àisài
showjumping

双套马车赛
shuāngtào mǎchēsài
carriage race

长途旅行 chángtú lǚxíng | **trail riding**

花式骑术 huāshìqíshù | **dressage**

马球 mǎqiú | **polo**

词汇 cíhuì • vocabulary

慢步 mànbù **walk**	慢跑 mànpǎo **canter**	跳跃 tiàoyuè **jump**	笼头 lóngtou **halter**	围场 wéichǎng **paddock**	无障碍赛马 wúzhàng'àisàimǎ **flat race**
小跑 xiǎopǎo **trot**	疾驰 jíchí **gallop**	马夫 mǎfū **groom**	马厩 mǎjiù **stable**	竞技场 jìngjìchǎng **arena**	赛马场 sàimǎchǎng **racecourse**

钓鱼 diàoyú • fishing

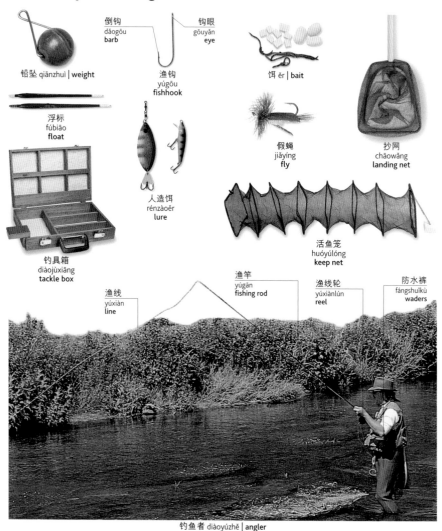

铅坠 qiānzhuì | weight

倒钩
dǎogōu
barb

钩眼
gōuyǎn
eye

渔钩
yúgōu
fishhook

饵 ěr | bait

浮标
fúbiāo
float

假蝇
jiǎyíng
fly

抄网
chāowǎng
landing net

人造饵
rénzàoěr
lure

钓具箱
diàojùxiāng
tackle box

活鱼笼
huóyúlóng
keep net

渔线
yúxiàn
line

渔竿
yúgān
fishing rod

渔线轮
yúxiànlún
reel

防水裤
fángshuǐkù
waders

钓鱼者 diàoyúzhě | angler

垂钓种类 chuídiào zhǒnglèi • types of fishing

淡水垂钓
dànshuǐ chuídiào
freshwater fishing

假蝇垂钓
jiǎyíng chuídiào
fly fishing

休闲垂钓
xiūxián chuídiào
sport fishing

深海垂钓
shēnhǎi chuídiào
deep sea fishing

激浪投钓
jīlàng tóudiào
surfcasting

活动 huódòng • activities

撒网
sāwǎng
cast (v)

捕捉
bǔzhuō
catch (v)

收线
shōuxiàn
reel in (v)

网捕
wǎngbǔ
net (v)

放生
fàngshēng
release (v)

词汇 cíhuì • vocabulary

装饵 zhuāng'ěr **bait (v)**	**钓具** diàojù **tackle**	**雨衣** yǔyī **waterproofs**	**钓鱼许可证** diàoyú xǔkězhèng **fishing license**	**渔篓** yúlǒu **creel**
咬钩 yǎogōu **bite (v)**	**线轴** xiànzhóu **spool**	**杆** gān **pole**	**海洋捕捞** hǎiyáng bǔlāo **marine fishing**	**渔叉捕鱼** yúchābǔyú **spearfishing**

滑雪 huáxuě · skiing

滑雪坡道
huáxuě pōdào
ski slope

缆车吊椅
lǎnchē diàoyǐ
chairlift

缆车
lǎnchē
cable car

滑雪服
huáxuěfú
ski suit

滑雪杖
huáxuězhàng
ski pole

手套
shǒutào
glove

雪道
xuědào
ski run

滑雪靴
huáxuěxuē
ski boot

安全护栏
ānquánhùlán
safety barrier

滑雪板
huáxuěbǎn
ski

板边
bǎnbiān
edge

滑雪者
huáxuězhě
skier

板尖
bǎnjiān
tip

项目 xiàngmù · events

高山速降
gāoshān sùjiàng
downhill skiing

旗门杆
qiméngān
gate

小回转
xiǎohuízhuǎn
slalom

跳台滑雪
tiàotái huáxuě
ski jump

越野滑雪
yuèyě huáxuě
cross-country skiing

冬季运动 dōngjì yùndòng · winter sports

攀冰
pānbīng
ice climbing

溜冰
liūbīng
ice skating

滑雪镜
huáxuějìng
goggles

冰鞋
bīngxié
skate

花样滑冰
huāyàng huábīng
figure skating

单板滑雪
dānbǎn huáxuě
snowboarding

长橇滑雪
chángqiāo huáxuě
bobsled

小型橇
xiǎoxíngqiāo
luge

机动雪橇
jīdòng xuěqiāo
snowmobile

乘橇滑行
chéngqiāo huáxíng
sledding

词汇 cíhuì · vocabulary

高山滑雪
gāoshān huáxuě
alpine skiing

大回转
dàhuízhuǎn
giant slalom

雪道外
xuědàowài
off-piste

冰上溜石
bīngshàng liūshí
curling

狗拉雪橇
gǒulā xuěqiāo
dogsledding

速滑
sùhuá
speed skating

冬季两项
dōngjì liǎngxiàng
biathlon

雪崩
xuěbēng
avalanche

其他运动 qítāyùndòng ● **other sports**

滑翔机
huáxiángjī
glider

悬挂式滑翔机
xuánguàshì
huáxiángjī
hang-glider

滑翔
huáxiáng
gliding

降落伞
jiàngluòsǎn
parachute

悬挂滑翔
xuánguà huáxiáng
hang-gliding

绳索
shéngsuǒ
rope

攀岩
pānyán
rock climbing

跳伞
tiàosǎn
parachuting

滑翔伞
huáxiángsǎn
paragliding

特技跳伞
tèjìtiàosǎn
skydiving

悬绳下降
xuánshéng xiàjiàng
abseiling

蹦极
bèngjí
bungee jumping

汽车拉力赛
qìchē lālìsài
rally driving

赛车
sàichē
auto racing

赛车手
sàichēshǒu
racing driver

摩托车越野赛
mótuōchē yuèyěsài
motocross

摩托车赛
mótuōchēsài
motorcycle racing

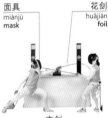

滑板
huábǎn
skateboard

轮滑鞋
lúnhuáxié
rollerskate

滑板运动
huábǎn yùndòng
skateboarding

滑旱冰
huáhànbīng
rollerskating

球棒
qiúbàng
stick

长曲棍球
cháng qūgùnqiú
lacrosse

面具
miànjù
mask

花剑
huājiàn
foil

击剑
jījiàn
fencing

保龄球瓶
bǎolíngqiú píng
pin

弓
gōng
bow

靶
bǎ
target

箭
jiàn
arrow

箭袋
jiàndài
quiver

射箭
shèjiàn
archery

射击
shèjī
target shooting

保龄球
bǎolíngqiú
bowling ball

保龄球运动
bǎolíngqiú yùndòng
bowling

美式台球
měishìtáiqiú
pool

台球
táiqiú
snooker

健身 jiànshēn • fitness

健身车
jiànshēnchē
exercise bike

健身器械
jiànshēn qìxiè
gym machine

长椅
chángyǐ
bench

力量训练器
lìliàng xùnliànqì
free weights

横杠
hénggàng
bar

健身房
jiànshēnfáng
gym

划船机
huáchuánjī
rowing machine

踏步机
tàbùjī
step machine

私人教练
sīrén jiàoliàn
personal trainer

跑步机
pǎobùjī
treadmill

交叉训练器
jiāochā xùnliànqì
cross-trainer

游泳池
yóuyǒngchí
swimming pool

桑拿浴
sāngnáyù
sauna

锻炼 duànliàn • exercises

紧身衣
jǐnshēnyī
tights

伸展腿
shēnzhǎntuǐ
stretch

弓箭步压腿
gōngjiànbù yātuǐ
lunge

俯卧撑
fǔwòchēng
push-up

哑铃
yǎlíng
dumbbell

蹲起
dūnqǐ
squat

仰卧起坐
yǎngwòqǐzuò
sit-up

二头肌训练
èrtóujī xùnliàn
biceps curl

蹬腿
dēngtuǐ
leg press

扩胸
kuòxiōng
chest press

运动鞋
yùndòngxié
athletic
shoes

重量训练
zhòngliàng xùnliàn
weight training

杠铃横杆
gànglíng
hénggǎn
weight bar

背心
bèixīn
vest

慢跑
mànpǎo
jogging

有氧运动
yǒuyǎng yùndòng
aerobics

词汇 cíhuì • vocabulary

训练 xùnliàn **train (v)**	原地跑 yuándìpǎo **run in place (v)**	伸展 shēnzhǎn **extend (v)**	普拉提 pǔlātí **Pilates**	循环训练法 xúnhuán xùnliànfǎ **circuit training**
热身 rèshēn **warm up (v)**	弯曲(四肢) wānqū (sìzhī) **flex (v)**	引体向上 yǐntǐ xiàngshàng **pull up (v)**	搏击操 bójīcāo **boxercise**	跳绳 tiàoshéng **jumping rope**

休闲 xiūxián
leisure

剧院 jùyuàn • theater

幕
mù
curtain

舞台侧翼
wǔtáicèyì
wings

布景
bùjǐng
set

观众
guānzhòng
audience

乐队
yuèduì
orchestra

舞台 wǔtái | stage

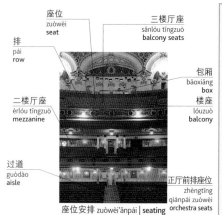

座位
zuòwèi
seat

三楼厅座
sānlóu tīngzuò
balcony seats

排
pái
row

包厢
bāoxiāng
box

二楼厅座
èrlóu tīngzuò
mezzanine

楼座
lóuzuò
balcony

过道
guòdào
aisle

正厅前排座位
zhèngtīng
qiánpái zuòwèi
orchestra seats

座位安排 zuòwèi'ānpái | seating

词汇 cíhuì • vocabulary

角色分配	剧本	首演
juésè fēnpèi	jùběn	shǒuyǎn
cast	**script**	**premiere**
男演员	背景幕布	幕间休息
nányǎnyuán	bèijǐngmùbù	mùjiānxiūxī
actor	**backdrop**	**intermission**
女演员	导演	节目
nǚyǎnyuán	dǎoyǎn	jiémù
actress	**director**	**program**
戏剧	制片人	乐池
xìjù	zhìpiānrén	yuèchí
play	**producer**	**orchestra pit**

中文 zhōngwén • english

音乐会 yīnyuèhuì | concert

音乐剧 yīnyuèjù | musical

戏装
xìzhuāng
costume

词汇 cíhuì • vocabulary

引座员
yǐnzuòyuán
usher

古典音乐
gǔdiǎn yīnyuè
classical music

乐谱
yuèpǔ
musical score

声带
shēngdài
soundtrack

鼓掌喝彩
gǔzhǎnghècǎi
applaud (v)

再来一次
zàiláiyícì
encore

演出什么时候开始？
yǎnchū shénme shíhòu kāishǐ?
What time does it start?

我想要两张今晚演出的票。
wǒ xiǎng yào liǎngzhāng jīnwǎn yǎnchūde piào.
I'd like two tickets for tonight's performance.

芭蕾舞 bālěiwǔ | ballet

歌剧 gējù | opera

电影院 diànyǐngyuàn • movies

爆米花
bàomǐhuā
popcorn

海报
hǎibào
poster

售票处
shòupiàochù
box office

大厅
dàtīng
lobby

电影放映厅
diànyǐng fàngyìngtīng
movie theater

银幕
yínmù
screen

词汇 cíhuì • vocabulary

喜剧片
xǐjùpiān
comedy

惊险片
jīngxiǎnpiān
thriller

恐怖片
kǒngbùpiān
horror movie

西部片
xībùpiān
Western

爱情片
àiqíngpiān
romance

科幻片
kēhuànpiān
science fiction movie

冒险片
màoxiǎnpiān
adventure

动画片
dònghuàpiān
animated film

乐队 yuèduì • orchestra

弦乐器 xiányuèqì • strings

竖琴
shùqín
harp

指挥
zhǐhuī
conductor

低音提琴
dīyīntíqín
double bass

小提琴
xiǎotíqín
violin

指挥台
zhǐhuītái
podium

中提琴
zhōngtíqín
viola

大提琴
dàtíqín
cello

乐谱
yuèpǔ
score

高音谱号
gāoyīn pǔhào
treble clef

音符
yīnfú
note

五线谱
wǔxiànpǔ
staff

低音谱号
dīyīn pǔhào
bass clef

Andante

rit.

记谱法 jìpǔfǎ | notation

钢琴 gāngqín | piano

词汇 cíhuì • vocabulary

序曲 xùqǔ overture	奏鸣曲 zòumíngqǔ sonata	休止符 xiūzhǐfú rest	升号 shēnghào sharp	本位号 běnwèihào natural	音阶 yīnjiē scale
交响乐 jiāoxiǎngyuè symphony	乐器 yuèqì instruments	音高 yīngāo pitch	降号 jiànghào flat	小节线 xiǎojiéxiàn bar	指挥棒 zhǐhuībàng baton

木管乐器 mùguǎnyuèqì • **woodwind**

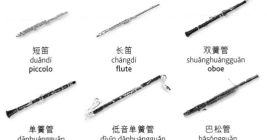
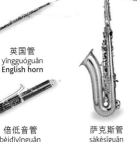

短笛	长笛	双簧管	英国管	
duǎndí	chángdí	shuānghuángguǎn	yīngguóguǎn	
piccolo	**flute**	**oboe**	**English horn**	

单簧管	低音单簧管	巴松管	倍低音管	萨克斯管
dānhuángguǎn	dīyīn dānhuángguǎn	bāsōngguǎn	bèidīyīnguǎn	sàkèsīguǎn
clarinet	**bass clarinet**	**bassoon**	**double bassoon**	**saxophone**

打击乐器 dǎjīyuèqì • **percussion**

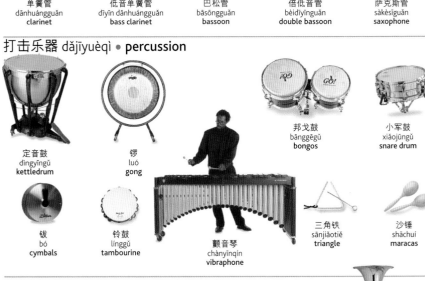

定音鼓
dìngyīngǔ
kettledrum

锣
luó
gong

邦戈鼓
bānggēgǔ
bongos

小军鼓
xiǎojūngǔ
snare drum

钹
bó
cymbals

铃鼓
línggǔ
tambourine

颤音琴
chànyīnqín
vibraphone

三角铁
sānjiǎotiě
triangle

沙锤
shāchuí
maracas

铜管乐器 tóngguǎn yuèqì • **brass**

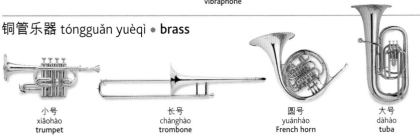

小号	长号	圆号	大号
xiǎohào	chánghào	yuánhào	dàhào
trumpet	**trombone**	**French horn**	**tuba**

音乐会 yīnyuèhuì • concert

主唱
zhǔchàng
lead singer

麦克风
màikèfēng
microphone

鼓手
gǔshǒu
drummer

吉他手
jítāshǒu
guitarist

歌迷
gēmí
fans

低音吉他手
dīyīn jítāshǒu
bass guitarist

扩音器
kuòyīnqì
speaker

摇滚音乐会 yáogǔn yīnyuèhuì | rock concert

乐器 yuèqì • instruments

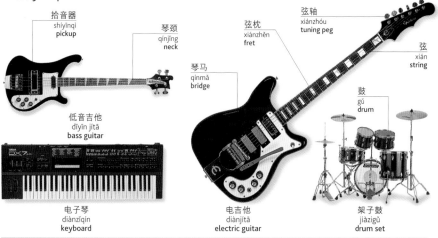

拾音器
shíyīnqì
pickup

琴颈
qínjǐng
neck

琴马
qínmǎ
bridge

低音吉他
dīyīn jítā
bass guitar

弦枕
xiánzhěn
fret

弦轴
xiánzhóu
tuning peg

弦
xián
string

鼓
gǔ
drum

电子琴
diànzǐqín
keyboard

电吉他
diànjítā
electric guitar

架子鼓
jiàzǐgǔ
drum set

音乐风格 yīnyuè fēnggé • musical styles

爵士乐 juéshìyuè | jazz

蓝调音乐 lándiào yīnyuè | blues

朋克音乐 péngkè yīnyuè | punk

民间音乐 mínjiān yīnyuè | folk music

流行音乐 liúxíng yīnyuè | pop

舞曲 wǔqǔ | dance

说唱音乐 shuōchàng yīnyuè | rap

重金属摇滚 zhòngjīnshǔyáogǔn
heavy metal

古典音乐 gǔdiǎn yīnyuè
classical music

词汇 cíhuì • vocabulary

歌曲 gēqǔ song	歌词 gēcí lyrics	旋律 xuánlǜ melody	节拍 jiépāi beat	雷盖音乐 léigài yīnyuè reggae	乡村音乐 xiāngcūn yīnyuè country	聚光灯 jùguāngdēng spotlight

观光 guānguāng • sightseeing

游客
yóukè
tourist

旅行路线
lǚxíng lùxiàn
itinerary

敞篷
chǎngpéng
open-top

观光巴士 guānguāngbāshì | tour bus

导游
dǎoyóu
tour guide

小雕像
xiǎodiāoxiàng
statuette

游览胜地 yóulǎn shèngdì | tourist attraction

团体旅游
tuántǐlǚyóu
guided tour

纪念品
jìniànpǐn
souvenirs

词汇 cíhuì • vocabulary

开门 kāimén open	旅行指南 lǚxíngzhǐnán guidebook	便携式摄像机 biànxiéshì shèxiàngjī camcorder	左 zuǒ left	…在哪里？ …zàinǎli? Where is…?
关门 guānmén closed	胶片 jiāopiàn film	照相机 zhàoxiàngjī camera	右 yòu right	我迷路了。 wǒ mílùle. I'm lost.
入场费 rùchǎngfèi admission charge	电池 diànchí batteries	(行路的)指引 (xínglùde) zhǐyǐn directions	直行 zhíháng straight ahead	你能告诉我到…的路吗？ nǐ néng gàosù wǒ dào…delù ma? Can you tell me the way to….?

名胜 míngshèng · attractions

绘画
huìhuà
painting

展品
zhǎnpǐn
exhibit

展览
zhǎnlǎn
exhibition

古迹
gǔjì
famous ruin

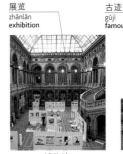

艺术馆
yìshùguǎn
art gallery

纪念碑
jìniànbēi
monument

博物馆
bówùguǎn
museum

历史建筑
lìshǐ jiànzhù
historic building

赌场
dǔchǎng
casino

庭园
tíngyuán
gardens

国家公园
guójiā gōngyuán
national park

游览信息 yóulǎnxìnxī · information

日程
richéng
times

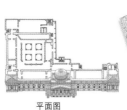

平面图
píngmiàntú
floor plan

地图
dìtú
map

时刻表
shíkèbiǎo
timetable

旅游问询处
lǚyóu wènxúnchù
tourist information

户外活动 hùwàihuódòng · outdoor activities

小道
xiǎodào
footpath

日晷
rìguǐ
sundial

咖啡馆
kāfēiguǎn
café

公园 gōngyuán | park

草坪
cǎopíng
grass

长椅
chángyǐ
bench

法式花园
fǎshì huāyuán
formal gardens

过山车
guòshānchē
roller coaster

游乐园
yóulèyuán
fairground

主题公园
zhǔtí gōngyuán
theme park

野生动物园
yěshēng dòngwùyuán
safari park

动物园
dòngwùyuán
zoo

活动 huódòng · activites

骑自行车
qízìxíngchē
cycling

慢跑
mànpǎo
jogging

滑板
huábǎn
skateboarding

滚轴溜冰
gǔnzhóu liūbīng
rollerblading

骑马专用道
qímǎ zhuānyòngdào
bridle path

食物篮
shíwùlán
hamper

观鸟
guānniǎo
bird watching

骑马
qímǎ
horse riding

远足
yuǎnzú
hiking

野餐
yěcān
picnic

游乐场 yóulèchǎng · playground

沙箱
shāxiāng
sandpit

儿童戏水池
értóng xìshuǐchí
paddling pool

秋千
qiūqiān
swings

跷跷板 qiāoqiāobǎn | seesaw

滑梯 huátī | slide

攀登架 pāndēngjià | climbing frame

海滩 hǎitān • beach

旅馆
lǚguǎn
hotel

遮阳伞
zhēyángsǎn
beach umbrella

海滩小屋
hǎitān xiǎowū
beach hut

沙
shā
sand

海浪
hǎilàng
wave

海
hǎi
sea

海滨游泳袋
hǎibīn yóuyǒngdài
beach bag

比基尼泳装
bǐjīníyǒngzhuāng
bikini

晒日光浴 shài rìguāngyù | sunbathe (v)

救生员
jiùshēngyuán
lifeguard

救生瞭望塔
jiùshēng liáowàngtǎ
lifeguard tower

防风屏
fángfēngpíng
windbreak

海滨步道
hǎibīn bùdào
promenade

轻便折叠躺椅
qīngbiàn zhédiétǎngyǐ
deck chair

太阳镜
tàiyángjìng
sunglasses

遮阳帽
zhēyángmào
sunhat

防晒油
fángshàiyóu
suntan lotion

防晒液
fángshàiyè
sunblock

浮水气球
fúshuǐqìqiú
beach ball

游泳圈
yóuyǒngquān
rubber ring

游泳衣
yóuyǒngyī
swimsuit

铲子
chǎnzi
spade

桶
tǒng
bucket

沙堡
shābǎo
sandcastle

贝壳
bèiké
shell

海滩浴巾
hǎitān yùjīn
beach towel

露营 lùyíng · camping

卫生间
wèishēngjiān
toilets

垃圾箱
lājīxiāng
waste disposal

浴室
yùshì
shower block

接电装置
jiēdiàn zhuāngzhì
electric hook-up

防雨罩
fángyǔzhào
flysheet

地钉
dìdīng
tent peg

防风绳
fángfēng shéng
guy rope

旅行拖车
lǚxíng tuōchē
caravan

露营地 lùyíngdì | campsite

词汇 cíhuì · vocabulary

露营
lùyíng
camp (v)

营地管理处
yíngdì guǎnlǐchù
site manager's office

自由宿营地
zìyóu sùyíngdì
pitches available

满
mǎn
full

宿营地
sùyíngdì
pitch

支帐篷
zhīzhàngpéng
pitch a tent (v)

帐篷杆
zhàngpénggān
tent pole

行军床
xíngjūn chuáng
camp bed

野餐长椅
yěcān chángyǐ
picnic bench

吊床
diàochuáng
hammock

野营车
yěyíngchē
camper van

拖车
tuōchē
trailer

木炭
mùtàn
charcoal

引火物
yǐnhuǒwù
firelighter

点火
diǎnhuǒ
light a fire (v)

营火
yínghuǒ
campfire

支架
zhījià
frame

铺地防潮布
pūdì fángcháobù
ground sheet

背包
bèibāo
backpack

保温瓶
bāowēnpíng
vacuum flask

水瓶
shuǐpíng
water bottle

帐篷
zhàngpéng
tent

驱虫剂
qūchóngjì
insect repellent

营地灯
yíngdìdēng
torch

蚊帐
wénzhàng
mosquito net

保暖内衣
bǎonuǎn nèiyī
thermals

徒步靴
túbùxuē
walking boots

雨衣
yǔyī
waterproofs

睡袋
shuìdài
sleeping bag

睡垫
shuìdiàn
sleeping mat

野营炉
yěyínglú
camping stove

烧烤架
shāokǎojià
barbecue

充气床垫 chōngqì chuángdiàn | air mattress

家庭娱乐 jiātíngyúlè • home entertainment

便携式CD播放机
biànxiéshì CD bōfàngjī
personal CD player

MD录放机
MD lùfàngjī
mini disk recorder

MP3播放机
MP3 bōfàngjī
MP3 player

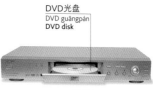

DVD光盘
DVD guāngpán
DVD disk

DVD播放机
DVD bōfàngjī
DVD player

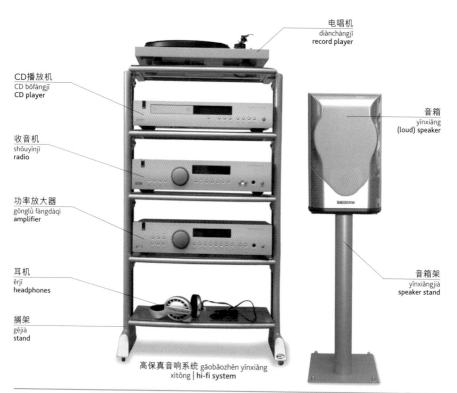

电唱机
diànchàngjī
record player

CD播放机
CD bōfàngjī
CD player

收音机
shōuyīnjī
radio

功率放大器
gōnglǜ fàngdàqì
amplifier

耳机
ěrjī
headphones

搁架
gējià
stand

音箱
yīnxiāng
(loud) speaker

音箱架
yīnxiāngjià
speaker stand

高保真音响系统 gāobǎozhēn yīnxiǎng
xìtǒng | **hi-fi system**

录像带
lùxiàngdài
video tape

显示屏
xiǎnshìpíng
screen

接目杯
jiēmùbēi
eyecup

录像机
lùxiàngjī
video recorder

便携式摄像机
biànxiéshì shèxiàngjī
camcorder

卫星电视天线
wèixīng diànshì tiānxiàn
satellite dish

宽屏电视
kuānpíng diànshì
widescreen television

控制台
kòngzhìtái
console

快进
kuàijìn
fast forward

暂停
zàntíng
pause

录制
lùzhì
record

音量
yīnliàng
volume

操纵手柄
cāozòng shǒubǐng
controller

倒带
dàodài
rewind

播放
bōfàng
play

停止
tíngzhǐ
stop

视频游戏 shìpín yóuxì | video game

遥控器 yáokòngqì | remote control

词汇 cíhuì • vocabulary

激光唱盘 jīguāng chàngpán compact disc	故事片 gùshìpiàn feature film	节目 jiémù programme	收费频道 shōufèi píndào pay per view channel	看电视 kàndiànshì watch television (v)
盒式录音带 héshì lùyīndài cassette tape	广告 guǎnggào advertisement	立体声 lìtǐshēng stereo	换频道 huàn píndào change channel (v)	关电视 guāndiànshì turn the television off (v)
盒式磁带录音机 héshì cídàilùyīnjī cassette player	数字式 shùzìshì digital	有线电视 yǒuxiàn diànshì cable television	开电视 kāidiànshì turn the television on (v)	调收音机 diàoshōuyīnjī tune the radio (v)

摄影 shèyǐng · photography

曝光记数器
bàoguāngjì shùqì
frame counter

快门键
kuàimén jiàn
shutter release

快门速度调节钮
kuàimén sùdù tiáojiéniǔ
shutter-speed dial

闪光灯
shǎnguāngdēng
flash

光圈调节环
guāngquān tiáojiéhuán
aperture dial

滤镜
lǜjìng
filter

镜头盖
jìngtóugài
lens caps

镜头
jìngtóu
lens

单镜头反光照相机 dānjìngtóu fǎnguāngzhàoxiàngjī | SLR camera

闪光灯
shǎnguāngdēng
flash gun

曝光表
bàoguāngbiǎo
lightmeter

变焦镜头
biànjiāo jìngtóu
zoom lens

三脚架
sānjiǎojià
tripod

相机种类 xiàngjī zhǒnglèi · types of camera

数码相机
shùmǎ xiàngjī
digital camera

一次成像全自动相机
yīcìchéngxiàng quánzìdòng
xiàngjī
APS camera

立拍立现相机
lìpāi lìxiàn xiàngjī
instant camera

一次性相机
yīcìxìng xiàngjī
disposable camera

照相 zhàoxiàng · photograph (v)

胶卷
jiāojuǎn
film spool

胶片
jiāopiān
film

调焦
tiáojiāo
focus (v)

冲洗
chōngxǐ
develop (v)

底片
dīpiān
negative

全景照
quánjǐngzhào
landscape

人像照
rénxiàngzhào
portrait

相片 xiàngpiān | photograph

相册
xiàngcè
photo album

相框
xiàngkuàng
photo frame

问题 wèntí · problems

曝光不足
pùguāng bùzú
underexposed

曝光过度
pùguāng guòdù
overexposed

调焦不准
tiáojiāo bùzhǔn
out of focus

红眼
hóngyǎn
red eye

词汇 cíhuì · vocabulary

取景器
qǔjǐngqì
viewfinder

相机盒
xiàngjīhé
camera case

曝光
pùguāng
exposure

暗室
ànshì
darkroom

样片
yàngpiàn
print

无光泽
wúguāngzé
mat

有光泽
yǒuguāngzé
gloss

放大
fàngdà
enlargement

请冲洗这个胶卷。
qǐng chōngxǐ zhège jiāojuǎn.
I'd like this film processed

游戏 yóuxì • games

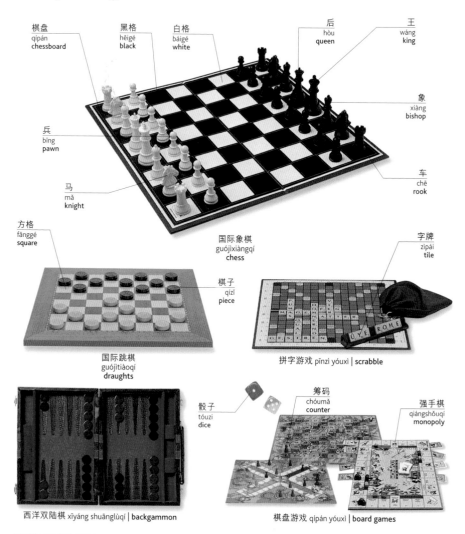

棋盘
qípán
chessboard

黑格
hēigé
black

白格
báigé
white

后
hòu
queen

王
wáng
king

象
xiàng
bishop

兵
bīng
pawn

车
chē
rook

马
mǎ
knight

方格
fānggé
square

国际象棋
guójìxiàngqí
chess

字牌
zìpái
tile

棋子
qízǐ
piece

国际跳棋
guójìtiàoqí
draughts

拼字游戏 pīnzì yóuxì | scrabble

骰子
tóuzi
dice

筹码
chóumǎ
counter

强手棋
qiángshǒuqí
monopoly

西洋双陆棋 xīyáng shuānglùqí | backgammon

棋盘游戏 qípán yóuxì | board games

集邮 jíyóu | stamp collecting

拼图 pīntú | jigsaw puzzle

多米诺骨牌 duōmǐnuò gǔpái dominoes

靶盘
bǎpán
dartboard

靶心
bǎxīn
bullseye

飞镖 fēibiāo | darts

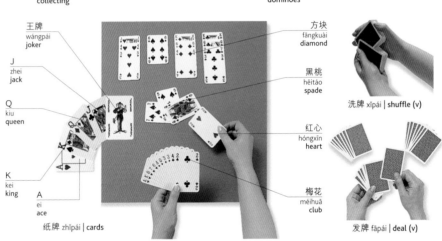

王牌
wángpái
joker

J
zhei
jack

Q
kiu
queen

K
kei
king

A
ei
ace

纸牌 zhǐpái | cards

方块
fāngkuài
diamond

黑桃
hēitáo
spade

红心
hóngxīn
heart

梅花
méihuā
club

洗牌 xǐpái | shuffle (v)

发牌 fāpái | deal (v)

词汇 cíhuì • vocabulary

走棋 zǒuqí move	赢 yíng win (v)	输家 shūjiā loser	点 diǎn point	桥牌 qiáopái bridge	掷骰子。 zhìtóuzi. **Roll the dice.**
玩 wán play (v)	赢家 yíngjiā winner	游戏 yóuxì game	得分 défēn score	一副牌 yífùpái pack of cards	该谁了？ gāishuíle? **Whose turn is it?**
玩家 wánjiā player	输 shū lose (v)	赌注 dǔzhù bet	扑克牌 pūkèpái poker	同花 tonghuā suit	该你了。 gāinǐle. **It's your move.**

工艺美术 1 gōngyìměishù yī · arts and crafts 1

画家 huàjiā artist

画 huà painting

画架 huàjià easel

画布 huàbù canvas

画笔 huàbǐ brush

调色板 tiáosèbǎn palette

(用颜料等)绘画 (yòng yánliào děng) huìhuà | painting

颜料 yánliào · paints

油画颜料 yóuhuà yánliào oil paints

水彩画颜料 shuǐcǎi huàyánliào watercolour paint

彩色蜡笔 cǎisèlàbǐ pastels

丙烯颜料 bǐngxī yánliào acrylic paint

广告颜料 guǎnggào yánliào | poster paint

颜色 yánsè · colours

红色 hóngsè | red

蓝色 lánsè | blue

黄色 huángsè yellow

绿色 lǜsè | green

橘色 júsè | orange

紫色 zǐsè | purple

白色 báisè | white

黑色 hēisè | black

灰色 huīsè | grey

粉红色 fěnhóngsè pink

褐色 hèsè | brown

靛青色 diànqīngsè indigo

中文 zhōngwén · english

其他工艺 qítā gōngyì · other crafts

素描簿
sùmiáobù
sketch pad

草图
cǎotú
sketch

油墨
yóumò
ink

铅笔
qiānbǐ
pencil

炭笔
tànbǐ
charcoal

素描 sùmiáo | drawing

印刷 yìnshuā | printing

版画 bǎnhuà | engraving

石头
shítou
stone

木槌
mùchuí
mallet

凿子
záozǐ
chisel

木头
mùtóu
wood

刮刀
guādāo
modelling tool

陶工转盘
yáogōng zhuànpán
potter's wheel

雕刻
diāokè
sculpting

木工
mùgōng
woodworking

黏土
niántǔ
clay

胶
jiāo
glue

纸板
zhǐbǎn
cardboard

拼贴 pīntiē | collage

陶艺 táoyì | pottery

珠宝制作
zhūbǎo zhìzuò
jewellery making

纸板制型
zhǐbǎnzhìxíng
papier-mâché

折纸
zhézhǐ
origami

模型制作
móxíng zhìzuò
model making

工艺美术 2 gōngyìměishùèr • arts and crafts 2

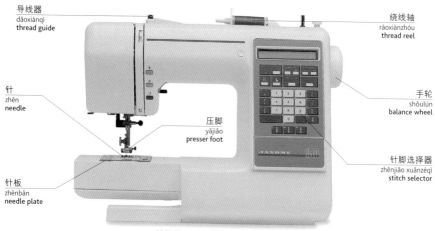

导线器
dǎoxiànqì
thread guide

绕线轴
ràoxiànzhóu
thread reel

针
zhēn
needle

手轮
shǒulún
balance wheel

压脚
yājiǎo
presser foot

针脚选择器
zhēnjiǎo xuǎnzéqì
stitch selector

针板
zhēnbǎn
needle plate

缝纫机 féngrènjī | sewing machine

剪刀
jiǎndāo
scissors

纸样
zhǐyàng
pattern

针垫
zhēndiàn
pincushion

卷尺
juǎnchǐ
tape measure

布料
bùliào
material

大头针
dàtóuzhēn
pin

针线筐 zhēnxiankuāng | sewing basket

线
xiàn
thread

领钩环
lǐnggōuhuán
eye

线轴
xiànzhóu
bobbin

领钩
lǐnggōu
hook

顶针
dǐngzhēn
thimble

划粉
huáfěn
tailor's chalk

人体模型
réntǐ móxíng
tailor's dummy

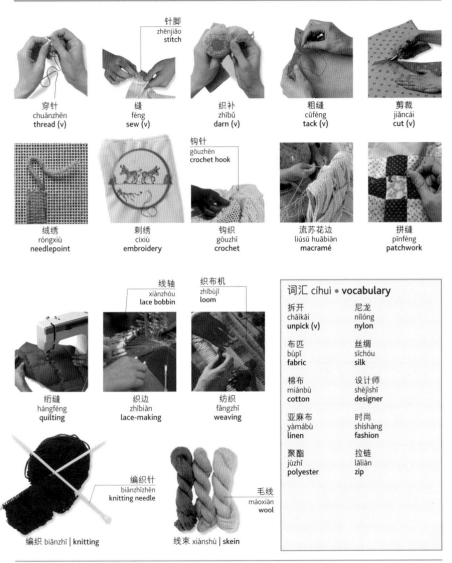

针脚
zhēnjiǎo
stitch

穿针
chuānzhēn
thread (v)

缝
féng
sew (v)

织补
zhībǔ
darn (v)

粗缝
cūféng
tack (v)

剪裁
jiǎncái
cut (v)

绒绣
róngxiù
needlepoint

刺绣
cìxiù
embroidery

钩针
gōuzhēn
crochet hook

钩织
gōuzhī
crochet

流苏花边
liúsū huābiān
macramé

拼缝
pīnféng
patchwork

线轴
xiànzhóu
lace bobbin

织布机
zhībùjī
loom

绗缝
hángféng
quilting

织边
zhībiān
lace-making

纺织
fǎngzhī
weaving

编织针
biānzhīzhēn
knitting needle

编织 biānzhī | knitting

线束 xiànshù | skein

毛线
máoxiàn
wool

词汇 cíhuì • vocabulary

拆开
chāikāi
unpick (v)

尼龙
nílóng
nylon

布匹
bùpǐ
fabric

丝绸
sīchóu
silk

棉布
miánbù
cotton

设计师
shèjìshī
designer

亚麻布
yàmábù
linen

时尚
shíshàng
fashion

聚酯
jùzhǐ
polyester

拉链
lāliàn
zip

环境 huánjìng
environment

宇宙空间 yǔzhòukōngjiān • space

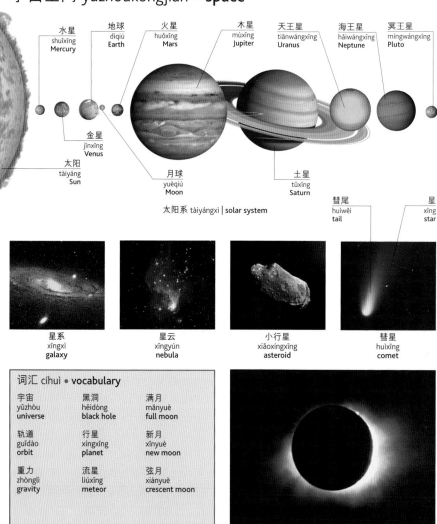

水星
shuǐxīng
Mercury

地球
dìqiú
Earth

火星
huǒxīng
Mars

木星
mùxīng
Jupiter

天王星
tiānwángxīng
Uranus

海王星
hǎiwángxīng
Neptune

冥王星
míngwángxīng
Pluto

金星
jīnxīng
Venus

太阳
tàiyáng
Sun

月球
yuèqiú
Moon

土星
tǔxīng
Saturn

太阳系 tàiyángxì | solar system

彗尾
huìwěi
tail

星
xīng
star

星系
xīngxì
galaxy

星云
xīngyún
nebula

小行星
xiǎoxíngxīng
asteroid

彗星
huìxīng
comet

词汇 cíhuì • vocabulary

宇宙 yǔzhòu universe	**黑洞** hēidòng black hole	**满月** mǎnyuè full moon
轨道 guǐdào orbit	**行星** xíngxīng planet	**新月** xīnyuè new moon
重力 zhònglì gravity	**流星** liúxīng meteor	**弦月** xiányuè crescent moon

(日、月)食 (rì, yuè) shí | eclipse

中文 zhōngwén • english

太空探索 tàikōngfú · space exploration

雷达
léidá
radar

航天飞机
hángtiān fēijī
space shuttle

助推器
zhùtuīqì
thruster

舱门
cāngmén
crew hatch

太空服
tàikōngfú
space suit

推进器
tuījìnqì
booster

宇航员 yǔhángyuán
astronaut

登月舱 dēngyuècāng | lunar module

发射架
fāshèjià
launch pad

发射
fāshè
launch

人造卫星
rénzàowèixīng
satellite

空间站
kōngjiān zhàn
space station

天文学 tiānwénxué · astronomy

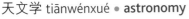

星座
xīngzuò
constellation

双筒望远镜
shuāngtǒng wàngyuǎnjīng
binoculars

天文望远镜
tiānwén
wàngyuǎnjīng
telescope

三脚架
sānjiǎojià
tripod

地球 dìqiú • Earth

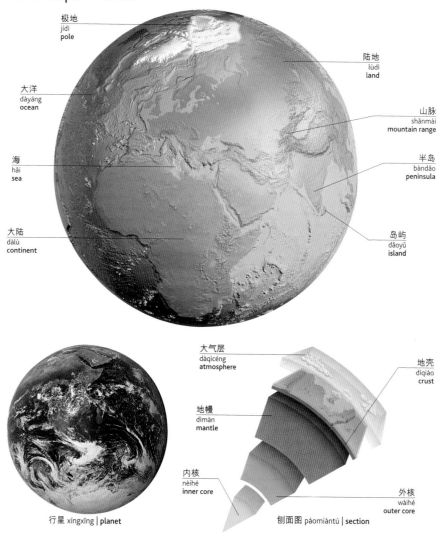

极地
jídì
pole

陆地
lùdì
land

大洋
dàyáng
ocean

山脉
shānmài
mountain range

海
hǎi
sea

半岛
bàndǎo
peninsula

大陆
dàlù
continent

岛屿
dǎoyǔ
island

大气层
dàqìcéng
atmosphere

地壳
dìqiào
crust

地幔
dìmàn
mantle

内核
nèihé
inner core

外核
wàihé
outer core

行星 xíngxīng | planet

刨面图 páomiàntú | section

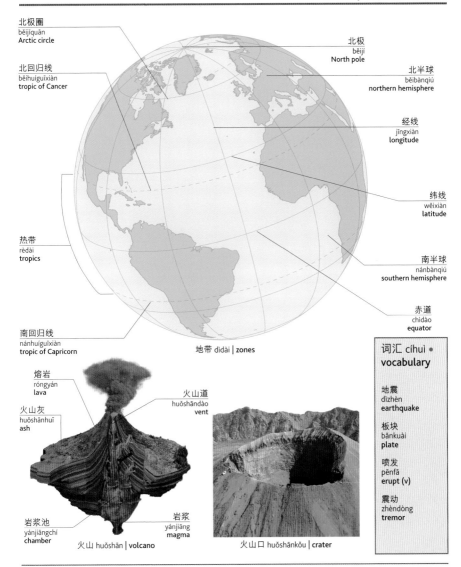

北极圈
běijíquān
Arctic circle

北极
běijí
North pole

北回归线
běihuíguīxiàn
tropic of Cancer

北半球
běibànqiú
northern hemisphere

经线
jīngxiàn
longitude

纬线
wěixiàn
latitude

热带
rèdài
tropics

南半球
nánbànqiú
southern hemisphere

赤道
chìdào
equator

南回归线
nánhuíguīxiàn
tropic of Capricorn

地带 dìdài | zones

熔岩
róngyán
lava

火山道
huǒshāndào
vent

火山灰
huǒshānhuī
ash

岩浆池
yánjiāngchí
chamber

岩浆
yánjiāng
magma

火山 huǒshān | volcano

火山口 huǒshānkǒu | crater

词汇 cíhuì · vocabulary

地震
dìzhèn
earthquake

板块
bǎnkuài
plate

喷发
pēnfā
erupt (v)

震动
zhèndòng
tremor

地貌 dìmào • landscape

山
shān
mountain

山坡
shānpō
slope

河岸
hé'àn
bank

河流
héliú
river

急流
jíliú
rapids

岩石
yánshí
rocks

冰河
bīnghé
glacier

山谷 shāngǔ | valley

丘陵
qiūlíng
hill

高原
gāoyuán
plateau

峡谷
xiágǔ
gorge

岩洞
yándòng
cave

平原 píngyuán | plain

沙漠 shāmò | desert

森林 sēnlín | forest

树林 shùlín | wood

雨林
yǔlín
rainforest

沼泽
zhǎozé
swamp

草场
cǎochǎng
meadow

草原
cǎoyuán
grassland

瀑布
pùbù
waterfall

溪流
xīliú
stream

湖
hú
lake

间歇喷泉
jiànxiē pēnquán
geyser

海岸
hǎi'àn
coast

悬崖
xuányá
cliff

珊瑚礁
shānhújiāo
coral reef

河口
hékǒu
estuary

天气 tiānqì • weather

外逸层
wàiyìcéng
exosphere

极光
jíguāng
aurora

热层
rècéng
thermosphere

阳光 yángguāng | sunshine

电离层
diànlícéng
ionosphere

中间层
zhōngjiāncéng
mesosphere

紫外线
zǐwàixiàn
ultraviolet rays

同温层
tóngwēncéng
stratosphere

风 fēng | wind

臭氧层
chòuyǎngcéng
ozone layer

大气层 dàqìcéng | atmosphere

对流层
duìliúcéng
troposphere

词汇 cíhuì • vocabulary

雨夹雪 yǔjiáxuě sleet	阵雨 zhènyǔ shower	热 rè hot	干燥 gānzào dry	多风 duōfēng windy	我热/冷。 wǒ rè/lěng. I'm hot/cold.
冰雹 bīngbáo hail	阳光明媚 yángguāng míngmèi sunny	冷 lěng cold	潮 cháo wet	狂风 kuángfēng gale	正在下雨。 zhèngzài xiàyǔ. It's raining.
雷 léi thunder	多云 duōyún cloudy	温暖 wēnnuǎn warm	湿润 shīrùn humid	温度 wēndù temperature	度… dù… It's … degrees.

云 yún | cloud

雨 yǔ | rain

闪电 shǎndiàn lightning

暴风雨 bàofēngyǔ | storm

霭 ǎi | mist

雾 wù | fog

彩虹 cǎihóng | rainbow

雪 xuě | snow

霜 shuāng | frost

冰 bīng | ice

冰柱 bīngzhù icicle

结冰 jiébīng | freeze

飓风 jùfēng | hurricane

龙卷风 lóngjuǎnfēng tornado

季风 jìfēng | monsoon

洪水 hóngshuǐ | flood

岩石 yánshí • rocks

火成岩 huǒchéngyán • igneous

花岗岩
huāgāngyán
granite

黑曜岩
hēiyàoyán
obsidian

玄武岩
xuánwǔyán
basalt

浮石
fúshí
pumice

沉积岩 chénjīyán • sedimentary

砂岩
shāyán
sandstone

石灰岩
shíhuīyán
limestone

白垩
bái'è
chalk

燧石
suìshí
flint

砾岩
lìyán
conglomerate

煤
méi
coal

变质岩 biànzhìyán • metamorphic

板岩
bǎnyán
slate

页岩
yèyán
schist

片麻岩
piànmáyán
gneiss

大理石
dàlǐshí
marble

宝石 bǎoshí • gems

红宝石
hóngbǎoshí
ruby

海蓝宝石
hǎilánbǎoshí
aquamarine

紫水晶
zǐshuǐjīng
amethyst

钻石
zuànshí
diamond

玉石
yùshí
jade

黑玉
hēiyù
jet

绿宝石
lǜbǎoshí
emerald

蛋白石
dànbáishí
opal

蓝宝石
lánbǎoshí
sapphire

月长石
yuèzhǎngshí
moonstone

石榴石
shíliúshí
garnet

黄玉
huángyù
topaz

电气石
diànqìshí
tourmaline

矿物 kuàngwù · minerals

石英
shíyīng
quartz

云母
yúnmǔ
mica

硫磺
liúhuáng
sulphur

赤铁矿
chìtiěkuàng
hematite

方解石
fāngjiěshí
calcite

孔雀石
kǒngquèshí
malachite

绿松石
lǜsōngshí
turquoise

缟玛瑙
gǎomǎnǎo
onyx

玛瑙
mǎnǎo
agate

石墨
shímò
graphite

金属 jīnshǔ · metals

金属
jīnshǔ
gold

银
yín
silver

铂
bó
platinum

镍
niè
nickel

铁
tiě
iron

铜
tóng
copper

锡
xī
tin

铝
lǚ
aluminium

汞
gǒng
mercury

锌
xīn
zinc

动物 1 dòngwùyī · **animals 1**
哺乳动物 bǔrǔ dòngwù · **mammals**

腮须
sāixū
whiskers

尾
wěi
tail

兔子
tùzǐ
rabbit

仓鼠
cāngshǔ
hamster

小家鼠
xiǎojiāshǔ
mouse

老鼠
lǎoshǔ
rat

刺猬
cìwèi
hedgehog

松鼠
sōngshǔ
squirrel

蝙蝠
biānfú
bat

浣熊
huànxióng
raccoon

狐狸
húli
fox

狼
láng
wolf

小狗
xiǎogǒu
puppy

小猫
xiǎomāo
kitten

小海豹
xiǎohǎibào
pup

狗
gǒu
dog

猫
māo
cat

水獭
shuǐtǎ
otter

海豹
hǎibào
seal

鳍状肢
qízhuàngzhī
flipper

喷水孔
pēnshuǐkǒng
blowhole

海狮
hǎishī
sea lion

海象
hǎixiàng
walrus

鲸
jīng
whale

海豚
hǎitún
dolphin

鹿角
lùjiǎo
antler

鬃毛
zōngmáo
mane

蹄
tí
hoof

驼峰
tuófēng
hump

鹿
lù
deer

斑马
bānmǎ
zebra

长颈鹿
chángjǐnglù
giraffe

骆驼
luòtuó
camel

象鼻
xiàngbí
trunk

长牙
chángyá
tusk

角
jiǎo
horn

河马
hémǎ
hippopotamus

象
xiàng
elephant

犀牛
xīniú
rhinoceros

虎
hǔ
tiger

鬃毛
zōngmáo
mane

狮子
shīzi
lion

猴子
hóuzi
monkey

大猩猩
dàxīngxing
gorilla

树袋熊
shùdài xióng
koala

育儿袋
yù'érdài
pouch

熊猫
xióngmāo
panda

爪
zhǎo
claw

袋鼠
dàishǔ
kangaroo

熊
xióng
bear

北极熊
běijí xióng
polar bear

动物 2 dòngwùèr · animals 2
鸟 niǎo · birds

尾
wěi
tail

金丝雀
jīnsīquè
canary

麻雀
máquè
sparrow

蜂鸟
fēngniǎo
hummingbird

燕子
yànzi
swallow

乌鸦
wūyā
crow

鸽子
gēzi
pigeon

啄木鸟
zhuómùniǎo
woodpecker

隼
sǔn
falcon

猫头鹰
māotóuyīng
owl

海鸥
hǎi'ōu
gull

鹰
yīng
eagle

鹈鹕
tíhú
pelican

火烈鸟
huǒlièniǎo
flamingo

鹳
guàn
stork

鹤
hè
crane

企鹅
qǐé
penguin

鸵鸟
tuóniǎo
ostrich

爬行动物 páxíng dòngwù · reptiles

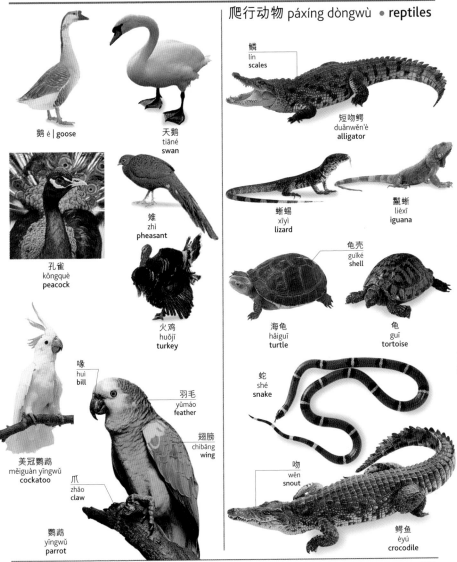

鹅 é | goose

天鹅
tiāné
swan

孔雀
kǒngquè
peacock

雉
zhì
pheasant

火鸡
huǒjī
turkey

美冠鹦鹉
měiguàn yīngwǔ
cockatoo

喙
huì
bill

羽毛
yǔmáo
feather

翅膀
chìbǎng
wing

爪
zhǎo
claw

鹦鹉
yīngwǔ
parrot

鳞
lín
scales

短吻鳄
duǎnwěn'è
alligator

蜥蜴
xīyì
lizard

鬣蜥
lièxī
iguana

龟壳
guīké
shell

海龟
hǎiguī
turtle

龟
guī
tortoise

蛇
shé
snake

吻
wěn
snout

鳄鱼
èyú
crocodile

动物 3 dòngwùsān · animals 3
两栖动物 liǎngqī dòngwù · amphibians

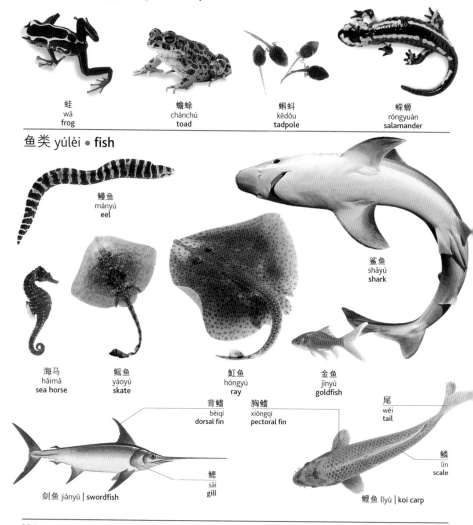

蛙
wā
frog

蟾蜍
chánchú
toad

蝌蚪
kēdǒu
tadpole

蝾螈
róngyuán
salamander

鱼类 yúlèi · fish

鳗鱼
mányú
eel

海马
hǎimǎ
sea horse

鳐鱼
yáoyú
skate

魟鱼
hóngyú
ray

鲨鱼
shāyú
shark

金鱼
jīnyú
goldfish

背鳍
bèiqí
dorsal fin

胸鳍
xiōngqí
pectoral fin

尾
wěi
tail

鳞
lín
scale

鳃
sāi
gill

剑鱼 jiànyú | swordfish

鲤鱼 lǐyú | koi carp

无脊椎动物 wújǐzhuī dòngwù · invertebrates

蚂蚁
mǎyǐ
ant

白蚁
báiyǐ
termite

蜜蜂
mìfēng
bee

黄蜂
huángfēng
wasp

甲壳虫
jiǎqiàochóng
beetle

蟑螂
zhāngláng
cockroach

蛾
é
moth

触角
chùjiǎo
antenna

蝴蝶
húdié
butterfly

茧
jiǎn
cocoon

毛虫
máochóng
caterpillar

蟋蟀 xīshuài | **cricket**

蚱蜢
zhàměng
grasshopper

螳螂
tángláng
praying mantis

蜇针
zhēzhēn
sting

蝎子
xiēzi
scorpion

蜈蚣
wúgōng
centipede

蜻蜓
qīngtíng
dragonfly

苍蝇
cāngyíng
fly

蚊子
wénzi
mosquito

瓢虫
piáochóng
ladybird

蜘蛛
zhīzhū
spider

蛞蝓
kuòyú
slug

蜗牛
wōniú
snail

蚯蚓 qiūyǐn | **worm**

海星
hǎixīng
starfish

贻贝
yíbèi
mussel

螃蟹 pángxiè | **crab**

龙虾 lóngxiā | **lobster**

章鱼 zhāngyú | **octopus**

鱿鱼 yóuyú | **squid**

水母 shuǐmǔ | **jellyfish**

植物 zhíwù • plants

树 shù • tree

叶
yè
leaf

树枝
shùzhī
branch

细枝
xìzhī
twig

树皮
shùpí
bark

柳树
liǔshù
willow

根
gēn
root

树干
shùgàn
trunk

橡树 xiàngshù | oak

白杨
báiyáng
poplar

桉树
ānshù
eucalyptus

落叶松
luòyèsōng
larch

山毛榉
shānmáojǔ
beech

桦树
huàshù
birch

松树
sōngshù
pine

雪松
xuěsōng
cedar

枫树
fēngshù
maple

榆树
yúshù
elm

椴树
duànshù
lime

冬青树
dōngqīngshù
holly

浆果
jiāngguǒ
berry

棕榈树
zōnglǘshù
palm

显花植物 xiǎnhuā zhíwù • flowering plant

花
huā
flower

雄蕊
xióngruǐ
stamen

花瓣
huābàn
petal

花萼
huā'è
calyx

叶梗
yègěng
stalk

主茎
zhǔjīng
stem

花蕾
huālěi
bud

毛茛
máogèn
buttercup

雏菊
chújú
daisy

蓟
jì
thistle

蒲公英
púgōngyīng
dandelion

石南花
shínánhuā
heather

罂粟
yīngsù
poppy

毛地黄
máodìhuáng
foxglove

忍冬
rěndōng
honeysuckle

向日葵
xiàngrìkuí
sunflower

苜蓿
mùxu
clover

野风信子
yěfēngxìnzǐ
bluebells

樱草
yīngcǎo
primrose

羽扇豆
yǔshàndòu
lupins

荨麻
qiánmá
nettle

城镇 chéngzhèn · town

街道
jiēdào
street

路沿
lùyán
kerb

街角
jiējiǎo
street corner

商店
shāngdiàn
shop

十字路口
shízìlùkǒu
intersection

单行道
dānhángdào
one-way system

人行道
rénxíngdào
pavement

办公楼
bàngōnglóu
office block

公寓楼
gōngyùlóu
apartment
block

小巷
xiǎoxiàng
alley

停车场
tíngchēchǎng
car park

路标
lùbiāo
street sign

安全岛护栏
ānquán dǎohùlán
bollard

路灯
lùdēng
street light

中文 zhōngwén · english

建筑物 jiànzhùwù · buildings

市政厅
shìzhèngtīng
town hall

图书馆
túshūguǎn
library

电影院
diànyǐngyuàn
cinema

剧院
jùyuàn
theatre

大学
dàxué
university

学校
xuéxiào
school

摩天大楼
mótiān dàlóu
skyscraper

区域 qūyù · areas

工业区
gōngyèqū
industrial estate

市区
shìqū
city

郊区
jiāoqū
suburb

村庄
cūnzhuāng
village

词汇 cíhuì · vocabulary

步行区 bùxíngqū pedestrian zone	小街 xiǎojiē side street	检修井 jiǎnxiūjǐng manhole	排水沟 páishuǐgōu gutter	教堂 jiàotáng church
林阴道 línyīndào avenue	广场 guǎngchǎng square	公共汽车站 gōnggòngqìchē zhàn bus stop	工厂 gōngchǎng factory	下水道 xiàshuǐdào drain

建筑 jiànzhù • architecture

建筑与结构 jiànzhù yǔ jiégòu • buildings and structures

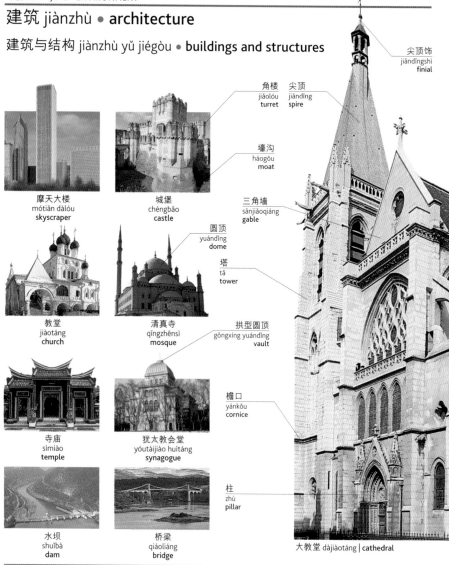

尖顶饰
jiāndǐngshi
finial

角楼
jiǎolóu
turret

尖顶
jiàndǐng
spire

壕沟
háogōu
moat

三角墙
sānjiǎoqiáng
gable

圆顶
yuándǐng
dome

塔
tǎ
tower

拱型圆顶
gǒngxíng yuándǐng
vault

檐口
yánkǒu
cornice

柱
zhù
pillar

摩天大楼
mótiān dàlóu
skyscraper

城堡
chéngbǎo
castle

教堂
jiàotáng
church

清真寺
qīngzhēnsì
mosque

寺庙
sìmiào
temple

犹太教会堂
yóutàijiào huìtáng
synagogue

水坝
shuǐbà
dam

桥梁
qiáoliáng
bridge

大教堂 dàjiàotáng | cathedral

建筑风格 jiànzhù fēnggé • styles

哥特式 gētèshì | gothic

柱顶楣梁
zhǔdǐng méiliáng
architrave

文艺复兴时期风格
wényìfùxīng shíqī fēnggé
Renaissance

巴洛克式
bāluòkèshì
baroque

拱
gǒng
arch

檐壁
yánbì
frieze

圣坛
shèngtán
choir

洛可可式
luòkěkěshì
rococo

三角楣
sānjiǎoméi
pediment

扶墙
fúqiáng
buttress

新古典主义风格
xīn gǔdiǎnzhǔyì fēnggé
neoclassical

新艺术风格
xīn yìshù fēnggé
art nouveau

装饰艺术风格
zhuāngshìyìshù fēnggé
art deco

日常便览 rìcháng biànlǎn
reference

时间 shíjiān • time

分针
fēnzhēn
minute hand

时针
shízhēn
hour hand

钟表
zhōngbiǎo
clock

词汇 cíhuì • vocabulary

秒
miǎo
second

分钟
fēnzhōng
minute

小时
xiǎoshí
hour

现在
xiànzài
now

以后
yǐhòu
later

半小时
bàn xiǎoshí
half an hour

一刻钟
yí kèzhōng
a quarter of an
hour

二十分钟
èrshí fēnzhōng
twenty minutes

四十分钟
sìshí fēnzhōng
forty minutes

几点了?
jǐ diǎn le?
What time is it?

三点了。
sāndiǎn le.
It's three o'clock.

一点五分
yìdiǎn wǔ fēn
five past one

一点十分
yìdiǎn shí fēn
ten past one

一点十五分
yìdiǎn shíwǔ fēn
quarter past one

一点二十分
yìdiǎn èrshí fēn
twenty past one

秒针
miǎozhēn
second hand

一点二十五分
yìdiǎn èrshíwǔ fēn
twenty five past one

一点半
yìdiǎnbàn
one thirty

一点三十五分
yìdiǎn sānshíwǔ fēn
twenty five to two

一点四十分
yìdiǎn sìshí fēn
twenty to two

一点四十五分
yìdiǎn sānshíwǔ fēn
quarter to two

一点五十分
yìdiǎn wǔshí fēn
ten to two

一点五十五分
yìdiǎn wǔshíwǔ fēn
five to two

两点钟
liǎngdiǎn zhōng
two o'clock

昼夜 zhòuyè • night and day

午夜 wǔyè | midnight

日出 rìchū | sunrise

拂晓 fúxiǎo | dawn

早晨 zǎochén | morning

日落
rìluò
sunset

正午
zhèngwǔ
noon

黄昏 huánghūn | dusk

傍晚 bàngwǎn | evening

下午 xiàwǔ | afternoon

词汇 cíhuì • vocabulary

早
zǎo
early

你来早了。
nǐ lái zǎo le.
You're early.

请准时些。
qǐng zhǔnshí xiē.
Please be on time.

几点结束？
jǐdiǎn jiéshù?
What time does it end?

准时
zhǔnshí
on time

你迟到了。
nǐ chídào le.
You're late.

待会儿见。
dàihuǐer jiàn.
I'll see you later.

天晚了。
tiān wǎnle.
It's getting late.

迟
chí
late

我马上就到。
wǒ mǎshàng jiùdào.
I'll be there soon.

几点开始？
jǐdiǎn kāishǐ?
What time does it start?

会持续多久？
huì chíxù duōjiǔ?
How long will it last?

日历 rìlì ● **calendar**

月
yuè
month

年
nián
year

一月
yīyuè
January

2010

日
rì
day

星期一	星期二	星期三	星期四	星期五	星期六	星期日
xīngqīyī	xīngqīèr	xīngqīsān	xīngqīsì	xīngqīwǔ	xīngqīliù	xīngqīrì
Monday	**Tuesday**	**Wednesday**	**Thursday**	**Friday**	**Saturday**	**Sunday**

工作日
gōngzuòrì
work day

星期
xīngqī
week

日期
rìqī
date

1	2	3	4	5	6	7
8	9	10	11	12	13	14
15	16	17	18	19	20	21

昨天
zuótiān
yesterday

今天
jīntiān
today

明天
míngtiān
tomorrow

周末
zhōumò
weekend

词汇 cíhuì ● **vocabulary**

一月	三月	五月	七月	九月	十一月
yīyuè	sānyuè	wǔyuè	qīyuè	jiǔyuè	shíyīyuè
January	**March**	**May**	**July**	**September**	**November**

二月	四月	六月	八月	十月	十二月
èryuè	sìyuè	liùyuè	bāyuè	shíyuè	shíèryuè
February	**April**	**June**	**August**	**October**	**December**

年 nián • years

1900   一九○○年 yījiǔlínglíng nián • nineteen hundred

1901   一九○一年 yījiǔlíngyī nián • nineteen hundred and one

1910   一九一○年 yījiǔyīlíng nián • nineteen ten

2000   二○○○年 èrlínglíng nián • two thousand

2001   二○○一年 èrlínglíngyī nián • two thousand and one

季节 jìjié • seasons

春天
chūntiān
spring

夏天
xiàtiān
summer

秋天
qiūtiān
fall

冬天
dōngtiān
winter

词汇 cíhuì • vocabulary

世纪 shìjì century	本周 běnzhōu this week	后天 hòutiān the day after tomorrow	今天几号？ jīntiān jǐhào? What's the date today?
十年 shínián decade	上周 shàngzhōu last week	每周 měizhōu weekly	今天是二○○二年二月七日。 jīntiān shì èrlínglíngèr nián èryuè qīrì. It's February seventh, two thousand and two.
千年 qiānnián millennium	下周 xiàzhōu next week	每月 měiyuè monthly	
两周 liǎngzhōu two weeks	前天 qiántiān the day before yesterday	每年 měinián annual	

数字 shùzì • **numbers**

0   零 líng • zero

1   一 yī • one

2   二 èr • two

3   三 sān • three

4   四 sì • four

5   五 wǔ • five

6   六 liù • six

7   七 qī • seven

8   八 bā • eight

9   九 jiǔ • nine

10   十 shí • ten

11   十一 shíyī • eleven

12   十二 shí'èr • twelve

13   十三 shísān • thirteen

14   十四 shísì • fourteen

15   十五 shíwǔ • fifteen

16   十六 shíliù • sixteen

17   十七 shíqī • seventeen

18   十八 shíbā • eighteen

19   十九 shíjiǔ • nineteen

20   二十 èrshí • twenty

21   二十一 èrshíyī • twenty-one

22   二十二 èrshí'èr • twenty-two

30   三十 sānshí • thirty

40   四十 sìshí • forty

50   五十 wǔshí • fifty

60   六十 liùshí • sixty

70   七十 qīshí • seventy

80   八十 bāshí • eighty

90   九十 jiǔshí • ninety

100   一百 yībǎi • one hundred

110   一百一十 yībǎiyīshí • one hundred and ten

200   二百 èrbǎi • two hundred

300   三百 sānbǎi • three hundred

400   四百 sìbǎi • four hundred

500   五百 wǔbǎi • five hundred

600   六百 liùbǎi • six hundred

700   七百 qībǎi • seven hundred

800   八百 bābǎi • eight hundred

900   九百 jiǔbǎi • nine hundred

1,000　一千 yīqiān • one thousand

10,000　一万 yīwàn • ten thousand

20,000　两万 liǎngwàn • twenty thousand

50,000　五万 wǔwàn • fifty thousand

55,500　五万五千五百 wǔwàn wǔqiān wǔbǎi • fifty-five thousand five hundred

100,000　十万 shíwàn • one hundred thousand

1,000,000　一百万 yībǎiwàn • one million

1,000,000,000　十亿 shíyì • one billion

第一 diyī first

第二 dì'èr second

第三 dìsān third

第四 dìsì • fourth

第五 dìwǔ • fifth

第六 dìliù • sixth

第七 dìqī • seventh

第八 dìbā • eighth

第九 dìjiǔ • ninth

第十 dìshí • tenth

第十一 dìshíyī • eleventh

第十二 dìshíèr • twelfth

第十三 dìshísān • thirteenth

第十四 dìshísì • fourteenth

第十五 dìshíwǔ • fifteenth

第十六 dìshíliù • sixteenth

第十七 dìshíqī • seventeenth

第十八 dìshíbā • eighteenth

第十九 dìshíjiǔ • nineteenth

第二十 dì'èrshi • twentieth

第二十一 dì'èrshíyī • twenty-first

第二十二 dì'èrshíèr • twenty-second

第二十三 dì'èrshísān • twenty-third

第三十 dìsānshí • thirtieth

第四十 dìsìshí • fortieth

第五十 dìwǔshí • fiftieth

第六十 dìliùshí • sixtieth

第七十 dìqīshí • seventieth

第八十 dìbāshí • eightieth

第九十 dìjiǔshí • ninetieth

第一百 dìyībǎi • one hundredth

度量衡 dùliánghéng • weights and measures

面积 miànjī • area

平方英尺
pīngfāng
yīngchǐ
square foot

平方米
píngfāng mǐ
square meter

距离 jùlí • distance

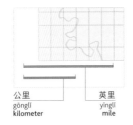

公里
gōnglǐ
kilometer

英里
yīnglǐ
mile

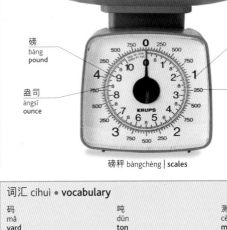

秤盘
chèngpán
pan

千克
qiānkè
kilogram

克
kè
gram

磅
bàng
pound

盎司
àngsī
ounce

磅秤 bàngchèng | scales

词汇 cíhuì • vocabulary

码 mǎ yard	**吨** dūn ton	**测量** cèliáng measure (v)
米 mǐ meter	**毫克** háokè milligram	**称重量** chēng zhòngliàng weigh (v)

长度 chángdù • length

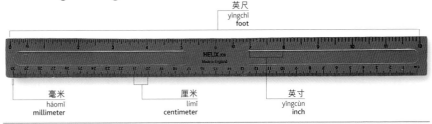

英尺
yīngchǐ
foot

毫米
háomǐ
millimeter

厘米
límǐ
centimeter

英寸
yīngcùn
inch

容量 róngliàng • volume

半升
bànshēng
half-liter

品脱
pīntuō
pint

容积
róngjī
volume

毫升
háoshēng
milliliter

量壶 liànghú | measuring cup

液体量器 yètǐ liángqì | liquid measure

容器 róngqì • container

袋
dài
bag

硬纸盒
yìngzhǐhé
carton

包
bāo
packet

瓶
píng
bottle

罐
guàn
can

塑料盒 sùliàohé | tub

广口瓶 guǎngkǒupíng | jar

罐头盒 guàntóuhé | can

喷水器 pēnshuǐqì | spray bottle

块
kuài
bar

软管
ruǎnguǎn
tube

卷
juǎn
roll

纸盒
zhǐhé
pack

喷雾罐
pēnwùguàn
spray can

世界地图 shìjiè dìtú · **world map**

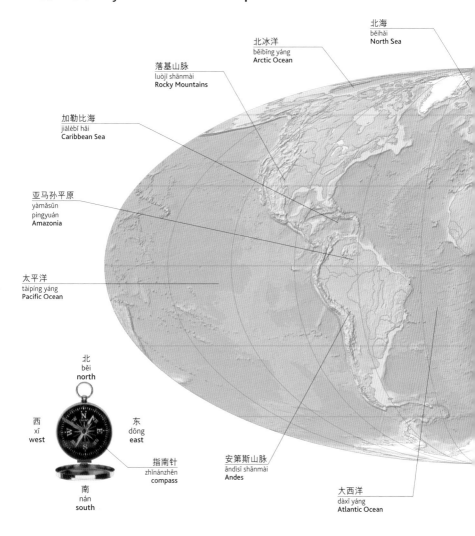

北海
běihǎi
North Sea

北冰洋
běibīng yáng
Arctic Ocean

落基山脉
luòjī shānmài
Rocky Mountains

加勒比海
jiālèbǐ hǎi
Caribbean Sea

亚马孙平原
yàmǎsūn
píngyuán
Amazonia

太平洋
tàipíng yáng
Pacific Ocean

北
běi
north

西
xī
west

东
dōng
east

指南针
zhǐnánzhēn
compass

南
nán
south

安第斯山脉
āndìsī shānmài
Andes

大西洋
dàxī yáng
Atlantic Ocean

中文 zhōngwén · **english**

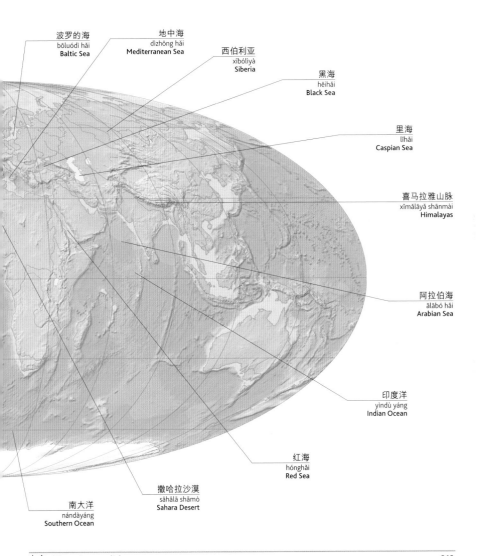

波罗的海
bōluódì hǎi
Baltic Sea

地中海
dìzhōng hǎi
Mediterranean Sea

西伯利亚
xībóliyà
Siberia

黑海
hēihǎi
Black Sea

里海
lǐhǎi
Caspian Sea

喜马拉雅山脉
xǐmǎlāyǎ shānmài
Himalayas

阿拉伯海
ālābó hǎi
Arabian Sea

印度洋
yìndù yáng
Indian Ocean

红海
hónghǎi
Red Sea

撒哈拉沙漠
sāhālā shāmò
Sahara Desert

南大洋
nándàyáng
Southern Ocean

北美洲 běiměizhōu · North and Central America

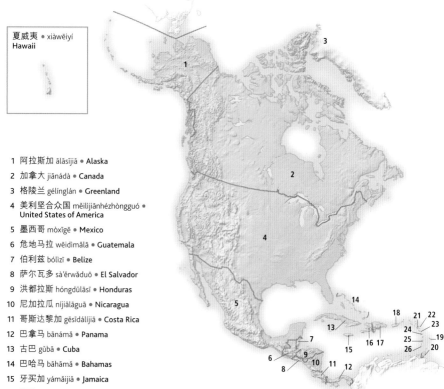

夏威夷 · xiàwēiyí
Hawaii

1 阿拉斯加 ālāsījiā · Alaska

2 加拿大 jiānádà · Canada

3 格陵兰 gélínglán · Greenland

4 美利坚合众国 měilìjiānhézhòngguó ·
   United States of America

5 墨西哥 mòxīgē · Mexico

6 危地马拉 wēidìmǎlā · Guatemala

7 伯利兹 bólìzī · Belize

8 萨尔瓦多 sà'ěrwǎduō · El Salvador

9 洪都拉斯 hóngdūlāsī · Honduras

10 尼加拉瓜 níjiālāguā · Nicaragua

11 哥斯达黎加 gēsīdálíjiā · Costa Rica

12 巴拿马 bānámǎ · Panama

13 古巴 gǔbā · Cuba

14 巴哈马 bāhāmǎ · Bahamas

15 牙买加 yámǎijiā · Jamaica

16 海地 hǎidì · Haiti

17 多米尼加 duōmǐníjiā · Dominican Republic

18 波多黎各 bōduōlígè · Puerto Rico

19 巴巴多斯 bābāduōsī · Barbados

20 特立尼达和多巴哥 tèlìnídá hé duōbāgē ·
    Trinidad and Tobago

21 圣基茨和尼维斯 shèngjīcí hé níwéisī ·
    St. Kitts and Nevis

22 安提瓜和巴布达 āntíguā hé bābùdá · Antigua and Barbuda

23 多米尼克 duōmǐníkè · Dominica

24 圣卢西亚 shènglúxīyà · St. Lucia

25 圣文森特和格林纳丁斯 shèngwénsēntè hé gélínnàdīngsī ·
    St. Vincent and the Grenadines

26 格林纳达 gélínnàdá · Grenada

南美洲 nánmĕizhōu · South America

1 委内瑞拉 wĕinèiruìlā · Venezuela

2 哥伦比亚 gēlúnbĭyà · Colombia

3 厄瓜多尔 èguāduōĕr · Ecuador

4 秘鲁 bìlŭ · Peru

5 加拉帕戈斯群岛 jiālāpàgēsī qúndăo
  · Galápagos Islands

6 圭亚那 guīyànà · Guyana

7 苏里南 sūlĭnán · Suriname

8 法属圭亚那 fǎshŭ guīyànà ·
  French Guiana

9 巴西 bāxī · Brazil

10 玻利维亚 bōlìwéiyà · Bolivia

11 智利 zhìlì · Chile

12 阿根廷 āgēntíng · Argentina

13 巴拉圭 bālāguī · Paraguay

14 乌拉圭 wūlāguī · Uruguay

15 福克兰群岛（马尔维纳斯群岛）fúkèlán
   qúndăo (mǎĕrwéinàsī qúndăo) · Falkland Islands

词汇 cíhuì · vocabulary

国家 guójiā country	省 shĕng province	地域 dìyù zone
民族 mínzú nation	领土 lĭngtŭ territory	行政区 xíngzhèngqū district
大陆 dàlù continent	殖民地 zhímíndì colony	地区 dìqū region
主权国家 zhŭquán guójiā state	公国 gōngguó principality	首都 shŏudū capital

欧洲 ōuzhōu • Europe

1 爱尔兰 ài'ěrlán • Ireland

2 英国 yīngguó • United Kingdom

3 葡萄牙 pútáoyá • Portugal

4 西班牙 xībānyá • Spain

5 巴利阿里群岛 bālìālǐ qúndǎo • Balearic Islands

6 安道尔 āndào'ěr • Andorra

7 法国 fǎguó • France

8 比利时 bǐlìshí • Belgium

9 荷兰 hélán • Netherlands

10 卢森堡 lúsēnbǎo • Luxembourg

11 德国 déguó • Germany

12 丹麦 dānmài • Denmark

13 挪威 nuówēi • Norway

14 瑞典 ruìdiǎn • Sweden

15 芬兰 fēnlán • Finland

16 爱沙尼亚 àishā'níyà • Estonia

17 拉脱维亚 lātuōwéiyà • Latvia

18 立陶宛 lìtáowǎn • Lithuania

19 加里宁格勒 jiālìnínggélè • Kaliningrad

20 波兰 bōlán • Poland

21 捷克 jiékè • Czech Republic

22 奥地利 àodìlì • Austria

23 列支敦士登 lièzhīdūnshìdēng • Liechtenstein

24 瑞士 ruìshì • Switzerland

25 意大利 yìdàlì • Italy

26 摩纳哥 mónàgē • Monaco

27 科西嘉岛 kēxījiādǎo • Corsica

28 撒丁岛 sādīngdǎo • Sardinia

29 圣马力诺 shèngmǎlìnuò • San Marino

30 梵蒂冈 fàndìgāng • Vatican City

31 西西里岛 xīxīlǐdǎo • Sicily

32 马耳他 mǎ'ěrtā • Malta

33 斯洛文尼亚 sīluòwénníyà • Slovenia

34 克罗地亚 kèluódìyà • Croatia

35 匈牙利 xiōngyálì • Hungary

36 斯洛伐克 sīluòfákè • Slovakia

37 乌克兰 wūkèlán • Ukraine

38 白俄罗斯 bái'éluósī • Belarus

39 摩尔多瓦 mó'ěrduōwǎ • Moldova

40 罗马尼亚 luómǎníyà • Romania

41 塞尔维亚 sài'ěrwéiyà • Serbia

42 波斯尼亚和黑塞哥维那(波黑) bōsīníyà hé hēisàigēwéinà(bōhēi) • Bosnia and Herzogovina

43 阿尔巴尼亚 ā'ěrbāníyà • Albania

44 马其顿 mǎqídùn • Macedonia

45 保加利亚 bǎojiālìyà • Bulgaria

46 希腊 xīlà • Greece

47 科索沃 kēsuǒwò (争议中 zhēngyìzhōng) • Kosovo (disputed)

48 黑山 hēishān • Montenegro

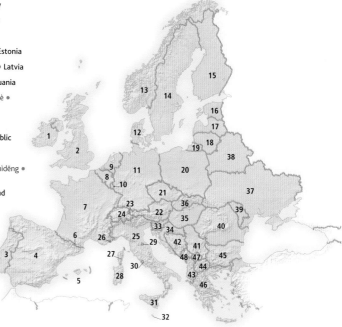

非洲 fēizhōu · **Africa**

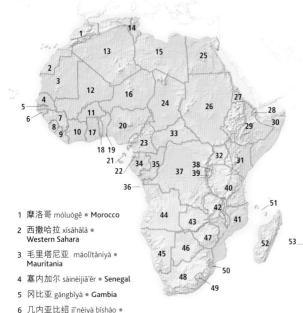

1 摩洛哥 móluògē · Morocco

2 西撒哈拉 xīsāhālā · Western Sahara

3 毛里塔尼亚 máolǐtǎníyà · Mauritania

4 塞内加尔 sàinèijiā'ěr · Senegal

5 冈比亚 gāngbǐyà · Gambia

6 几内亚比绍 jǐ'nèiyà bǐshào · Guinea-Bissau

7 几内亚 jǐ'nèiyà · Guinea

8 塞拉利昂 sàilāliáng · Sierra Leone

9 利比里亚 lìbǐlǐyà · Liberia

10 科特迪瓦 kētèdíwǎ · Ivory Coast

11 布基纳法索 bùjīnà fǎsuǒ · Burkina Faso

12 马里 mǎlǐ · Mali

13 阿尔及利亚 ā'ěrjílìyà · Algeria

14 突尼斯 tūnísī · Tunisia

15 利比亚 lìbǐyà · Libya

16 尼日尔 nírìěr · Niger

17 加纳 jiānà · Ghana

18 多哥 duōgē · Togo

19 贝宁 bèiníng · Benin

20 尼日利亚 nírìlìyà · Nigeria

21 圣多美和普林西比 shèngduōměi hé pǔlínxībǐ · São Tomé and Principe

22 赤道几内亚 chìdàojǐnèiyà · Equatorial Guinea

23 喀麦隆 kāmàilóng · Cameroon

24 乍得 zhàdé · Chad

25 埃及 āijí · Egypt

26 苏丹 sūdān · Sudan

27 厄立特里亚 èlìtèlǐyà · Eritrea

28 吉布提 jíbùtí · Djibouti

29 埃塞俄比亚 āisài'ébǐyà · Ethiopia

30 索马里 suǒmǎlǐ · Somalia

31 肯尼亚 kěnníyà · Kenya

32 乌干达 wūgāndá · Uganda

33 中非共和国 zhōngfēi gònghéguó · Central African Republic

34 加蓬 jiāpéng · Gabon

35 刚果 gāngguǒ · Congo

36 卡奔达(安哥拉) kǎbēndá (āngēlā) · Cabinda (Angola)

37 刚果民主共和国 gāngguǒ mínzhǔ gònghéguó · Democratic Republic of the Congo

38 卢旺达 lúwàngdá · Rwanda

39 布隆迪 bùlóngdí · Burundi

40 坦桑尼亚 tǎnsāngníyà · Tanzania

41 莫桑比克 mòsāngbǐkè · Mozambique

42 马拉维 mǎlāwéi · Malawi

43 赞比亚 zànbǐyà · Zambia

44 安哥拉 āngēlā · Angola

45 纳米比亚 nàmǐbǐyà · Namibia

46 博茨瓦纳 bócíwǎnà · Botswana

47 津巴布韦 jīnbābùwéi · Zimbabwe

48 南非 nánfēi · South Africa

49 莱索托 láisuǒtuō · Lesotho

50 斯威士兰 sīwēishìlán · Swaziland

51 科摩罗群岛 kēmóluóqúndǎo · Comoros

52 马达加斯加 mǎdájiāsíjiā · Madagascar

53 毛里求斯 máolǐqiúsī · Mauritius

中文 zhōngwén · english

亚洲 yàzhōu • Asia

1 俄罗斯联邦 éluósīliánbāng • Russian Federation

2 格鲁吉亚 gélǔjíyà • Georgia

3 亚美尼亚 yàměiníyà • Armenia

4 阿塞拜疆 ā'sàibàijiāng • Azerbaijan

5 伊朗 yīlǎng • Iran

6 伊拉克 yīlākè • Iraq

7 叙利亚 xùlìyà • Syria

8 黎巴嫩 líbānèn • Lebanon

9 以色列 yǐsèliè • Israel

10 约旦 yuēdàn • Jordan

11 沙特阿拉伯 shātè'ālābó • Saudi Arabia

12 科威特 kēwēitè • Kuwait

13 卡塔尔 kǎtǎ'ěr • Qatar

14 阿拉伯联合酋长国 ālābó liánhé qiúzhǎngguó • United Arab Emirates

15 阿曼 āmàn • Oman

16 也门 yěmén • Yemen

17 哈萨克斯坦 hāsàkèsītǎn • Kazakhstan

18 乌兹别克斯坦 wūzībiékèsītǎn • Uzbekistan

19 土库曼斯坦 tǔkùmànsītǎn • Turkmenistan

20 阿富汗 āfùhàn • Afghanistan

21 塔吉克斯坦 tǎjíkèsītǎn • Tajikistan

22 吉尔吉斯坦 jíěrjísītǎn • Kyrgyzstan

23 巴基斯坦 bājīsītǎn • Pakistan

24 印度 yìndù • India

25 马尔代夫 mǎ'ěrdàifū • Maldives

26 斯里兰卡 sīlǐlánkǎ • Sri Lanka

27 中国 zhōngguó • China

28 蒙古 měnggǔ • Mongolia

29 朝鲜 cháoxiǎn • North Korea

30 韩国 hánguó • South Korea

31 日本 rìběn • Japan

32 尼泊尔 níbó'ěr • Nepal

33 不丹 bùdān • Bhutan

34 孟加拉国 mèngjiālāguó • Bangladesh

35 缅甸 miǎndiàn • Burma (Myanmar)

36 泰国 tàiguó • Thailand

37 老挝 lǎowō • Laos

38 越南 yuènán • Vietnam

39 柬埔寨 jiǎnpǔzhài • Cambodia

40 马来西亚 mǎláixīyà • Malaysia

41 新加坡 xīnjiāpō • Singapore

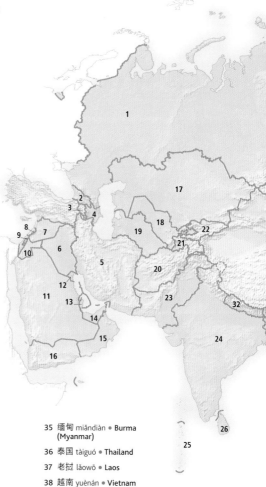

中文 zhōngwén • english

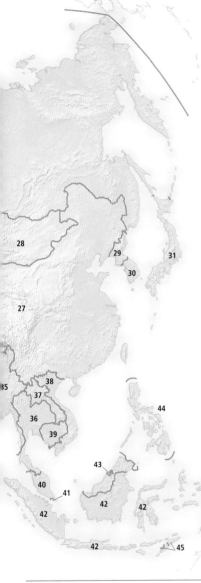

大洋洲 dàyángzhōu • Australasia

1 澳大利亚 àodàliyà • Australia

2 塔斯马尼亚(岛) tǎsīmǎníyà(dǎo) • Tasmania

3 新西兰 xīnxīlán • New Zealand

42 印度尼西亚 yìndùníxīyà • Indonesia

43 文莱 wénlái • Brunei

44 菲律宾 fēilǜbīn • Philippines

45 东帝汶 dōngdìwèn • East Timor

46 巴布亚新几内亚 bābùyà xīnjǐnèiyà • Papua New Guinea

47 所罗门群岛 suǒluómén qúndǎo • Solomon Islands

48 瓦努阿图 wǎnǔātú • Vanuatu

49 斐济 fěijì • Fiji

小品词与反义词 xiǎopǐncí yǔ fǎnyìcí · particles and antonyms

到...去 dào...qù **to**	从...来 cóng...lái **from**	为 wèi **for**	向...方向 xiàng...fāngxiàng **toward**
在...上方 zài...shàngfāng **over**	在...下方 zài...xiàfāng **under**	沿着... yánzhe... **along**	越过 yuèguò **across**
在...前面 zài...qiánmian **in front of**	在...后面 zài...hòumian **behind**	连同 liántóng **with**	没有... méiyǒu... **without**
在...上 zài...shàng **onto**	到...里 dào...lǐ **into**	在...之前 zài...zhīqián **before**	在...之后 zài...zhīhòu **after**
在...里 zài...lǐ **in**	在...外 zài...wài **out**	不迟于... bùchíyú... **by**	直到... zhídào... **until**
在...上面 zài...shàngmian **above**	在...下面 zài...xiàmian **below**	早 zǎo **early**	迟 chí **late**
在...里面 zài...lǐmiàn **inside**	在...外面 zài...wàimiàn **outside**	现在 xiànzài **now**	以后 yǐhòu **later**
向上 xiàngshàng **up**	向下 xiàngxià **down**	一直 yìzhí **always**	从不 cóngbù **never**
在 zài **at**	超出 chāochū **beyond**	经常 jīngcháng **often**	很少 hěnshǎo **rarely**
穿越 chuānyuè **through**	在...周围 zài...zhōuwéi **around**	昨天 zuótiān **yesterday**	明天 míngtiān **tomorrow**
在...之上 zài...zhīshàng **on top of**	在...旁边 zài...pángbiān **beside**	第一 dìyī **first**	最后 zuìhòu **last**
在...之间 zài...zhījiān **between**	在...对面 zài...duìmiàn **opposite**	每... měi... **every**	一些 yìxiē **some**
在...附近 zài...fùjìn **near**	离...远 lí...yuǎn **far**	关于 guānyú **about**	准确地 zhǔnquèdì **exactly**
这里 zhèlǐ **here**	那里 nàlǐ **there**	一点儿 yìdiǎn'er **a little**	很多 hěnduō **a lot**

大 dà **large**	小 xiǎo **small**	热 rè **hot**	冷 lěng **cold**
宽 kuān **wide**	窄 zhǎi **narrow**	开 kāi **open**	关 guān **closed**
高大 gāodà **tall**	矮小 ǎixiǎo **short**	满 mǎn **full**	空 kōng **empty**
高 gāo **high**	低 dī **low**	新 xīn **new**	旧 jiù **old**
厚 hòu **thick**	瘦 shòu **thin**	轻 qīng **light**	黑暗 hēiàn **dark**
轻 qīng **light**	重 zhòng **heavy**	容易 róngyì **easy**	困难 kùnnán **difficult**
硬 yìng **hard**	软 ruǎn **soft**	空闲 kòngxián **free**	忙碌 mánglù **occupied**
潮湿 cháoshī **wet**	干燥 gānzào **dry**	强壮 qiángzhuàng **strong**	虚弱 xūruò **weak**
好 hǎo **good**	坏 huài **bad**	胖 pàng **fat**	瘦 shòu **thin**
快 kuài **fast**	慢 màn **slow**	年轻 niánqīng **young**	年老 niánlǎo **old**
正确 zhèngquè **correct**	错误 cuòwù **wrong**	更好 gènghǎo **better**	更差 gèngchà **worse**
干净 gānjìng **clean**	脏 zāng **dirty**	黑色 hēisè **black**	白色 báisè **white**
好看 hǎokàn **beautiful**	丑 chǒu **ugly**	有趣 yǒuqù **interesting**	厌恶 yànwù **boring**
贵 guì **expensive**	便宜 piányì **cheap**	生病的 shēngbìngde **sick**	健康的 jiànkāngde **well**
安静 ānjìng **quiet**	吵闹 chǎonào **noisy**	开始 kāishǐ **beginning**	结束 jiéshù **end**

中文 zhōngwén • **english**

常用语 cháng yòngyǔ • useful phrases

基本用语 jīběn yòngyǔ • essential phrases

是
shì
Yes

不
bù
No

也许
yěxǔ
Maybe

请
qǐng
Please

谢谢
xièxiè
Thank you

不用谢
búyòngxiè
You're welcome

抱歉；打扰一下
bàoqiàn, dǎrǎoyíxià
Excuse me

对不起
duìbuqǐ
I'm sorry

不要
búyào
Don't

好
hǎo
OK

很好
hěnhǎo
That's fine

正确
zhèngquè
That's correct

不对
búduì
That's wrong

问候 wènhòu • greetings

你好
nǐ hǎo
Hello

再见
zàijiàn
Goodbye

早上好
zǎoshang hǎo
Good morning

下午好
xiàwǔ hǎo
Good afternoon

晚上好
wǎnshang hǎo
Good evening

晚安
wǎn'ān
Good night

你好吗?
nǐ hǎo ma?
How are you?

我叫…
wǒ jiào…
My name is…

您怎么称呼?
nín zěnme chēnghu?
What is your name?

他/她叫什么名字?
tā/tā jiào shénme míngzi?
What is his/her name?

我介绍一下…
wǒ jièshào yíxià…
May I introduce…

这是…
zhèshì…
This is…

很高兴见到你
hěngāoxìng jiàndào nǐ
Pleased to meet you

待会儿见
dài huì'er jiàn
See you later

标志 biāozhì • signs

游客问询处
yóukè wènxúnchù
Tourist information

入口
rùkǒu
Entrance

出口
chūkǒu
Exit

紧急出口
jǐnjí chūkǒu
Emergency exit

推
tuī
Push

危险
wēixiǎn
Danger

禁止吸烟
jìnzhǐxīyān
No smoking

故障
gùzhàng
Out of order

开放时间
kāifàng shíjiān
Opening times

免费入场
miǎnfèi rùchǎng
Free admission

全天开放
quántiān kāifàng
Open all day

减价
jiǎnjià
Reduced price

打折
dǎshé
Sale

进前敲门
jìnqiánqiāomén
Knock before entering

禁止践踏草坪
jìnzhǐ jiàntàcǎopíng
Keep off the grass

求助 qiúzhù • help

你能帮帮我吗?
nǐ néng bāngbāng wǒ ma?
Can you help me?

我不懂
wǒ bù dǒng
I don't understand

我不知道
wǒ bù zhīdào
I don't know

你说英语吗?
nǐ shuō yīngyǔ ma?
Do you speak English?

你说中文吗?
nǐ shuō zhōngwén ma?
Do you speak Chinese?

我会说英语
wǒ huì shuō yīngyǔ
I speak English

我会说西班牙语
wǒ huì shuō xībānyáyǔ
I speak Spanish

请说得再慢些
qǐng shuōdé zài màn xiē
Please speak more slowly

请帮我写下来
qǐng bāng wǒ xiě xiàlái
Please write it down for me

我丢了…
wǒ diūle…
I have lost…

方向 fāngxiàng ·
directions

我迷路了
wǒ mílùle
I am lost

...在哪里?
zàinǎli
Where is the...?

最近的...在哪里?
zuìjìnde...zàinǎli?
Where is the nearest...?

洗手间在哪儿?
xǐshǒujiān zàinǎer?
Where is the restroom?

我怎么去...?
wǒ zěnme qù...?
How do I get to...?

右转
yòuzhuǎn
To the right

左转
zuǒzhuǎn
To the left

向前直行
xiàngqián zhíháng
Straight ahead

到...有多远?
wǒ zěnme qù...?
How far is...?

交通标志 jiāotōng
biāozhì · road signs

各方通行
gèfāng tōngxíng
All directions

谨慎驾驶
jǐnshèn jiàshǐ
Caution

禁入
jìnrù
Do not enter

减速
jiǎnsù
Slow down

绕行
ràoxíng
Detour

靠右侧行驶
kào yòucè xíngshǐ
Keep right

高速公路
gāosùgōnglù
Freeway

禁止停车
jìnzhǐ tíngchē
No parking

禁止通行
jìnzhǐ tōngxíng
No through road

单行道
dānxíngdào
One-way street

其他方向通行
qítāfāngxiàng tōngxíng
Other directions

只限本区居民(停车)
zhǐxiànběnqūjūmín (tíngchē)
Residents only

道路管制
dàolùguǎnzhì
Roadworks

危险弯道
wēixiǎnwāndào
Dangerous bend

住宿 zhùsù ·
accommodations

我订了房间
wǒ dìng le fángjiān
I have a reservation

餐厅在哪儿?
cāntīng zàinà'er
Where is the dining room?

我的房间号是...
wǒ de fángjiān hào shì...
My room number is ...

几点吃早餐?
jǐdiǎn chī zǎocān?
What time is breakfast?

我将在...点回来
wǒ jiāng zài...diǎn huílái
I'll be back at ... o'clock

我明天离开
wǒ míngtiān líkāi
I'm leaving tomorrow

饮食 yǐnshí · eating
and drinking

干杯!
gānbēi
Cheers!

好吃极了
hàochījíle
It's delicious

难吃死了
nánchīsǐle
It's awful

我不喝酒
wǒ bù hējiǔ
I don't drink

我不抽烟
wǒ bù chōuyān
I don't smoke

我不吃肉
wǒ bù chīròu
I don't eat meat

够了,谢谢
gòule, xièxiè
No more for me,
thank you

请再来点儿
qǐng zàilái diǎn'er
May I have some more?

我们要结账
wǒmen yào jiézhàng
May we have the
check?

请开张收据
qǐng kāi zhāng shōujù
Can I have a receipt?

禁烟区
jìnyānqū
No-smoking area

健康 jiànkāng · health

我不舒服
wǒ bù shūfu
I don't feel well

我难受
wǒ nánshòu
I feel sick

离这儿最近的医生
电话是多少?
lí zhè'er zuìjìn de yīshēng
diànhuà shì duōshǎo?
What is the telephone
number of the nearest
doctor?

我这儿疼
wǒ zhè'er téng
It hurts here

我发烧了
wǒ fāshāole
I have a temperature

我怀孕...个月了
wǒ huáiyùn...gè yuèle
I'm ... months pregnant

我需要...处方
wǒ xūyào...chǔfāng
I need a prescription for ...

我通常服用...
wǒ tōngcháng fúyòng...
I normally take ...

我对...过敏
wǒ duì...guòmǐn
I'm allergic to ...

他好吗?
tā hǎoma?
Will he be all right?

她好吗?
tā hǎoma?
Will she be all right?

中文索引 zhōngwén suǒyǐn • Chinese index

中文
索引

中
文
索
引

中
文
索
引

中
文
索
引

中
文
索
引

中文索引

中文 zhōngwén • english

中
文
索
引

中文
索引

中
文
索
引

中文 索引

中文索引

中文
索
引

英文索引 yīngwén suǒyǐn · English index

wire strippers 81
wires 60
with 320
withdrawal slip 96
without 320
witness 180
wok 69
wolf 290
woman 23
womb 52
women's clothing 34
women's wear 105
wood 79, 233, 275, 285
wood glue 78
wood shavings 78
wooden spoon 68
woodpecker 292
woodstain 79
woodwind 257
woodworking 275
work 172
workbench 78
workday 306
workshop 78
world map 312
worm 295
worried 25
wound 46
wrap 155
wrapping 111
wreath 111
wrench 80, 81, 203
wrestling 236
wrinkle 15
wrist 13, 15
wristband 230
writ 180
write v 162

X

X-ray 48
X-ray film 50
X-ray machine 212
X-ray viewer 45

Y

yacht 215, 240
yam 125
yard 310
yarn 277
yawn v 25
year 163, 306
yeast 138
yellow 274
yellow card 223
Yemen 318
yes 322
yesterday 306
yoga 54
yogurt 137
yolk 137, 157
you're welcome 322
Yugoslavia 316

Z

Zambia 317
zebra 291
zero 308
zest 126
Zimbabwe 317
zinc 289
zipper 277
ZIP code 98
zone 315
zones 283
zoo 262
zoology 169
zoom lens 270
zucchini 125

鸣谢 míngxiè • acknowledgments

DORLING KINDERSLEY would like to thank Tracey Miles and Christine Lacey for design assistance, Georgina Garner for editorial and administrative help, Sonia Gavira, Polly Boyd, and Cathy Meeus for editorial help, and Claire Bowers for compiling the DK picture credits.

The publisher would like to thank the following for their kind permission to reproduce their photographs:
Abbreviations key:
t = top, b = bottom, r = right, l = left, c = center
Abode: 62; **Action Plus:** 224bc; **alamy. com:** 154t; A.T. Willett 287bcl; Michael Foyle 184bl; Stock Connection 287bcr; **Allsport/Getty Images:** 238cl; **Alvey and Towers:** 209 acr, 215bcl, 215bcr, 241cr; **Peter Anderson:** 188cbr, 271br. **Anthony Blake Photo Library:** Charlie Stebbings 114cl; John Sims 114tcl; **Andyalte:** 98tl; **apple mac computers:** 268tcr; **Arcaid:** John Edward Linden 301bl; Martine Hamilton Knight, Architects: Chapman Taylor Partners, 213cl; Richard Bryant 301br; **Argos:** 41tcl, 66cbl, 66cl, 66br, 66bcl, 69cl, 70bcl, 71t, 77tl, 269tc, 270bl; **Axiom:** Eitan Simanor 105bcr; Ian Cumming 104; Vicki Couchman 148cr; **Beken Of Cowes Ltd:** 215cbc; **Bosch:** 76tcr, 76tc, 76tcl; **Camera Press:** 27c, 38tr, 256t, 257cr; Barry J. Holmes 148tr; Jane Hanger 159cr; Mary Germanou 259bc; **Corbis:** 78b; Anna Clopet 247tr; Bettmann 181tl, 181tr; Bo Zauders 156t; Bob Rowan 152bl; Bob Winsett 247cbl; Brian Bailey 247br; Carl and Ann Purcell 162l; Chris Rainer 247ctl; ChromoSohm Inc. 179tr; Craig Aurness 215tbl; David H.Wells 249cbr; Dennis Marsico 274bl; Dimitri Lundt 236bcr; Duomo 211tl; Gail Mooney 277ctcr; George Lepp 248c; Gunter Marx 248cr; Jack Fields 210b; Jack Hollingsworth 231bl; Jacqui Hurst 277cbr; James L. Amos 247bl, 191ctr, 220bcr; Jan Butchofsky 277cbc; Johnathan Blair 243cr; Jon Feingersh 153tr; Jose F. Poblete 191br; Jose Luis Pelaez.Inc 153tc, 175tl; Karl Weatherly 220bl, 247tcr; Kelly Mooney Photography 259tl; Kevin Fleming 249bc; Kevin R. Morris 105tr, 243tl, 243tc; Kim Sayer 249tcr; Lynn Goldsmith 258t; Macduff Everton 231bcl; Mark Gibson 249bl; Mark L. Stephenson 249tcl; Michael Pole 115tr; Michael S. Yamashita 247ctcl; Mike King 247cbl; Neil Rabinowitz 214br; Owen Franken 112t; Pablo Corral 115bcr; Paul A. Sounders 169br, 249ctcl; Paul J. Sutton 224c, 224br;

Peter Turnley 105tcr; Phil Schermeister 227b, 248tr; R. W Jones 309; R.W. Jones 175tr; Richard Hutchings 168b; Rick Doyle 241ctr; Robert Holmes 97br, 277ctc; Roger Ressmeyer 169tr; Russ Schleipman 229; Steve Raymer 168cr; The Purcell Team 211ctr; Tim Wright 178; Vince Streano 194t; Wally McNamee 220br, 220bcl, 224bl; Yann Arhus-Bertrand 249tl; **Demetrio Carrasco / Dorling Kindersley (c) Herge / Les Editions Casterman:** 112ccl; **Dixons:** 270cl, 270cr, 270bl, 270bcl, 270bcr, 270ccr; **Education Photos:** John Walmsley 26tl; **Empics Ltd:** Adam Day 236br; Andy Heading 243c; Steve White 249cbc; **Getty Images:** 48bcl, 100t, 114bcr, 154bl, 287tr; 94tr; **Dennis Gilbert:** 106tc; **Hulsta:** 70t; **Ideal Standard Ltd:** 72r; **The Image Bank/Getty Images:** 58; **Impact Photos:** Eliza Armstrong 115cr; John Arthur 190tl; Philip Achache 246t; **The Interior Archive:** Henry Wilson, Alfie's Market 114bl; Luke White, Architect: David Mikhail, 59tl; Simon Upton, Architect: Phillippe Starck, St Martins Lane Hotel 100bcr, 100br; **Jason Hawkes Aerial Photography:** 216t; **Dan Johnson:** 26cbl, 35r; **Kos Pictures Source:** 215cbl, 240tc, 240tr; David Williams 216b; **Lebrecht Collection:** Kate Mount 169bc; **MP Visual. com:** Mark Swallow 202t; **NASA:** 280cr, 280ccl, 281tl; **P&O European Cruises:** 214bl; **P A Photos:** 181br; **The Photographers' Library:** 186bl, 186bc, 186t; **Plain and Simple Kitchens:** 66t; **Powerstock Photolibrary:** 169tl, 256t, 287tc; **Rail Images:** 208c, 208 cbl, 209br; **Red Consultancy:** Odeon cinemas 257br; **Redferns:** 259br; Nigel Crane 259c; **Rex Features:** 106br, 259tc, 259tr, 259bl, 280b; Charles Ommaney 114tcr; J.F.F Whitehead 243cl; Patrick Barth 101tl; Patrick Frilet 189cbl; Scott Wiseman 287bl; **Royalty Free Images:** Getty Images/Eyewire 154bl; **Science & Society Picture Library:** Science Museum 202b; **Skyscan:** 168t, 182c, 298; Quick UK Ltd 212; **Sony:** 268bc; **Robert Streeter:** 154br; **Neil Sutherland:** 82tr, 83tl, 90t, 118, 188ctr, 196tl, 196tr, 299cl, 299bl; **The Travel Library:** Stuart Black 264t; **Travelex:** 97cl; **Vauxhall:** Technik 198t, 199tl, 199tr, 199cl, 199cr, 199ctcl, 199ctcr, 199tcl, 199tcr, 200; **View Pictures:** Dennis Gilbert, Architects: ACDP Consulting, 106t; Dennis Gilbert, Chris Wilkinson Architects, 209tr; Peter

Cook, Architects: Nicholas Crimshaw and partners, 208t; **Betty Walton:** 185br; **Colin Walton:** 2, 4, 7, 9, 10, 28, 42, 56, 92, 95c, 99tl, 99tcl, 102, 116, 120t, 138t, 146, 150t, 160, 170, 191ctcl, 192, 218, 252, 260br, 260l, 261tr, 261c, 261cr, 271cbl, 271cbr, 271ctl, 278, 287br, 302, 401.

DK PICTURE LIBRARY:
Akhil Bahkshi; Patrick Baldwin; Geoff Brightling; British Museum; John Bulmer; Andrew Butler; Joe Cornish; Brian Cosgrove; Andy Crawford and Kit Hougton; Philip Dowell; Alistair Duncan; Gables; Bob Gathany; Norman Hollands; Kew Gardens; Peter James Kindersley; Vladimir Kozlik; Sam Lloyd; London Northern Bus Company Ltd; Tracy Morgan; David Murray and Jules Selmes; Musée Vivant du Cheval, France; Museum of Broadcast Communications; Museum of Natural History; NASA; National History Museum; Norfolk Rural Life Museum; Stephen Oliver; RNLI; Royal Ballet School; Guy Ryecart; Science Museum; Neil Setchfield; Ross Simms and the Winchcombe Folk Picture Museum; Singapore Symphony Orchestra; Smart Museum of Art; Tony Souter; Erik Svensson and Jeppe Wikstrom; Sam Tree of Keygrove Marketing Ltd; Barrie Watts; Alan Williams; Jerry Young.

Additional Photography by Colin Walton.

Colin Walton would like to thank:
A&A News, Uckfield; Abbey Music, Tunbridge Wells; Arena Mens Clothing, Tunbridge Wells; Burrells of Tunbridge Wells; Gary at Di Marco's; Jeremy's Home Store, Tunbridge Wells; Noakes of Tunbridge Wells; Ottakar's, Tunbridge Wells; Selby's of Uckfield; Sevenoaks Sound and Vision; Westfield, Royal Victoria Place, Tunbridge Wells.

All other images are Dorling Kindersley copyright. For further information see www. dkimages.com